GLYPH-BREAKER

STEVEN ROGER FISCHER

GLYPH-BREAKER

COPERNICUS
AN IMPRINT OF SPRINGER-VERLAG

Published in the United States by Copernicus, an imprint of Springer-Verlag New York, Inc.

Copernicus
Springer-Verlag New York, Inc.
175 Fifth Avenue
New York, NY 10010

Library of Congress Cataloging-in-Publication Data
Fischer, Steven R.
    Glyphbreaker / Steven Roger Fischer.
      p.   cm.
    Includes bibliographical references and index.
    ISBN 0-387-98241-8 (hardcover : alk. paper)
    1. Extinct languages.   I. Title.
P901.F57 1997
417'.7—DC21   97-11633

Manufactured in the United States of America.
Printed on acid-free paper

9 8 7 6 5 4 3 2 1

ISBN 0-387-98241-8   SPIN 10576265

To Taki

CONTENTS

PREFACE

A "glyph" (short for hiero*glyph*) is a sign in a script. And a "breaker" is a person who cracks a script's code. A "glyph-breaker" is then a decipherer, someone who lets us read the unreadable, that linguistic magician who gives voice to the mute past.

Until 1984 no one had been able to read Crete's 3600-year-old Phaistos Disk, Europe's earliest literature and greatest written enigma. Until 1994 no one could make sense of Easter Island's mysterious *rongorongo* writing, Oceania's only script predating the twentieth century. No one had ever deciphered two wholly different historical scripts before. Until now.

This is the true story of these two achievements.

With the Aegean adventure, a gold talent of gratitude will forever be owed to the remarkable Joseph Judge, former associate editor of the *National Geographic* in Washington, DC, poet, and historian, who died of cancer only one month before these lines were written; Joseph Judge's inspiration and support were Homeric. The Polynesian challenge succeeded because of the wisdom and encouragement of the eminent ethnologist Thomas S. Barthel of Tübingen, Germany; the American archaeologist Georgia Lee of Los Osos, California; and the British archaeologist Paul Bahn of Hull, England. There were scores of other colleagues and helpmates, too, from St. Petersburg, Russia, to Hangaroa, Rapanui (Easter Island), who each contributed a valuable piece to either of the two epigraphic puzzles. This is their achievement, too. My gratitude goes to them all.

I am especially grateful to my wife Taki. She was the one who made the impossible possible. And shared every peak and valley.

There's no secret so hidden that it cannot be found, no voice so mute that it cannot be heard.

Steven Roger Fischer
Waiheke Island, New Zealand
May 1996

CHAPTER 1

IN ODYSSEUS'S WAKE

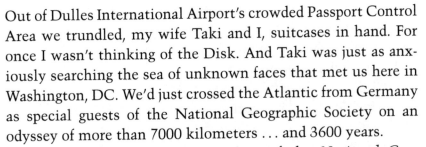

Out of Dulles International Airport's crowded Passport Control Area we trundled, my wife Taki and I, suitcases in hand. For once I wasn't thinking of the Disk. And Taki was just as anxiously searching the sea of unknown faces that met us here in Washington, DC. We'd just crossed the Atlantic from Germany as special guests of the National Geographic Society on an odyssey of more than 7000 kilometers ... and 3600 years.

"See anyone holding up a copy of the *National Geographic?*"

"What's that sign over there?"

An attractive woman of graceful years was flaunting some sort of brownish-orange homemade sign. I glanced at its curious "letters." Then I did a double-take, having recognized in the colorful pictograms the syllables *we-le-ko-me si-ti-we-ne* in a form of writing whose sound values hadn't been read since 1600 B.C.

It was "Welcome, Steven" in the script of ancient Crete's Phaistos Disk.

"Hi, I'm Joe Judge," said a friendly greying gentleman alongside the woman with the extraordinary sign, extending his hand in greeting. "And this is my wife Phyllis. What do you think of the sign? Could you read it?"

"Hello, I'm George Stuart," said another man resembling a big panda, just as eagerly shaking my hand. "Welcome to Washington. Let me tell you, we're all very much excited about your decipherment."

The folks from the Geographic couldn't have been nicer.

The long drive into the District, as we soon learned Washington proper is called by the locals, was made pleasantly short by amicable conversation and rushing images of a tree-and-jogger-lined canal and verdant woods and colonial-style white wooden houses this sundrenched summer of 1984. Chauffeured to the elegant Jefferson Hotel in downtown Washington, just opposite the National Geographic headquarters, Taki and I first freshened up and then rejoined our three hosts downstairs for drinks. The elegantly appointed hotel boasted Bacchus's own bar—but failed to offer my long-craved root beer, which had always been unavailable in Europe, too, where Taki and I had been living for four years.

"Tell me, when did you know that you'd successfully done it?" asked Joe Judge, then the associate editor of the *National Geographic*, eager to return to the reason for our visit.

"I suppose not until late March or early April of this year, 1984," I replied, sipping on a cold soft drink. "Only once all the sound values of the Disk's glyphs had finally been retrieved, I guess."

"Is it really Europe's earliest attested language and literature?"

"That's right."

"How many languages did you have to use to do it?"

"About twenty."

"How long did the decipherment take you, Dr. Fischer?"

The question came from a senior staff member of the National Geographic Society, a lovely and eloquent woman called Mary. It was the next day, at our special round-table luncheon in the wood-paneled executive dining room of the brand new "Mayan Temple" M Street Building of the National Geographic. Senior staff had gathered here to commend my decipherment.

I was answering so many questions by now, left, right, and center, that I scarcely had time to swallow. Several of those seated at the table were grinning in sympathy.

"I began the decipherment work back in 1982," I replied. "Most of the first year was spent in just trying to figure out a valid approach. Each decipherment has its own particular means of solution, you see. It takes a long time to find what the right approach is. Then came the internal analysis of the Phaistos Disk, using only numbers. I did that to work out the structure of the inscription, independent of any sounds. That took several months of pretty hard work. But the phonetic assignations were the hardest part. That was putting the proper sounds to the 45 glyphs on the Disk. Once I was finally on the right track, it went relatively quickly. Up to now it's been two full years."

"*Why* did you do it?"

This now from a distinguished-looking white-haired gentleman in blue serge with vest. I found out later that he was Mary's husband Tom. He pursed his lips and lifted his head.

I smiled. "Because it was there."

"You mean it was a personal challenge," offered Mary.

"That's right. Some men feel they have to climb mountains. Others sail single-handedly around the world. The Phaistos Disk said something to me. It was my sincere belief that its decipherment was theoretically possible. And so I got to work."

I got to work.... It all sounded so horribly easy. But how could anyone begin to understand? That brain-splitting, three-dimensional game of archaeological word-chess that comes to possess you so utterly that it becomes all you breathe, eat, and sleep, twenty-four hours a day, seven days a week. Until there's no other thought in your mind but Disk, *Disk*, DISK! and your right hand starts shaking uncontrollably and can't stop ... and never will stop again for the rest of your life.

But I had done it. With Taki right at my side all the way. For which unique achievement we were to be feted in Washington, DC, in the many rootbeer-and-cake days that followed, iced with a special reception at the exclusive Cosmos Club, candled with intimate and memorable dinners, and cherried-on-the-top with congratulatory handshakes from some of America's finest journalists and epigraphers (experts in the study of ancient inscriptions).

By deciphering ancient Crete's Phaistos Disk, I had indeed recovered Europe's earliest attested language and literature—the Minoan language, almost four thousand years old. This had revealed itself to be a very early East Hellenic dialect. In other words, Minoan was closely related to the contemporaneous Mycenaean language that was spoken by the early Greeks on the mainland at Mycenae, Pylos, Tiryns, and elsewhere. Half a millennium before the Trojan War.

And over a millennium and a half before the Man from Galilee.

"*He saw the cities of many peoples and learnt their ways,*" sang Homer of Odysseus, that earliest of globetrotters, back in the eighth century B.C. Yet the blind bard might also have been singing of the odyssey that eventually led me to the island world of the prehistoric Aegean after years of wandering in which I, too, saw the cities of many peoples and learnt their ways....

I'd never heard of either Odysseus or Homer when a schoolchild in Los Angeles, California, where I was born in 1947. But in 1956, now in Tacoma, Washington, my parents gave me a book for my ninth birthday—*The Wonderful World of Archaeology* by Ronald Jessup—in which, among many fascinating things, I read all about Sir Arthur Evans. Sir Arthur had discovered and excavated the ruins of Knossos, Europe's first capital city, on the island of Crete in the Aegean just south of mainland Greece. And I read about Michael Ventris, too, who had deciphered the Linear B script of ancient Greece in 1953, proving the prehistoric Aegean's "chicken-scratch" to be written, wonder of wonders, in an early Greek language. This was the hour of the glyphbreaker, a philological achievement that my children's book called "the Everest of Greek archaeology" because in the same year Hillary and Tenzing had scaled Mt. Everest.

And there was a small picture in the book of Crete's enigmatic Phaistos Disk, too, along with this caption: "No-one has yet read the inscription on the Cretan Disc of Phaestos...."

I cherished *The Wonderful World of Archaeology* and always kept it close at hand in the many wanderings over the globe that followed.

Later that same year my family moved to the island of Okinawa, south of Japan. And it was here that I learned my first foreign language, Japanese. While other kids were gleefully scraping their shins at baseball and football and roller-skating and biking, I was learning old tales in Japanese; exploring for artifacts in the thick, dank jungle just behind my grammar school; and often, to the utter horror of Mom and Dad, returning home with unexploded shells and rusting hand grenades and even human bones from the Pacific's bloodiest battlefield in World War II.

This total immersion in a foreign culture at such an impressionable age, acquiring a second tongue and meeting and learning another race and their ways, forever altered my life, I now appreciate in retrospect, forty years later. It was the single most formative experience of my life. It was a baptism of the first order: into a born-again citizen of the world.

By 1959, once back in Los Angeles, I was hopelessly devoted to collecting anything that had the aura of glorious "oldness" about it for my private museum: such Crown Jewels as shed snakeskins, halfpenny stamps, Roman coins and Indian-head pennies, turn-of-the-century automobile advertisements, scratched phonograph records as thick as my little finger. And especially old crumbling books, the more decrepit the better. Preferably in Latin and French and thus certain to reek of antiquity or foreignness.

My first year at high school found me eagerly enrolling—as a result of the post-Sputnik fervor for foreign languages that swept over America in the early 1960s—in the Russian class that was being offered for the first time. Thus Russian became my second foreign tongue, at 14. It proved to be absolutely essential over thirty years later in my extensive dealings with Russian colleagues in solving the riddle of Easter Island's *rongorongo* script. Whereupon French was discovered, probably because my huge pile of dusty old French books, still unread, reminded me daily that herein lay the key to an entire world of culture and tradition called *Europe* . . . so very far removed from Southern Californian teenagers in the middle of the twentieth century.

Graduation night, 1965, found me crossing the continental United States by car for a New York rendezvous with the celebrated cruise liner *Queen Mary* and two months Euro-railing with a friend, then still a rare experience for young Americans. Only weeks after my return to Los Angeles, I was signed as a singer-composer by a Hollywood record company and even cut a popular record that played on the air in Los Angeles and Honolulu in that memorable summer of 1965. Yet I realized that an important life decision had to be made then: either show business or a university education.

I bought my course books and never shed a tear.

At the University of California at Santa Barbara I majored, of course, in foreign languages. And after meeting a very special young woman from Germany named Dagmar ("Taki") in the summer of 1966 and falling forever in love, I immediately enrolled in German classes, too. In addition to the daily French and Russian.

When in my senior year I eventually left America for Germany on a one-year university exchange program, Taki joined TWA as an international stewardess so as to be able to visit me regularly abroad. At TWA's Hostess Training College, one of the things she learned was quickly to seek out a safe spot for any sudden difficulty that might arise during takeoffs and landings. The lesson wasn't forgotten. On one of the very first flights of her six-year flying career, she managed to get my own university charter flight to Germany and, at Boston's Logan International Airport, quickly sought out the safest-looking spot for an unexpectedly quick takeoff: her own fiancé's lap!

We married six months later, in January 1969. It was a proper *Studentenhochzeit* (student wedding) in the romantic old university town of Heidelberg, where I was studying languages. This occurred at the height of Germany's student protest movement, an exciting if confusing time of loud debate and louder demonstrations, of water cannons and painted banners ... and sweet love on wintry honeymoon nights in gingerbread-and-lattice-work Rothenburg ob der Tauber, Germany's famous medieval town.

Back in the States by mid-summer, I commenced postgraduate school at UCLA while Taki flew out of Los Angeles International Airport. A Master's degree in German followed within the year. While we toured the world every three months on free airline passes, I taught German classes at UCLA, crammed for my impending Ph.D. exams, and then began preparing my doctoral dissertation.

Finally, in 1973, I was awarded a Ph.D. in Philology and Linguistics from UCLA.

During this intensely rich and active period of study and travel, I had acquired a working knowledge of some 15 additional tongues, old and new. Unbeknownst to me at the time, I was soon to need every one of them.

When a post-doctoral fellowship was generously offered to me by the University Grants Committee of New Zealand, Taki and I felt we couldn't refuse the rare honor. And so, in the summer of 1975, down we flew into the Antipodean winter, to Christchurch on New Zealand's South Island, where for the next five years I was busy teaching, researching, and writing historical books while Taki assumed the responsibilities of Head Secretary at Christchurch's venerable Canterbury Public Library.

After several years there I proudly took out New Zealand citizenship (but kept my American citizenship), so certain was I that I had at last found my Shangri-la. New Zealand is a wondrous pearl of a country. It boasts a clean, healthy, robust society, with a resourceful and self-confident people—mostly of British and Māori descent—and a bountiful, relatively uncontaminated natural environment. It's our planet's last refuge.

It was at this time, in 1978, that I read an engrossing article in the *National Geographic* by Joseph Judge—the same senior journalist who with his wife Phyllis would meet Taki and me at Dulles International Airport six years later—about the Minoans and Mycenaeans of ancient Greece. The article reproduced a life-size color photograph of the Phaistos Disk. This at once recalled my children's book, *The Wonderful World of Archaeology*. A caption accompanied the photograph:

> *Impressed with 241 pictogram seals, this 3600-year-old clay disk holds the earliest known example of printing. Covering both sides, 61 "words"—separated by lines and arranged in spiral form—perhaps express a hymn to a divinity.*

My eyes lingered on the haunting artifact for the longest time, I recall.

That same article eventually inspired Taki and me to fly down to Crete for a study tour two years after we had moved to Europe in 1980. Our years in New Zealand had shown us that it was necessary to be in Europe for a few years in order to profit from better access to research materials that simply weren't available in the South Pacific. I had books to write, and these particular works could only see the light of day under the European sun. So we moved to Nuremberg, Germany, the medieval walled city of Hans Sachs and Albrecht Dürer. This ultimately made possible our second trip to Greece and our first-ever visit to Crete.

And so it was that in 1982 I was finally standing in front of the original Phaistos Disk itself, cool and enigmatic inside its special glass case there in Crete's stiflingly hot and crowded Heraklion Museum....

The Minoans of the second millennium B.C.—the ancient world's most famous seafaring folk who ruled the Mediterranean's "wine-dark sea" from North Africa in the south to Troy in the north, and from Ugarit in the east to perhaps as far as Sicily in the west—are celebrated in scholarship not only as the founders of the Western world's first high civilization.... but also as ancient Europe's greatest mystery.

Until relatively recently, their very existence was little more than myth.

In the last days of the nineteenth century, the Englishman Sir Arthur Evans bought a "rather messy little hill" just three miles southeast of Crete's present-day capital of Heraklion on the island's central north coast. On March 23, 1900, Sir Arthur's host of Cretan laborers began digging. And on that same day they discovered what the famous British archaeologist would later call the "Palace of Minos." For Evans and his laborers had awakened from its millennia-long slumber Knossos ... Europe's first capital city.

In the almost four decades that followed, Sir Arthur directed and privately financed, out of his own personal fortune, the archaeological excavations at Knossos. His work and that of an army of subsequent archaeologists from many nations—at a score of island sites—have since revealed the remains of a remarkably advanced civilization, hitherto wholly unknown, that here on Crete had raised magnificent palace-shrine complexes as early as 2000 B.C. while fostering extensive trade with ancient Egypt and the Levant.

Knossos and other Minoan centers boasted sophisticated indoor lead-pipe plumbing and riotous frescoes and red-columned loggias and jetting fountains and vast "bull-springing" courtyards for the Minoan ritual sport of vaulting over a charging bull's back. The Minoans' famed "hundred cities" of myth maintained networks of paved highways, and there were countless ports redolent of tar and cedar and oakum for the vast Minoan fleet, sprawling vineyard villas and sheep farms, and hundreds of cult caves and peak sanctuaries exalting the sacred. And everywhere, it seems, there loomed the ubiquitous double-axe and double-horns—fashioned of gold or bronze or stone or clay—that were the enduring female-male symbols of a proud and bold people who lived as long before the Roman Empire as the Romans lived before us.

And who still remain unidentified today.

No one truly knows what race of people these marvelous Minoans of ancient Crete belonged to. No one knows what language they spoke. What they called themselves. Where they came from. What really prompted them, about the middle of the second millennium B.C., gradually to yield their sovereignty—over many years and apparently in non-violent fashion—to the northern mainlanders, the Mycenaean Greeks.

As Europe's greatest mystery, the Minoans are the historian's greatest challenge.

All that we know of these Minoans—a name that Sir Arthur Evans himself coined after Minos, the legendary ruler of Knossos—is what has percolated down through the millennia in lachrymal myth, more poetic fancy than historical fact. And what we have more recently learned through archaeological surgery. From western Khania to Rethymnon, from central Tylissos to Knossos, from eastern Mallia to Gournia, and from southern Phaistos to Zakros, the only voice we have had to tell us anything about these brash pioneers of Europe's frontier days is that of their rare architecture, art, and artifacts.

And that of their even rarer scripts....

"Here in Case 41," I overheard an attractive Cretan tour guide, midnight-haired and scimitar-browed, explaining to her party of British tourists here in the Heraklion Museum—a stroll through whose holdings, a friend once wrote, is like leafing through the first family album of Western man—"we see the famous clay Disk of Phaistos, whose palace ruins on the south coast we'll be visiting tomorrow. The Disk dates from the beginning of the New Palace Period, or about 1600 before Christ. As you can see, both sides of the Disk carry hieroglyphic signs. These were impressed using stamps or sealstones—like those just over there in that showcase to your right—onto the clay while it was still wet. Therefore, what we have here in the Phaistos Disk is in fact the world's first example of printing. A *Minoan* invention."

Oohs and aahs.

"The two inscriptions on either side of the Disk proceed spirally inward, from the outer edge to the center. The 'words' are formed by groupings of symbols that are separated by vertical lines. In all, there are 45 separate symbols represented on the Disk, many repeating themselves often. Each symbol most likely reproduces an individual open syllable of speech—*ko, no, so,* and so forth. The symbols, also called pictograms, include animal and human figures, tools, weapons, flowers and plants, and various other objects of everyday Minoan life."

"Is the Disk from here, from Crete?"

"There is no doubt that the script and the unknown language of the Phaistos Disk," the latter-day Helen replied with a grin, quoting, I noticed, the official Museum Guide, "were also the script and language of the Minoans of this period. This has been proved by the later discovery, at Arkalokhori, also here on Crete, of an inscribed axe bearing similar pictograms, and by the discovery of a clay bar from Mallia, too, on Crete's north coast, with a similar script."

"What does the Phaistos Disk say?"

"No one knows. It's the greatest mystery of the Heraklion Museum. Whoever reads it will have solved the riddle of the Minoan people. Anyone keen to try?" A bevy of chuckles. "And now, everyone, over here in Case 40 you can also see from Phaistos a rather lovely collection of intricately inscribed...."

The Britons shuffled to one side.

Whereupon I could finally ease myself closer to get a better look at the Phaistos Disk.

It was a nape-chilling object, hand-sized and muddy brown. I felt awe. I quietly took a photo of it. Then I moved on, turning round once, then twice, to steal another glance.

Later, I felt myself drawn back again, just to stand there in front of it in silent veneration, like a Cretan villager before a beloved icon. (Indeed, to me the artifact will always be imbued with something akin to holiness.) Only with the greatest reluctance did I finally tear myself away, again swept along by the press of tourists in the oppressively hot and malodorous hall.

The next day, over at the whitewashed, mountain-hugging hamlet of Kritsá in the east, on a whim I bought an inexpensive replica of the Phaistos Disk.

"What are we going to do with that?" asked Taki.

"Read it."

We both laughed.

CHAPTER 2
LOGOS

It's the third day of July 1908, and over in London the international athletes are already arriving for the Fourth Olympic Games, which are to commence in just ten days. It will be a British triumph. Only three days ago, in Switzerland, one female and three male balloonists successfully traversed the Alps for the first time, having attained a head-spinning altitude of almost 6000 meters. The great Russian composer Rimsky-Korsakov died a week and a half ago; three days later, former U.S. President Grover Cleveland passed away. And this very week the American Wilbur Wright is flaunting before astounded crowds in Europe his new improved "flying machine."

Yet here on isolated Crete, 34-year-old Italian archaeologist Luigi Pernier has heard nothing of this. Small, stout Pernier and his two younger landsmen Minto and Aurigemma—in dark khaki with stiff collars, black ties, and high leather boots, sporting handlebar moustaches—enjoy precious little contact with the outside world. And they have something else on their minds at the moment. Huddled over their outdoor work table in the purple gloaming of a Mediterranean sunset, they are excitedly exchanging smiles about an extraordinary artifact they've just pried out of the earth here at the Minoan ruins of the Phaistos palace-shrine on the island's remote south coast.

It had happened in the early evening. Work had almost been halted for the day. As usual, the sun had seared hearth-hot until sweat was purling down cracked, red cheeks. Double-horned Mt. Ida in the north was still dancing in the convection currents high over the abundant Messara Plain. Now "Apollo's chariot"—the sun—resembled a squished orange as it descended onto the off-shore isles of Nisi Paximadia in the west, causing the Libyan Sea to "sparkle like burnished bronze," as Homer would have sung.

It's hotter here at Phaistos than anywhere else on Crete. Pernier's Italian colleague, old Halbherr, had already discovered that when first excavating the ruins of Phaistos's majestic palace-shrine eight years earlier. (That was the same year that Sir Arthur Evans had first set his spade to Knossos just over the mountains on Crete's much cooler north coast.) And Pernier can never get used to it. It's an insidious heat. A nose-bleeding and lip-cracking heat that has one grabbing for the canteen far too often.

But for once the canteen lies forgotten.

A Cretan workman had reported finding something *"poly thavmasios!"* ("most wondrous!") in Building 40/101 just northeast of Phaistos's Great Central Court, only a few strides from the so-called "Queen's Megaron," or royal hall. Hurriedly donning their white pith helmets, Pernier and his assistants had left the command tent to investigate.

And there it had lain. A sort of earthen-brown clay disk. With curious stamped figures on its dusty convex face.

After recording the object's exact position in his work log, Pernier carefully whisk-brushed away the last remnants of earth. Then, with the tip of his knife, ever so cautiously he eased the relic from its silent grave.

"Fantastico," he muttered. His companions watched in silent awe.

Never in his career had Pernier seen anything like it. And never again would he experience such a moment.

Other objects were found in the vicinity. A clay accounting tablet in the script Sir Arthur Evans was calling Linear A. Ceramic dating to Late Middle Minoan 3b, or about 1600–1580 B.C. Some ashes. And some carbonized bones of the sacred bull.

There had obviously been a horrendous fire....

Every field scientist has a "peak experience." For the Briton Howard Carter, it was the moment he was finally able to unseal Pharaoh Tutankhamun's unplundered tomb in Egypt's Valley of the Kings. For the Kenyans Louis and Mary Leakey, it was brushing away the loose soil about the upper jaw of the fractured skull of their now-legendary *Zinjanthropus boisei (Australopithecus boisei)* in the Olduvai Gorge, Tanzania. And for the American historian-adventurer Hiram Bingham, it was ascending an all but inaccessible mountain range in Peru to behold the Incas' glorious Machu Picchu, that noble city in the clouds.

Luigi Pernier's peak experience was disinterring the stunning Phaistos Disk. Though a long and distinguished career as one of Italy's foremost archaeologists would follow, no subsequent adventure in his life would ever provide the same rare exhilaration of that baking midsummer's evening in 1908 when he lifted the precious relic from the earth and gazed for the first time on that other-worldly spiral of symbols hauntingly calling to him in the Minoan language—a tongue that hadn't been heard in the Mediterranean since the pinnacle of Minoan power and glory 3500 years earlier.

Sharing birthdays with Crete's celebrated "Snake Priestess" statuette, the Phaistos Disk, Pernier realized, doubtless held ancient Europe's greatest riddle. A complete prehistoric text ... "printed" 400 years before Moses led the Children of Israel to the Promised Land!

Clutching it like a mother her child, Pernier brought the relic back to the work table alongside the tent. The next day he carefully cleaned and photographed the treasure. Then he began to pen a detailed description, which would appear the

following year as a 47-page article in the archaeological journal
Ausonia.

The Phaistos Disk was 2.1 cm thick. Its diameter averaged
16 cm, a hand's length, Pernier would write in that article. And
it had been fire-hardened by the conflagration that had devas-
tated the northeast complex of the Phaistos palace-shrine
sometime around 1600 B.C. Both sides of the relic were
imprinted with inward-spiraling pictograms. Side A, facing
upward when found, displayed a "rosette" sign in its center and
31 pictogram groupings, or "fields," separated by vertical lines.
Side B had 30 such fields. In all, the 45 identified signs or pictograms were used 241 times: 122 on Side A and 119 on Side B.

Of immeasurable importance for cultural history, as
Pernier pointed out in the same article, was the fact that the
relic represented the world's earliest known example of "printing"—if by printing one means the use of movable stamps to
produce an unlimited number of texts. It was also conceivable,
Pernier reasoned further, that the ancient Minoans had
employed this same process not only with soft clay, as here for
the Phaistos Disk, but also with dyes and cuttlefish ink on
papyrus and fabrics and other perishable materials. In this way,
entire libraries might easily have been printed on Minoan
Crete. Prehistoric libraries. Printed by prehistoric Europeans.

Understandably, Pernier was eager to learn the Phaistos
Disk's message. So he proceeded to "identify" each pictogram
on the Disk, believing that the inscription—which the fields of
signs had to constitute—was made up at least in part of phonetic (sound) characters that were being used with a syllabic
value (*ko, no, so* for "Knossos," for example). Pernier thought
he could detect in the pictograms a crested warrior, a shield, a
tree, a walking man, a cat's head, a bee, a tunny (fish), an
oxhide, a priestess, a flying bird, and so forth.

However, because the origin and therefore the language of
the Minoan people were unknown, Pernier had no point of reference with which to continue his investigation.

And that was the end of Pernier's modest decipherment
attempt.

Of course Sir Arthur Evans, whose host of Cretan laborers had been digging on Evans's privately owned Knossos site for the preceding eight years, soon learned of the find and hastened to study Pernier's remarkable artifact. Evans immediately included his own observations on the Disk among the galley sheets to his tome *Scripta Minoa I*, which was to appear the following year in Oxford, England (Figure 2.1).

Sir Arthur disagreed with the Italian Pernier on many points. How can one be sure that the Phaistos Disk is of Minoan provenance? he testily countered. It could just as well be an Anatolian import, from the area that encompasses modern-day

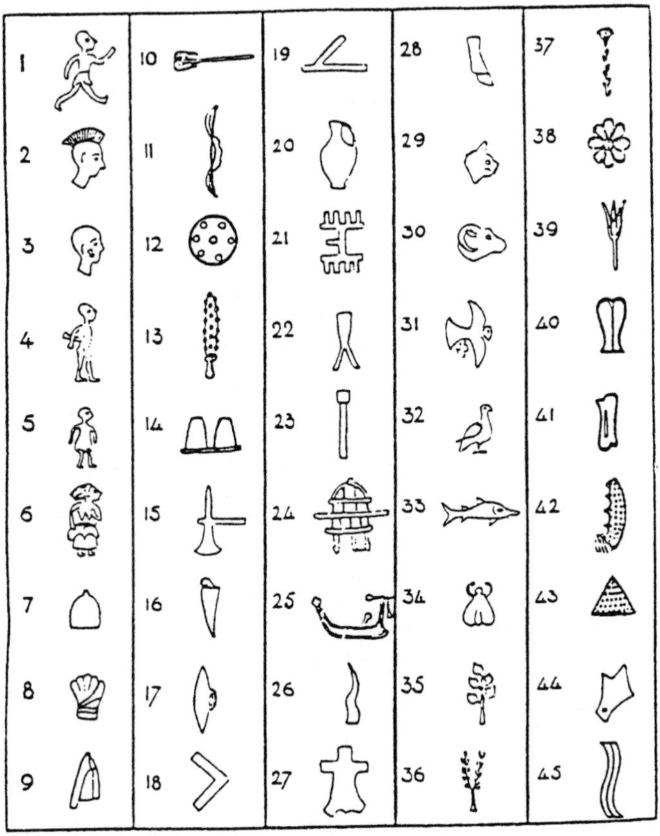

FIGURE 2.1
The 45 pictograms of the Phaistos Disk.
(From A. Evans, *Scripta Minoa I*, Oxford, 1909)

Turkey. In his published report, Evans appeared to be depreciating the importance of his rival's unparalleled discovery.

At the same time, Sir Arthur did agree with Pernier that "The general character of the hieroglyphic script [of the Phaistos Disk] presents, in any case, a close parallel with the Minoan and a certain proportion of the signs are identical."

A contradiction? Perhaps.

Sir Arthur concurred, too, that many of the signs possessed a phonetic (sound) rather than ideographic (pictorial) quality. The pictograms of the Phaistos Disk were to be *spoken*, in other words. They weren't just symbolizing the idea of a thing or action.

Evans also attempted to "identify" most of the pictograms, just as Pernier had done.

But this led to a similar dead end.

For there was still no point of reference. The people who produced the relic were unknown, as was their language. Hence one couldn't justify putting sound to sign.

With nothing to go on, and therefore nothing to lose, a horde of well-meaning dilettanti now descended on the Phaistos Disk with a Minos's own quiverful of feathered fancy. In the succeeding eight decades, florid imagination has midwifed a plethora of so-called "decipherment methods" designed to unravel the mystery of the Phaistos Disk's inscription.

The most presumptuous of these methods has perhaps been to assume a country of origin for the Minoan people and their language and then simply to proclaim a text. It often seemed to be of little significance to these weekend decipherers how much a language can change over mere centuries, to say nothing of millennia. (Just look at the difference between American English and British English, separated for only about 300 years!)

An offshoot of this same method has been to name each glyph (sign) on the Phaistos Disk, again ignoring the realities of word histories and time-depth, and then to piece together the first syllables of each of these names so as to form a coherent text in the arbitrarily appointed tongue. Using this method, one overweening enthusiast proffered the first field or group of glyphs on Side A as ancient Greek:

> Ana, Saō; kōō, thea, Rē
> *Arise, Savior! Listen, Goddess, Rhea!*

Not only is this *not* the sort of archaic Greek one might expect for 1600 B.C., but the naive presumption of declaring a specific derivation and assuming one glyph equal to one word, with no scientific evidence for either speculation, invalidates any arbitrary result that may emerge.

A particularly rampant distemper of this ilk in regard to deciphering the Phaistos Disk has been the "ideographic" approach—that is, seeing each glyph as a symbolic picture and interpreting each in an eloquent series of statements. By ignoring Pernier's and Evans's mature observation that the ancient text is probably written both phonetically (that is, reproducing sounds, not images) and syllabically (reproducing in-di-vi-du-al syllables), the self-styled glyphbreakers enriched posterity with such immortal renderings of the Phaistos Disk as

> ... the lord walking on wings the breathless path, the
> star-smiter, the foaming gulf of waters, dogfish smiter
> on the creeping flower; the lord, smiter of the horse-
> hide ...

One doesn't have to be an expert in ancient Aegean epigraphy to recognize here that something has gone horribly amiss. All the same, it's a decipherment method that still claims its annual victims, much to the chagrin of serious scholars who in such circumstances more often than not find themselves battling a nine-headed Hydra.

It can hardly come as a surprise, then, to learn that in such ways the language of the Phaistos Disk has been "identified" as Northwest Semitic, Hittite, Egyptian, Greek, Luvian, Basque, and many other tongues. Its text has also been "translated" as a contract listing witnesses, a treaty, a liturgical calendar, the itinerary of a pilgrimage, an astronomical text, a sort of prehistoric passport, a service register of naval officers, an amulette written in "hieroglyphic cryptography," a musical score, a religious hymn (the most common interpretation), and so on *ad absurdum.*

Hundreds of articles and books have been published on Crete's famous Phaistos Disk, most offering similar extravagant interpretations.

For there has been no point of reference.

Until now. . . .

"In the beginning was the *logos,*" says the Gospel according to John. In Old Greek, *logos* meant "account, ratio, reason, argument, discourse, saying." (Only rarely did it signify "word.") And the historical *logos* suggests that the tribe called the Hellenes—that is, the people we know better under their "prehistoric" (according to Aristotle) name "Greeks"—first appeared on the scene as early as 2200 B.C.

Or so modern archaeology tells us. It records the sudden incursion, into the geographical area roughly described by today's Hellenic Republic (Greece), of a new and bellicose people who used their own special kind of pottery and rode a small, shaggy-haired breed of horse.

What tongue were these first Hellenes speaking? Certainly not Greek. Neither Zorbas's Cretan Greek nor even Homer's ancient Ionian Greek. On their arrival, and before their dispersion, the Hellenes were doubtless speaking a common dialect of a Proto Indo-European tongue.

This Indo-European is the world's most widely dispersed family of languages. For hundreds of years Indo-European languages were spoken from Iceland to northern India. Now, with the more "recent" migrations of the sixteenth to nineteenth centuries, Indo-European spans the Americas and South Africa and even Australia, New Zealand, and many smaller Pacific islands as well. Indo-European is our own language family. English is Indo-European.

How do we know that Indo-European ever existed as an autonomous language (or grouping of similar languages) so long before cassette recorders or books or even the written word itself? Well, a good deal of this hypothesized ancient language can be linguistically "reconstructed" by comparing all of Indo-European's daughter languages.

For example, we would be able to reconstruct a good deal of the Latin language even if none of the Latin-speaking Romans' texts had survived. This we could do simply by comparing the various daughter languages of Latin that are now called French, Spanish, Italian, Portuguese, Rumanian, and Rhaeto-Romanic (Switzerland) and finding their common elements—the things they share. Latin had all of these features; each daughter language retains some of them. It's sort of like piecing together a jigsaw puzzle so as to reconstruct a never-before-viewed picture ... but using sounds and grammar rules instead of cardboard.

Now when this splinter tribe of Proto Indo-Europeans arrived in the New Land to the south—later to be called Hellas or Greece—they encountered an indigenous population, as all migrants do. Thucydides, Europe's first reliable historian, speaks of a pre-Greek Carian presence in the Aegean. These were an enigmatic folk who later in historical times occupied southwestern Anatolia (now Turkey). Their language and origins are still unclear. Other early writers tell of the insular Pelasgians.

But even on the Greek mainland itself, we know from ancient place names that are clearly not Greek—*Athānai* (Athens), *Korinthos* (Corinth), *Mukānai* (Mycenae), and many more—that people speaking a language entirely different from that of the invading Proto Indo-Europeans were already living here at the time. Their place names were then simply taken over by the invaders. (In exactly the same way, the Anglo-Saxon Americans simply took over such non-English place or personal or tribal names as Chicago, Seattle, Honolulu, and, to complicate matters further, Los Angeles—a name borrowed from earlier Spanish invaders.)

These same indigenous folk of Hellas were apparently living on Crete, too. This is evidenced by the island's non-Greek place names *Knōsos* and *Amnisos* and *Tulisos* and some two hundred others. Crete had been known to the ancient Egyptians as *Keftiu*. The Hebrews of the Old Testament called it *Caphtor*. And the Mesopotamians of Mari referred to Crete as *Kaptara*. Crete's ancient indigenous population—the conjectured "Caphtori"—is even more obscure than the Carians of the more northern islands.

The fact that the Hebrews later called the Caphtorim the Kuretim (as is supposed) suggests a possible invasion into Crete of another ethnic group in prehistoric times.

What happened in Hellas once the Proto Indo-European pony riders faced and eventually subjugated this native population, both on the mainland and in the islands of the Aegean? Exactly the same thing that happened when the German tribes migrated south and southwest into Germania and, pointing at the great river, asked the natives what its name was.

"River," replied the Celts. Or, in their language, *Rhine*.

Our Aegean invaders experienced a similar irony ... only 2500 years earlier.

The Hellenes borrowed the names of many things that were unfamiliar to them, features and objects and inventions that they hadn't known in the plains of central Asia (if this is truly where they came from). Trees and plants and vegetables. Medicines. Animals and fishes. New types of pottery. Topographical designations such as "brae" and "crag" and "burg." Concepts of architecture and construction engineering, like *megaron* (a type of small hall), *thalamos* (an inner room), *plinthos* (a brick or tile). Even the bathtub (*asaminthos*) and the domed beehive (*simblos*). And, of course, the names of those countless local deities venerated in the New Land.

Daily (mis)pronouncing these strange new words, the Hellenes gradually modified their Proto Indo-European dialect until it became an autonomous Proto-Greek. This is just what happened with English, too. The English language gemmated on English soil and not elsewhere as a result of Germanic invaders adopting a plethora of Scandinavian, French, Latin, and Celtic words and creating new grammatical rules until the original tongue became unrecognizable. Fifteen hundred years later, the cousin of English that evolved on the continent is even taught in schools as a foreign language: German.

Such linguistic processes can tell us a lot about early Hellas.

The names of two trees provide a marvelous example. The cypress and the turpentine tree can't grow in areas subject to hard frost, so we know that the Hellenes couldn't have brought them or their names with them from the north. The cypress— Greek *kyparissos* and *kyparittos*—reveals an *ss/tt* split in the later Greek dialects. This is found in many other words, too, including those for "sea": *thalassa* and *thalatta*. Such a linguistic split proves that the Hellenes arrived as a single people from an area that lacked such things as cypresses and a sea.

And it proves that only after their arrival did the Hellenes' once-common tongue, a dialect of Proto Indo-European, divide into the many historical dialects of ancient Greek as the invaders dispersed within the geographical boundaries of Hellas—with its wealth of new experiences and objects and arts and new words for all of these.

"In the beginning was the *logos*...."

And for every advanced society there must also be the *written word*. How else is one to account for the hundredweight sack of wheat to Melos and talents of bronze from Cyprus and the wine and gold-work to Mycenae and Pylos and the longships full of priceless medicines and purple cloth and carved ivories and salted mutton destined for the rich Egyptian market at Avaris? How else is a Minos to know what reserves he possesses? How else are the taxmen to calculate what each of the hundred towns of Crete owes the Labyrinth at Knossos?

And so, out of economic necessity, a script is born.

Scholarship acknowledges three major and four minor scripts in the ancient Aegean and neighboring eastern Mediterranean. Linear A appears from the eighteenth to the fifteenth century B.C. on pottery fragments, clay seals and tablets, and other objects of bronze, gold, silver, and stone on Crete and nearby islands. Linear B, dating from 1450 to about 1200 B.C., is found overwhelmingly on seals and tablets on the Greek mainland and also at Knossos on Crete. And the Linear C script, up to a thousand years later, was used on the island of Cyprus in the east.

The four minor scripts? These are the Minoan hieroglyphic script that was used from about 1900 to 1625 B.C.; the Eteo-Cretan script and its probable predecessor Cyprian-Minoan; and the related Cretan pictographic script that is evidenced by the Phaistos Disk, the Arkalokhori bronze axe, and the Mallia clay bar—all to be dated around 1600 B.C., or contemporaneous with Crete's Linear A script.

The first of these to be deciphered, back in the 1870s, was the Linear C script of Cyprus (Figure 2.2). The Cypriots used this script with intentional conservatism—like the E pluribus unum on an American dollar bill—to adorn coins and monuments from the seventh to the second century B.C.

The combined efforts of treasure hunter Hamilton Lang, British consul at Larnaka, Cyprus; George Smith, cuneiform expert at the British Museum, London; and especially the Hellenic expert Moritz Schmidt of Germany showed Linear C to comprise an open syllabic script reproducing the Cyprian Greek language. The decipherment of Linear C was first made possible by locating, on coins from different towns, the word "king" each time followed by a second group of Linear C signs. Lang reasoned with ordered common sense that this second group had to give the actual name of each respective king. And he was right.

The origin of the Cyprian script, according to the first experts, lay in a mixture of known Phoenician and Lykian and Egyptian signs. Or it came directly from the Hittite hieroglyphs, as many assumed once the existence of the latter was known. However, when Sir Arthur Evans disinterred the Bronze Age scripts of Crete, all debate promptly ceased. It was

	a	e	i	o	u
	a	*e*	*i*	*o*	*u*
k	*ka*	*ke*	*ki*	*ko*	*ku*
t	*ta*	*te*	*ti*	*to*	*tu*
p	*pa*	*pe*	*pi*	*po*	*pu*
l	*la*	*le*	*li*	*lo*	*lu*
r	*ra*	*re*	*ri*	*ro*	*ru*
m	*ma*	*me*	*mi*	*mo*	*mu*
n	*na*	*ne*	*ni*	*no*	*nu*
j	*ja*	–	–	*jo*	–
w	*wa*	*we*	*wi*	*wo*	–
s	*sa*	*se*	*si*	*so*	*su*
z	*za*	–	–	*zo*	–
x	–	*xe*	–	–	–

FIGURE 2.2
The Linear C or classical Cyprian syllabary.

manifestly clear that on the gods' own isle lay not only Zeus's cradle but that of the Cyprian script too, Linear C.

The Linear C script of Cyprus is now recognized to be the last fruit on that gnarled olive tree of Aegean scripts used by Europe's first citizens.

With this discovery, too, Sir Arthur Evans put out a fire only to start an inferno.

Evans had initially gone to Crete in 1894—after a career as a foreign correspondent for the *Manchester Guardian* in Dubrovnik and as director of the Ashmolean Museum in Oxford, England—to ferret out more traces of what he was convinced had to be an autonomous, prehistoric Aegean script. He reasoned that the high level of civilization revealed by Heinrich Schliemann's recent findings at Mycenae, Orchomenos, and Tiryns on the Greek mainland could not be reconciled with the lack of any detectable system of writing in the area. Sir Arthur was positive that this evidence was to be found in the region's hieroglyphic-like seal stones; his collection at Oxford included several. It was obviously a case of "man before writing," as he put it, a confirmed Darwinist. The most primitive stage in the evolutionary growth of writing advanced first into "proper" hieroglyphics, he believed, such as that of the Egyptians. Then it developed into "sophisticated" alphabetic writing, such as that of the Phoenicians and classical Greeks.

Sir Arthur Evans's subsequent findings in this regard indulged this misconception, and his many later pontifications on the subject dominated Minoan-Mycenaean scholarship, for better or worse, for the next fifty years.

Yet it was also Sir Arthur Evans who at Knossos had unearthed and named the two different types of Cretan "linear" tablets, never seeing in them anything but different evolutionary "stages" of the same language. (We now know that one is Minoan and the other is Mycenaean Greek.) He called them linear because their glyphs were line-bound and non-pictographic. And he was convinced they were stages because they obviously displayed more developed forms representing two systems of writing that were independent of that of the pictogram seals used to mark goods on ancient Crete, many examples of which graced Evans's Oxford and Knossos collections. Indeed, Sir Arthur soon came to believe that Crete's two linear scripts were even more developed than Mesopotamia's cuneiform script or glorious Egypt's hieroglyphs.

And so Evans arrived at a formal classification of the three Cretan scripts: hieroglyphic or conventionalized pictographic, the linear script of Class A (that is, Linear A), and the linear script of Class B (Linear B). It was an historic achievement.

The classification still obtains today.

Naturally the Grand Old Man of Cretan archaeology wished to tap the maximum from what he had brewed. As early as 1900, in his first year of excavations at Knossos, Evans offered an astute observation. He persuaded himself that the 70 most common glyphs of the "advanced linear script" B had to be syllabic. By this he meant that its underlying language was written with an *in-di-vi-du-al* glyph for each spoken syllable (exactly what he was to say eight years later about the Phaistos Disk). When he was in his eighties, in the fourth volume of his wonderful *Palace of Minos* (1935), Evans even elaborated on his colleague Cowley's 1927 suggestion....

Cowley had said that the Cyprian Linear C glyphs *ta, to, lo, pa, u*, and *se*—being identical to the earlier Linear B glyphs (Figure 2.3)—probably shared the latter's sound values, regardless of whether they shared the same underlying language. Cowley had also pointed out that in a Linear B list of what appeared to be men's names, using these Cyprian correspondences yields a conspicuous number of these names that seemingly ended in *-o*. This hinted at an inflecting language, one in which the endings of words embody aspects of the language's grammar....

Sir Arthur Evans accepted this evidence. He also endorsed Cowley's additional observations. The Old Man even pointed out himself two further glyphs that appeared to alternate on the end of otherwise identical sign groups. Of this Sir Arthur wrote, "We have here, surely, good evidence of declension." (Declension is the marking of different cases of nouns, pronouns, and adjectives.)

Evans was on the right track. Had he pursued this line of brilliant reasoning, then he himself might very well have deciphered the Linear B script in the 1930s and identified the early Greek dialect it concealed.

But Sir Arthur Evans didn't pursue it. Despite his obvious astuteness, he could never exorcise the arbitrary conviction that the *form* of each glyph also had to be a bearer of meaning. For example, in the glyph that was later found simply to represent

Cyprian	Phonetic Value	Linear B
⊢	*ta*	⊢
+	*lo*	+
ⲧ	*to*	ⲧ
⊔	*se*	⊔
‡	*pa*	‡
⊤	*na*	⊼
⋀	*ti*	⋀

FIGURE 2.3

Comparison of Cyprian Greek Linear C with Mycenaean Linear B.

the sound *a*, Sir Arthur envisaged a double-axe that had to carry a religious connotation wherever it appeared. In the *o* he saw a throne that naturally bestowed a regal significance. And so forth.

Such fundamentalism was of course wholly incompatible with the more modern phonetic-syllabic explanation that held the correct solution. Unable to reconcile the two, Evans rigidly fixed his own epigraphic mooring lines.

And never sailed further.

Yet Sir Arthur Evans *had* discovered the scripts. And classified them. And, together with Cowley, pointed the way toward their successful decipherment. For 40 years Evans hoarded his private Linear A and Linear B tablets, refusing others permission to reproduce or even study them. Perhaps this was not out of selfishness or arrogance, as many have alleged. Perhaps Evans cherished a profound belief that one had to be in possession of *all* the evidence in order to address the Minoan culture and scripts "properly." And who commanded that totality better than the tablets' owner, Sir Arthur himself?

Seven weeks after Hitler's Wehrmacht troops parachuted onto Crete and appropriated Sir Arthur Evans's famous villa "Ariadne" at Knossos as the island's German Command Headquarters, the Grand Old Man of Cretan archaeology died, on July 11, 1941, at his peaceful Oxford retreat at the age of 90.

Eleven years later Linear B, freed at last, was successfully deciphered.

It was an American woman, Dr. Alice Kober, who unsealed the Cretan scripts' tomb for us—though she herself would not live to step inside. Hers was a decipherment method no less phenomenal than it was disarmingly ingenious.

Until then, almost every historical decipherment had proceeded from the identification, in the investigated script, of proper names. This was usually followed by the trial-and-error assigning of sound values for each of the script's glyphs. However, Kober's unique contribution to decipherment lay in first determining the *relationships* among the phonetic values of the glyphs ... on an abstract level.

Both Evans and Cowley had supposed that the language underlying Linear B was "inflectional." That is, the individual words of the language had to be modified in some way in order to show grammatical relationships. This is what Alice Kober proved in a series of penetrating essays published between 1943 and 1950, when she died of cancer at the age of 43.

Kober succeeded by addressing the "unknown script in an unknown language" *structurally*. Kober argued that given a sufficient amount of text in a language that inflects (showing grammar changes), as this Linear B appeared to be doing, a person can always find isolated linguistic units recurring in fixed positions as prefixes (*in*-vincible) or suffixes (invinc-*ible*) or even infixes (invi-*n*-cible, these words all being derived from the Latin root *vic*-). Such statistical periodicity or frequency can tell us what language we are dealing with. Or it can suggest phonetic values for these isolated units, enabling us to reconstruct the language if we can't identify it.

At least theoretically, Kober asserted, a decipherment of Linear B—the script that Kober first autopsied because its stock of (eventually) 57,000 glyphs offered a far more promising chance of success than Linear A's paltry 7000—should then be possible.

Alice Kober proceeded to identify three separate case endings in Linear B. A case ending is something that appears at the end of a word and shows this word's grammatical relationship to other words in a sentence; such as using *whom* instead of *who* and *Bob's* instead of *Bob*. A case ending shows how a word is temporarily functioning in a given statement. Kober reasoned that if the Linear B script consisted at least in part of open syllables like the Cyprian Linear C, as Evans and Cowley had suggested, then one could also say of four of the glyphs' phonetic values, by virtue of their changing endings in the texts, that two had to shoulder the same consonant (*p*- or *t*- or *k*- or *m*- and so forth) whereas two had to be yoked to the same vowel (-*a*, -*e*, -*i*, -*o*, or -*u*).

However, further progress in this promising vein was prevented by lack of textual material. No one had published the Linear B tablets in their entirety. No one had been allowed to.

Because of Sir Arthur.

Seeing how Alice Kober—by piecing together small bits of Evans's early publications like a patchwork quilt—was able to achieve such penetrating insights about the grammar of the language underlying the Linear B script, one can only bow in admiration. Still, these bits just weren't enough to go on. A complete decipherment of Linear B was obviously impossible.

Whereupon a 28-year-old Londoner astonished the world by accomplishing the "impossible."

By the beginning of 1951, the Briton Michael Ventris—who at 14 had been inspired by Sir Arthur Evans's lecture at London's Burlington House in 1936 and at 18 had published in the *American Journal of Archaeology* an essay on the "Minoan language" (supposedly "related to Etruscan," the teenage Ventris then wrote), an RAF navigator during World War II and now a promising London architect—was drafting his first Linear B "grid."

Syllable charts (see Figure 2.2 for the Cyprian syllable chart), that register vowels (*a, e, i, o,* and *u*) on the horizontal line and consonants (*m, n, p, t,* and so forth) on the vertical line so that the first can intersect with the second, had existed since the scientifically awakened seventeenth century. More recently, the German Moritz Schmidt had doubtless used just such a syllable chart in his successful decipherment of the Cyprian syllabic script, Linear C.

But Ventris's "grid" was something altogether different and innovative (Figure 2.4). It was based on an idea that originated with Alice Kober. Unlike a syllable chart, the grid does not offer respective vowel or consonant values but rather abstracts the vowels' and consonants' apparent interrelations as found in similar or dissimilar positions on the hundreds of Linear B tablets.

"It is risky to guess what the consonants (or vowels) actually are," wrote Ventris in that very first Work Note of January 28, 1951. "But one can predict that when at least half the signs of the syllabary have been securely fixed on the grid, it will need only a small number of inspired pieces of linguistic deduction to solve the whole simultaneous equation."

In the course of the next 18 months, the London architect circulated his Work Notes to the same 12 international scholars (later to three times this number) whom he'd initially queried in 1950 in order to define the state of Linear B scholar-

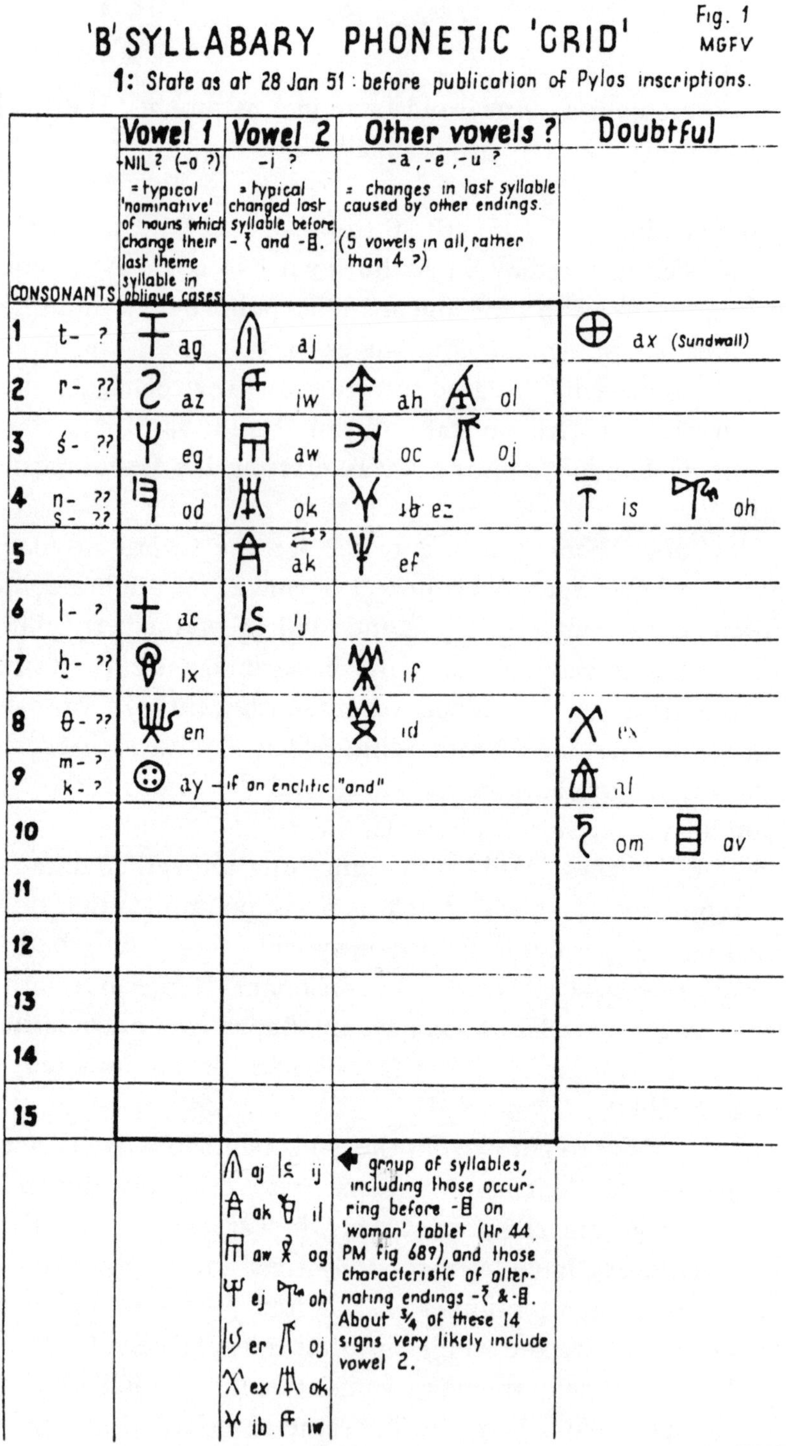

'B' SYLLABARY PHONETIC 'GRID'

Fig. 1
MGFV

1: State as at 28 Jan 51 : before publication of Pylos inscriptions.

CONSONANTS	Vowel 1 +NIL? (-o?) = typical 'nominative' of nouns which change their last theme syllable in oblique cases	Vowel 2 -i? = typical changed last syllable before -ʔ and -目.	Other vowels? -a, -e, -u? = changes in last syllable caused by other endings. (5 vowels in all, rather than 4?)		Doubtful	
1 t- ?	ag	aj			⊕ ax (Sundwall)	
2 r- ??	az	iw	ah	ol		
3 ś- ??	eg	aw	oc	oj		
4 n- ?? s- ??	od	ok	ɪb eʒ		is	oh
5		ak	ef			
6 l- ?	ac	ɪj				
7 ḥ- ??	ix		ɪf			
8 θ- ??	en		ɪd		ex	
9 m- ? k- ?	ay — if an enclitic "and"				al	
10					om	av
11						
12						
13						
14						
15						

aj | ij
ak | ɪl
aw | og
ej | oh
er | oj
ex | ok
ɪb | iw

◀ group of syllables, including those occurring before -目 on 'woman' tablet (Hr 44, PM fig 689), and those characteristic of alternating endings -ʔ & ·目. About ¾ of these 14 signs very likely include vowel 2.

FIGURE 2.4
Michael Ventris's first phonetic "grid,"
included in his Work Note of January 28, 1951.

ship. His abstract grid of vowel and consonant positions proved indispensable in the process of linguistic retrieval. It ultimately allowed or confirmed the assigning of specific phonetic values for each inscrutable Linear B glyph.

How could the English battle so victoriously so soon after the American Alice Kober had had to retreat because she lacked sufficient ammunition?

Well, the English didn't, actually. Not at first, that is. That initial grid was a "dud." Not only had the American archaeologist Carl Blegen's Linear B tablets from his 1939 excavation at Pylos on the southwestern Peloponnese not been available for study. But also Ventris, still assuming that Linear B's underlying language had to be Etruscan—that unidentified tongue of "the first Italians"—had failed to entertain the possibility of alternating differences in gender (masculine, feminine, and neuter) in the word endings. This is what we still (though rarely) find in English with *poet/poetess, aviator/aviatrix, hero/heroine*, and the like, where zero alternates with *-ess, -or* with *-rix*, and so on. Thus Ventris's earliest hazarded vowels lay far from their true values.

However, with dogged perseverence and an almost Jasonian conviction that the linguistic fleece could be fetched despite the daunting odds, Ventris struggled on. And once the Pylos Linear B tablets were published in 1951, Michael Ventris accepted the undeniable evidence in these ancient inscriptions that their underlying language reflected a difference in gender—a difference that was manifest in the final vowels of the tablets, just as Cowley had suggested twenty-four years earlier.

Whereupon other rounds of ammunition began to emerge.

Either Linear B had nearly every word in its language ending in a vowel (which was highly unlikely) or its spelling rules had to be quite different from those of the related Cyprian syllabic script, Ventris concluded. And if Linear B's spelling rules *were* different, given a new set of rules evidenced by what the tablets' glyphs were displaying in their positions and frequency, then the emerging language in which these tablets were written ...

Could only be an extremely early dialect of Greek!

Michael Ventris was bowled over. As odd as this might sound today, Greek certainly wasn't the language that any reputable scholar of the time had been expecting to find in the Linear B tablets of Knossos and the Greek mainland. The Greeks just couldn't have been on Crete in the second millennium B.C. That was far too early. Such a claim loosed an arrow at four centuries of inviolable Greek scholarship . . .

And struck it smack in the heel.

Because the proof was there. Perhaps most persuasive was Ventris's identification of proper names on the Linear B tablets. The location of proper names had played a crucial role in nearly every decipherment in the past, from the Egyptian hieroglyphs to the Persian cuneiforms. . . .

Ventris joined the BBC for an informal chat on the first of July 1952 to mark the long-overdue, posthumous publication of Sir Arthur Evans's *Scripta Minoa II*, the book that finally made available to scholars Evans's personal collection of Linear B tablets. "During the last few weeks," he remarked, "I have come to the conclusion that the Knossos and Pylos tablets must, after all, be written in Greek—a difficult and archaic Greek, seeing that it is five hundred years older than Homer and written in a rather abbreviated form, but Greek neverthe-less."

Ventris had just circulated his now-famous Work Note 20. In it he had demonstrated beyond reasonable doubt that a cer-tain category of words in Linear B on the Knossos tablets from Crete—a category that earlier had been thought to belong to a larger division or clan or territory—corresponded instead almost exactly to those categories listing towns and corpora-tions on the relatively contemporaneous Ugarit tablets from the Syrian coast. Could these Linear B words from Crete also be local place names? Ventris dared to ask.

They could indeed. Ventris studied the pre-Greek names around Knossos—pre-Greek because a Greek presence still couldn't be accepted. And on the Linear B tablets he was able to identify the place names Amnissos and Tylissos and even Knossos itself by using a combination of methods. The *a* he had retrieved from its frequency at the beginning of words. The *ni* had emerged from the consonant series in the abstract grid. With *?-no-so*, it could be logically deduced, given that this register contained names in the first place, that the first syllable was *ko-*, making *ko-no-so* or "Knossos" ... because the grid appeared to confirm Linear B glyph 70's *-o* in the *k-* consonantal column. And so forth.

All these might well be the historical Cretan names, Ventris argued, *if* word-final *-s*, in contrast to the Cyprian Linear C script, was truly ignored by the ancient Cretan scribes.

Subsequent evidence confirmed that word-final *-s* was indeed being ignored in this writing system. It also showed that all syllables ending in *-s*, *-m*, *-n*, *-l*, and *-r* were also ignored if they occurred before a consonant inside a word. In this way, Ventris was able to prove that *pa-i-to* spelled "Phaistos," that *ka-ko* was in fact *khalkos* ("bronze"), that *pe-ma* represented *sperma* ("seed"), and so on.

In addition, Ventris found that the vowels *a* and *e* and *o* and *u* could also stand for the diphthongs *ai* and *ei* and *oi* and *ui*—all of which the later Cyprian Linear C script had written out in full.

Thus Ventris was able to claim that the ancient scribes of Linear B, who were writing up to 1200 years before their Cyprian colleagues, used only one syllable-glyph to represent whatever could be pronounced as one syllable.

A logical conclusion. Especially for so primitive a script.

The glyphbreaking chain reaction had begun, and soon Linear B had exploded forth in its entirety....

In the end, the evidence was conclusive that Linear B indeed constituted an incredibly early dialect of Greek and that the Mycenaean Greeks had been the ones writing the Linear B tablets on Crete as well as on the northern mainland.

It was a discovery of historic magnitude.

Yet who would believe Michael Ventris, the architect? So many amateurs had abused the Greek hypothesis in the past in order to "decipher" the various Cretan scripts that the university experts heard only "Wolf!" in Ventris's BBC announcement. To say that the announcement fell on deaf ears would be an understatement. This might well have been the end of the Michael Ventris story ... and of the solution of Linear B.

Had it not been for John Chadwick. Then a young classicist at Oxford, Chadwick happened to have heard the radio interview and grew curious. He borrowed from Sir Arthur Evans's old friend Sir John Myres at Oxford those mimeographed Work Notes that Ventris had been posting to the experts (at his own expense and hitherto to no avail). Soon Chadwick was persuaded by their clarity of thought and linguistic soundness, and he duly congratulated Ventris in a letter.

He also offered his professional help.

For Ventris it was the miracle he had been waiting for. It had been a sobering experience—to work so hard for so long and accomplish so much, only to find that no one even listened, much less believed. Ventris wrote to Chadwick on July 28, 1952: "Every other day I get so doubtful about the whole thing that I'd almost rather it was someone else's."

He gratefully accepted the extended hand.

So the architect and the philologist combined their talents, and by November of the same year they had completed the scientific account of the decipherment of Linear B: "Evidence for Greek Dialect in the Mycenaean Archives." They experienced the incredible good fortune of having their article appear the very next year in the *Journal of Hellenic Studies*. Phonetic values for 65 Linear B glyphs were offered in that 1953 article (see Figure 2.5). Since then, only six of these values have required alteration; seven new ones have been added.

Whereupon another miracle occurred.

At the beginning of 1953, with "Evidence" yet to appear, the American archaeologist Carl Blegen, excavating again at Pylos,

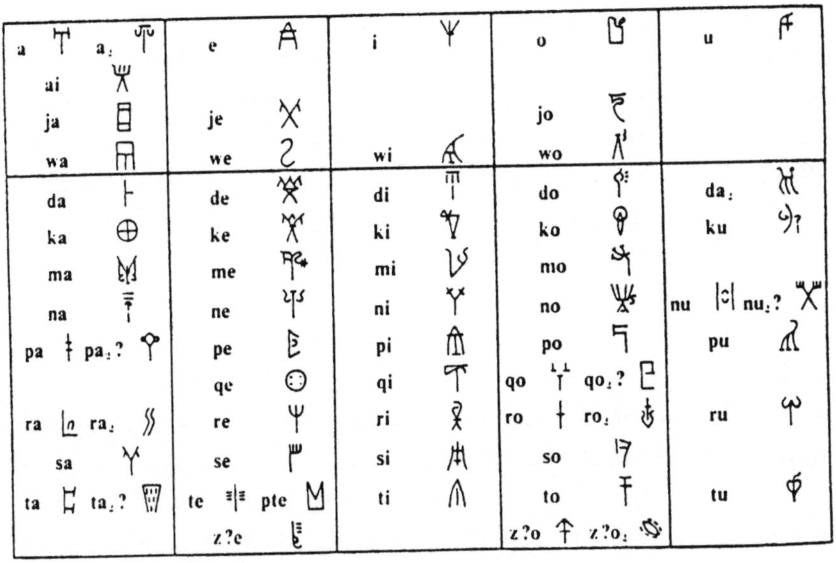

a	⊤	a:		e	Ä	i	Ψ	o	⬚	u	Ƒ
ai	⋎										
ja	🖯			je	✕			jo	⪫		
wa	🞔			we	⌇	wi	🝆	wo	🝊		
da	⊦			de	⛎	di	🝌	do	🝏	da:	🝑
ka	⊕			ke	🝕	ki	🝗	ko	🝙	ku	🝛
ma	🝞			me	🝡	mi	🝣	mo	🝥		
na	⨪			ne	🝨	ni	🝪	no	🝬	nu	🝮	nu:	🝯
pa	⊹	pa:	🝲	pe	🝵	pi	🝷	po	🝹	pu	🝻
				qe	☉	qi	⟙	qo	🝿	qo:	🞁		
ra	🞃	ra:	🞅	re	Ψ	ri	🞈	ro	⊦	ro:	🞊	ru	🞌
sa	⋎			se	🞐	si	🞒	so	🞔		
ta	🞖	ta:?	🞘	te	☰	pte	M	ti	⋀	to	�╪	tu	φ
				z?e	🞞			z?o	⟙	z?o:	🞡		

FIGURE 2.5
The Mycenaean Greek Linear B "Experimental Syllabary"
of Michael Ventris and John Chadwick as first announced
in the Journal of Hellenic Studies 63 (1953).

brought to the world's attention a newly unearthed Linear B tablet that dispelled any remaining doubt about Ventris's decipherment. Applying the deciphered glyph values, Blegen could syllabically sound out with no difficulty the glyphs *ti-ri-po* for "tripod" and *ti-ri-po-de* for "two tripods" and *di-pa* for "cup," as well as a succession of other words. Each was qualified on the tablet with the proper Greek adjectival forms for "-eared." Each was prefixed with the Greek word "without-" or "three-" or "four-." And each was followed by an ideogram depicting the very object with precisely the described number of "ears," or handles!

It was an external archaeological confirmation the like of which the world had never seen.

"All this seems too good to be true," Blegen excitedly wrote to Ventris in May 1953. "Is coincidence excluded?"

For many it wasn't. Though a sprinkling of scholars recognized almost at once what had been achieved here, the vast ocean of experts remained unconvinced. Some of them even waxed antagonistic. Failing to understand the step-by-step process of decipherment, they argued that this "invented" language of Ventris and Chadwick's wasn't even "proper Classical Greek." Which it wasn't, granted. It was Mycenaean Greek, a language that had thrived more than half a millennium before Homer.

Chaucer's English was hardly Hemingway's, one could point out.

Others, particularly the Germans, grumbled that such an ambiguous script allowing so many possible readings—*e-ke* alone yielded as many as 21 plausible Greek words—would make comprehension quite impossible.

Ventris and Chadwick calmly responded that those writing the Linear B tablets daily, as well as those reading them daily in their proper context, would have known precisely what the script meant. Just as L.A., N.Y., and U.S.A. are, in the correct context, readily understandable to any modern citizen of the world, though the abbreviations are, theoretically, replete with ambiguity.

Despite the nay-sayers, support for the decipherment of Linear B grew. Articles were written by others. Congresses were held. More evidence accumulated to support those first tenuous findings. Meanwhile, Ventris and Chadwick collaborated on a massive tome accounting for all of the Linear B tablets then known, which they finished in 1955.

Queen Elizabeth awarded Michael Ventris the O.B.E.—the Order of the British Empire—"for services to Mycenaean palaeography."

Then tragedy struck. Only weeks before *Documents in Mycenaean Greek* was published by Cambridge University Press, Michael Ventris, apparently having fallen asleep at the wheel on his way home south to London after an evening lecture, crashed into a lorry on the Great North Road near Hatfield and was killed instantly.

He was 34.

It was September 6, 1956, just two days before my parents gave me for my ninth birthday *The Wonderful World of Archaeology*, that inspiring book that called Ventris's achievement "the Everest of Greek archaeology."

Michael Ventris's legacy lives on. Within the two years after his tragic death, 432 articles, pamphlets, and books by 152 authors from 23 nations appeared on the subject of Mycenaean Linear B. And forty years later, at the end of the twentieth century, the field of Mycenaean Studies, that hallowed temple of prehistoric Aegean research whose pillars rest firmly on the plinth of Ventris's decipherment, now forms a major branch of classical studies and is found in the curriculum of nearly every major university in the world. Entire journals are devoted to research in Greek Linear B. Thousands of articles and books are now available. One can say without exaggeration that Ventris's singular achievement revolutionized our understanding of the ancient world.

The Greeks wrote the Linear B tablets.

The Aegean of the middle of the second millennium B.C. was Hellenic.

There's a reason why the decipherment of Mycenaean Greek Linear B features here in such detail. It's because this historic achievement ultimately also unlocked the door to the hitherto undeciphered scripts of the ancient Aegean ... including the Phaistos Disk's. However, though the door lay open, access to these other scripts has been difficult, obstructed, and hotly contested at every stage.

Michael Ventris's successful decipherment of the Linear B script initially inspired some scholars immediately to apply his grid approach to the kindred Linear A script of prehistoric Crete. If Ventris's method and results had been correct for Mycenaean Greek Linear B, reasoned these scholars optimistically, one should be able to decipher Minoan Linear A, too. This might then reveal at last who the Minoan people—those living at Knossos and elsewhere on Crete and the nearby isles before the Mycenaean Greek "intrusion"—really were.

Now, Minoan Linear A is *not* the writing on the Phaistos Disk (see Figure 2.6.) It is a different script. Like the Minoan hieroglyphic or pictographic scripts that existed on Crete at the same time, about 1600 B.C., Minoan Linear A reproduces the Minoan language syllabically—that is, each glyph of Linear A would signify *ko, no, so,* and so forth. Unlike the contemporary hieroglyphic or pictographic scripts, however, which in most cases depict an easily identifiable object, Minoan Linear A shares with later Mycenaean Greek Linear B a syllabary of highly simplified glyphs wherein graphic details are reduced to a minimum. In most cases, each glyph is so simplified as to render unrecognizable its original Minoan hieroglyph and/or pictogram.

For example, a Minoan pictogram of the tall, vase-shaped, Aegean hearth 𝘈 might have reproduced the sound *wa*, deriving, as I was later able to determine in my own research, from the first syllable (*was-*) of the Minoan word for "hearth." (In a similar development, our letter *a* in the English alphabet originated over three thousand years ago from the symbol of an ox or *aleph*.) In the Minoan hieroglyphic script and in the simplified scripts of Minoan Linear A and Mycenaean Greek Linear B, however, this identifiable pictogram of the vase-shaped hearth has been contracted to an unrecognizable square or rectangle on four or three stubby legs. Minoan hieroglyphic 𝘔, Minoan Linear A 𝗛, and Mycenaean Linear B 𝗛 all reproduce the same sound *wa*. For this object and sound *wa*, Cyprian Linear C has)(, which more closely resembles the Minoan pictogram from which it originated.

Although Minoan Linear A's simplified syllabary is conspicuously similar to that of the later Mycenaean Greek Linear B, the language underlying the Minoan Linear A script is certainly *not* the Mycenaean Greek language. It is the language of the Minoan people, who evidently were using several different, though closely related, scripts—the Linear A, hieroglyphic, and

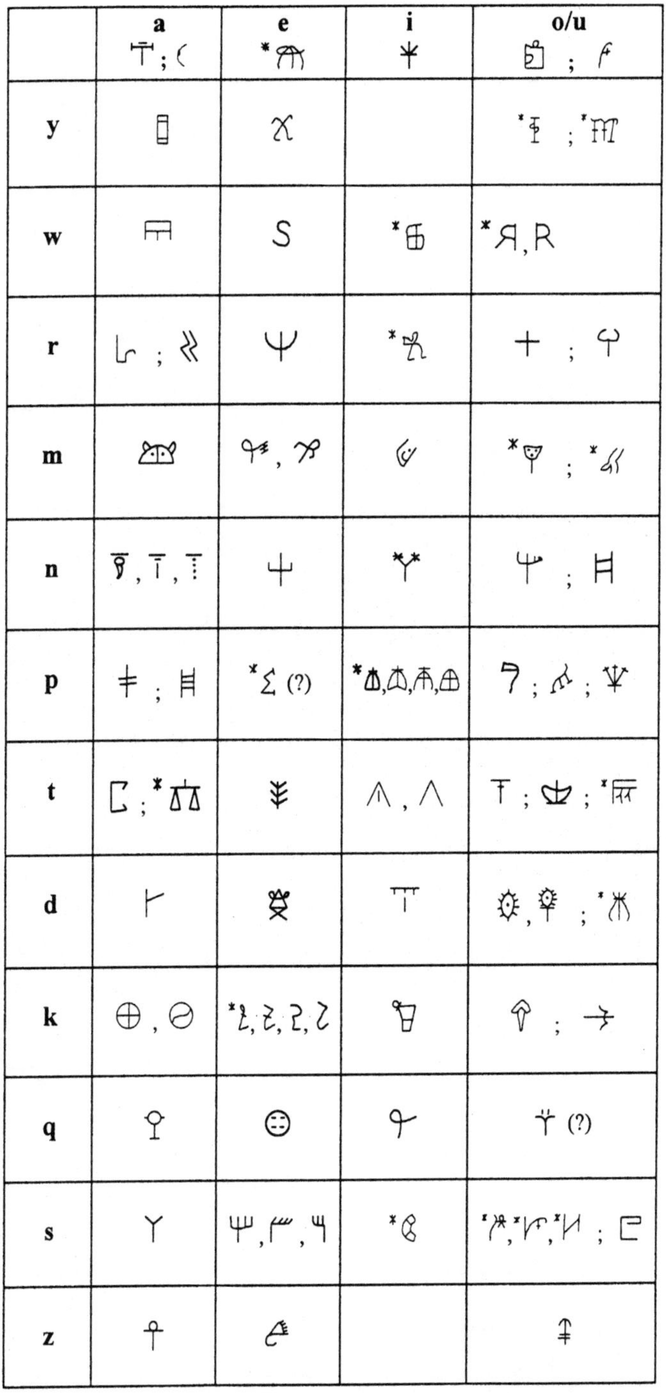

	a	e	i	o/u
y				
w				
r				
m				
n				
p				
t				
d				
k				
q				
s				
z				

FIGURE 2.6

Minoan Crete's Linear A syllabary with the phonetic values
proposed by Prof. Paul Faure of France in 1973.

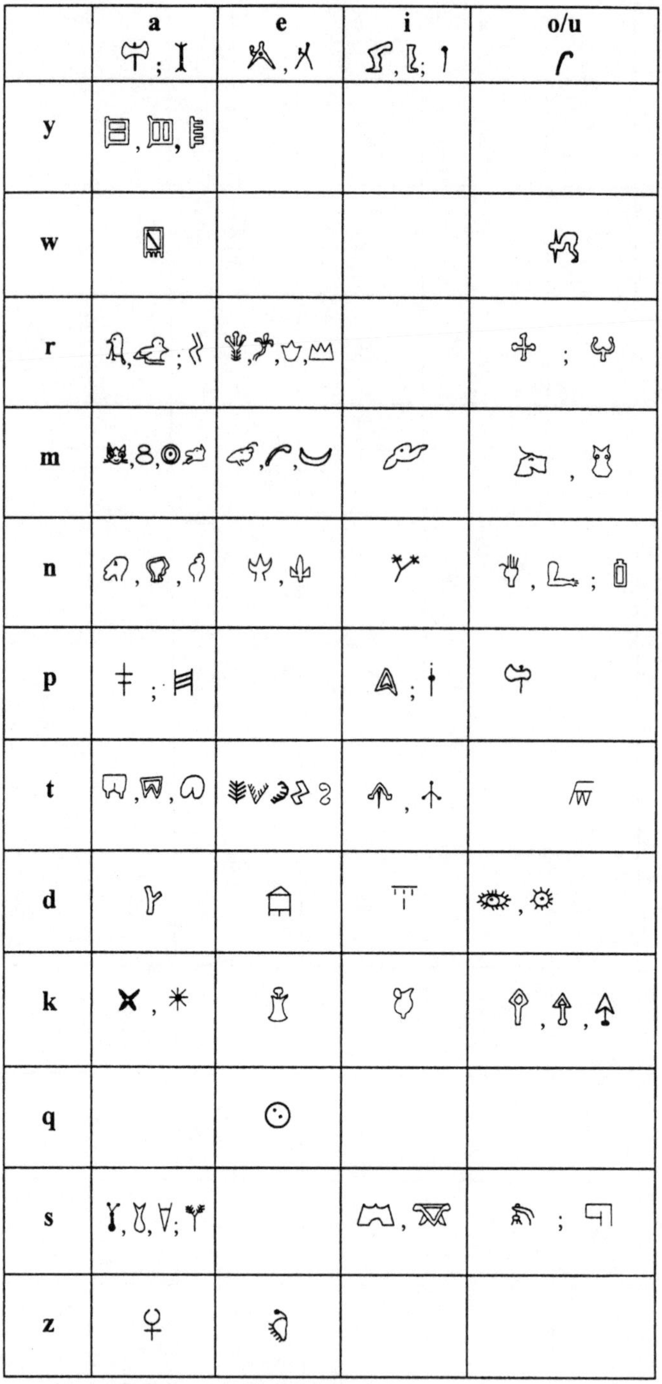

FIGURE 2.7
Minoan Crete's hieroglyphic syllabary with the phonetic values
proposed by Prof. Paul Faure of France in 1973.

pictographic scripts—in order to write their Minoan language on Crete and the neighboring isles.

Perhaps here in the Linear A script lay the key to the entire Minoan world, many scholars believed once Linear B had been successfully deciphered. Michael Ventris's grid approach wasn't applicable to Linear A after all, as it happened; only one-eighth of the amount of Mycenaean Greek Linear B's 57,000-glyph inventory was available for Minoan Linear A. Statistically, this has never been enough to sanction setting up an abstract grid of consonant-vowel relationships such as the one Michael Ventris had used to decipher Linear B.

However, because the Linear B glyphs were so close in their outward form to the Linear A glyphs, and because the sound values of the Linear B glyphs were now known, the epigraphic method that best suggested itself, as of the mid-1950s, was to transfer the Linear B sound values to their corresponding Linear A glyphs—and then simply to read Minoan Linear A!

If only it were that easy.

Foremost among the epigraphically valid approaches to reading the Minoan Linear A inscriptions since Michael Ventris's historic accomplishment of deciphering Linear B has indeed been the formal comparison of the speaking Linear B glyphs with the mute Linear A glyphs; this comparison has always been closely coupled with statistical surveys and structural analyses. All such undertakings have certainly contributed an impressive fund of knowledge to our understanding of the Minoan Linear A script. But by the beginning of the 1980s, no one could yet understand the Linear A inscriptions, though the sound values of most of the individual Linear A glyphs had been successfully retrieved. This inability to read Linear A stemmed from three basic problems: The Linear A inscriptions were too brief, too few, and—most important—written in an unidentifiable tongue.

Be that as it may, tremendous progress has been made in understanding the sound values of the Minoan Linear A glyphs.

Sir Arthur Evans's *Scripta Minoa* appeared as early as 1909, but this work was far too incomplete to make possible a decipherment of either Linear B or Linear A at the time. (Though Linear B was later considered the priority script, Evans's posthumous sequel *Scripta Minoa II*, containing only the Linear B archives from Knossos, didn't appear until 1952!) In the first half of the twentieth century, many objects inscribed with various Linear A glyphs were illustrated in publications by such distinguished European archaeologists as Halbherr, Sundwall, Doro Levi, and, most significantly, the Italian Pugliese Carratelli.

It was especially Pugliese Carratelli's 1945 contribution in the series *Monumenti Antichi* that, together with the successful decipherment of Mycenaean Greek Linear B in 1952, urged cross-script glyph recognition between the two similar linear scripts of B and A. As early as 1956, then, several Minoan Linear A syllabaries—based on obvious similarities to Linear B—had already been offered by Pugliese Carratelli (80 glyphs), Goold and Pope (70 glyphs), Meriggi (70 glyphs), and Furumark (58 glyphs).

By 1959 even John Chadwick approved, if guardedly, of 47 of these correspondences between Linear B and Linear A glyphs, acknowledging that the same sound values of Linear B held for similar glyphs in Linear A. In fact, Chadwick claimed at the time that Minoan Linear A differed from Mycenaean Greek Linear B about as much as the Greek alphabet differed from the Roman alphabet. Today, however, scholars can reliably say that it is rather more like the difference between the English and French alphabets. It's a script gap of only about 10 to 15 percent.

Linear A and Linear B, in other words, are almost identical scripts.

This recognition has come about as the result of intensive research into the nature of the Minoan Linear A corpus that has been conducted most notably in Europe and America since the 1950s. In 1961, William Brice of England published all the known Linear A inscriptions for the first time, allowing scholars a hitherto unknown access to the Linear A treasury. The American David Packard, in his 1967 Harvard doctoral dissertation and thereafter, proved through the spelling alternations in Linear A that deciphering this script through transferring Michael Ventris's Linear B glyph values offered results that were statistically far better than one might expect through chance alone. On purely analytical grounds, Packard was also able to suggest Linear A glyph readings that were not otherwise transparent. In 1971, two of the world's most dedicated Linear A scholars, Jacques Raison of France and Maurice Pope of South Africa (later Oxford), jointly published the much-expanded corpus and indexes of the Linear A material in exemplary fashion. The linguistic analyses of the Linear A material by Yves Duhoux of the Linguistic Institute of Louvain, Belgium, made possible the isolation of characteristic traits of the underlying Minoan language. (Duhoux also published the best description and documentation of the Phaistos Disk.) By the early 1980s, the corpus of Linear A inscriptions amounted to more than twice what Pugliese Carratelli had compiled in 1945, and over several years the French School of Athens published five stunning volumes by Louis Godart and Jean-Pierre Olivier that included photographs and transcriptions of all known Linear A texts, with exhaustive details of each inscribed artifact.

By this time, a number of Linear A scholars were claiming that *everything* one finds in Minoan A can also be found in Mycenaean Greek B. Others were asserting that these two Aegean writing systems described languages that shared the same general phonology—that is, languages that had to be closely related to one another. With a "long consecutive text" in the Minoan Linear A script—not just fragments of clay accounting tablets and short dedications and manufacturers' signs on discrete objects, which is all that is left today—the mystery of Linear A, and of the ethnic identity of the phenomenal Minoan empire it described, might soon be solved, these experts were alleging.

However, though the sound values of most of its glyphs were now known, the Linear A script still could not be understood, primarily because its underlying language, Minoan, remained unidentified. The only longer inscription that survives from the ancient Aegean—in the same language as that of Minoan Linear A, but in a different script—is the pictographic inscription of the Phaistos Disk.

If Linear A could not be comprehended through Linear B, then perhaps it could be understood through the Phaistos Disk itself ... that "long consecutive text" that enshrined the Minoans' identity in fired clay.

In the summer of 1982, once back from that fascinating trip to Crete and utterly enthralled by everything I had just seen and learned, I began research for a historical book I planned to write the following year about the Minoans and their amazing civilization. At the same time, I was beginning to learn the "flow" of the inscription on the Phaistos Disk as I rotated my replica counterclockwise, analyzing the individual glyphs and acquainting myself with the conspicuous repetitions of select glyphs in key positions and of entire fields of glyphs. I spent countless evening hours in this way, communing with my mute witness to Europe's cradle days.

Yet I felt the same frustration Luigi Pernier himself must have known. I realized that the *logos* was here, too. Certainly we might one day be able to hear the petrified voice of the past in this most ancient of all European CDs, but not until we developed the hardware to play it. And the prospects for this seemed bleak.

I didn't know at the time that my own "peak experience" was waiting.

CHAPTER 3

THE NEW
LABYRINTH

"*Ekue, Kurwītis Deneoi-que....*"

"Hear ye, Cretans and Greeks, my great, my quick!
Hear ye, Danaïdans, the great, the worthy! Hear ye, all
blacks, and hear ye, Pudaan and Libyan immigrants!"

*Commanding the theater-like staircase of Phaistos's
majestic palace-shrine, a pigtailed herald lifts the royal
Minos's proclamation disk aloft for all those present to see:
white, barebreasted priestesses in colorful flounced skirts;
tanned, muscular officers in back-aprons and penis sheaths;
naked children; black Nubian guards with bronze-tipped
lances erect. All crowd closer to learn the portentous news
from Knossos, their faces etched with apprehension. It is a
fateful moment in history in one of the most opulent centers of
European civilization, 1600 years before the birth of Christ....*

The ugly growl of an automobile—a rare sound where I was
then living, in a small village just outside of Nuremberg, Germany—wrenched me back into the present. I frowned at the
sudden intrusion and checked my watch. Two in the morning.
A cold and snowy February morning in 1984.

A.D.

My prehistoric CD was finally playing! After a year and a half of extreme effort, I had managed to construct that linguistic hardware and had retrieved the ghost-like voice from its Cretan maze.

I had not only fought this Minotaur right there in his own Labyrinth of Knossos. I had wrenched out his very tongue....

Minoan.

Ancient myth tells us, in one of the most famous stories in the history of the world, that the god of the sea Poseidon presented Minos of Knossos with a great white bull, which the King of Crete was instructed to sacrifice on the blood altar. But dazzled by the animal's strength and beauty, King Minos sent the bull to his herd instead, sacrificing another in its place.

Enraged, Poseidon vowed revenge.

The god caused Minos's queen Pasiphaë to lust after the holy beast with an unnatural desire. And when Pasiphaë ordered Daidalos to aid her, the court architect had little choice but to design and fashion for her a hollow wooden cow that he covered with a skin and then placed Pasiphaë inside. In this guise the Queen of Crete mated with the divine bull of Poseidon, and the issue of their union was the Minotaur ... a creature with a bull's head and a man's body.

Utterly horrified, King Minos commanded Daidalos to build the Labyrinth, a great maze near the royal palace in which the king then sequestered this monster-child his queen had shamelessly borne.

Soon thereafter, King Minos's son Prince Androgeos was killed at a sporting event in Athens. Blaming the Athenians, the King of Crete demanded that every nine years, seven Athenian youths and seven Athenian maidens be sent to him as tribute. These he would then sacrifice to the Minotaur in his dread Labyrinth, from which there was no exit.

Too weak to refuse, the Athenians complied.

Yet when the time for tribute approached again nine years later, Theseus, Prince of Athens, vowed to his parents that he would personally slay the Minotaur and, to this end, hid himself among the 13 other hostages who sailed south from Athens with lamentation. And at Knossos Theseus met and fell in love with Princess Ariadne, King Minos's daughter.

The handsome prince bared his heart to Ariadne and revealed who he really was and that he had come to kill her half-brother the Minotaur. And, joy of joys, Ariadne confessed her love for him, too, and agreed to help—*if* Theseus promised to carry her back with him to Athens as his wedded wife. Theseus promised, with impassioned kisses.

Whereupon Ariadne clandestinely secured from Daidalos a magical skein of wool, later instructing her beloved prince, in the dark of night, to begin unwinding it as he entered the inescapable Labyrinth and then simply to follow it out again once he had slain the Minotaur.

And this is just what happened. At least according to the ancient myth.

Yet what had been my magical skein? What had led me out of the philological maze in which I had been battling another sort of Cretan monster since the summer of 1982? Ordered common sense. An anything-but-magical methodology. One that was based on the scientific contributions of many gifted scholars from many nations.

And it was an adventure in its own way no less exciting than the mythical Theseus's, no less fraught with adversity than Sir Arthur Evans's, and no less replete with personal challenge—and gratification—than Michael Ventris's.

Let us now relive that first adventure, before turning to the white sands of Polynesia and an altogether different challenge. Let's follow the Phaistos Disk's ancient skein together, step by step, in general outline. (The more curious reader can learn about this in greater detail in the original scientific publications listed in "Suggested Reading" at the back of this book.) And by the time you emerge from the New Labyrinth you'll not only understand how it was accomplished but will also be prepared to embrace an Ariadne of a different kind:

Europe's first literature.

That initial year of informal investigation saw little con-
structive progress. Certainly, negative results are still results,
and they can even be informative. But they are frustrating and
seldom conducive to celebration. All I could say for certain
about the Phaistos Disk, according to the general consensus of
scholarship and my own conclusions, was that the Disk

- was authentic.

- comprised an inscription.

- was to be read right to left from the outside spiraling in.
  Proof for such a reading lay in the many printing overcuts
  showing how the scribe had impressed several glyphs over
  parts of others that had already been printed.

- contained a script that was phonetic. This meant that the
  glyphs in no way held a symbolic, emblematic, or pictorial
  significance but rather—*in each instance*—reproduced a
  sound meant to be spoken aloud.

- contained a script that was syllabic. This fact could be
  deduced from the overall number of 45 attested—and 60-
  odd conjectured—glyphs in the script's total inventory.
  This is too many for an alphabetic script (*a, b, c*) such as
  English with 26 letters. But it's far too few for an ideographic script such as Chinese with up to 50,000 signs.

Still, I appreciated that an entire living language had to be
contained here in the Disk, too. Hidden somewhere behind these
curious little pictures was a language as intricate and grammatical as any living language of today. Yet how could one begin to
"read" these glyphs if one didn't even know what language they
were written in, let alone their individual sound values?

Somehow I had to reduce—as the American epigrapher
Alice Kober enjoined back in 1948 when addressing the Linear B
script—one of these two "unknowns": either the unknown of
language or the unknown of script. One of the twain had to give.

Or we'd never learn what the Disk was saying.

The initial reduction of unknowns commenced with the
formal internal analysis of the Phaistos Disk in the autumn of
1983. I assigned each glyph a number according to Sir Arthur

Evans's numeration (Figure 2.1) in order to establish language relationships that could be seen independently of each glyph's potential sound value. Next I rewrote the entire text, both sides, left to right this time to facilitate reading, but using only these assigned numbers, with vertical field dividers (represented here by /).

And this is how the text of the Phaistos Disk then looked:

RETRIEVAL STAGE 1

Side A: 02-12-13-01-18 , / 24-40-12 / 29-45-07 , / 29-29-34 (,) / 02-12-04-40-33 / 27-45-07-12 / 27-44-08 (,) / 02-12-06-18-(-)(,) / 31-26-35 (,) / 02-12-41-19-35 / 01-41-40-07 (,) / 02-12-32-23-38 , / 39-11 / 02-27-25-10-23-18 / 28-01 , / 02-12-31-26 , / 02-12-27-27-35-37-21 / 33-23 (,) / 02-12-31-26 , / 02-27-25-10-23-18 / 28-01 , / 02-12-31-26 , / 02-12-27-14-32-18-27 / 06-18-17-19 / 31-26-12 / 02-12-13-01 / 23-19-35 , / 10-03-38 / 02-12-27-27-35-37-21 / 13-01 / 10-03-38 °

Side B: 02-12-22-40-07 / 27-45-07-35 / 02-37-23-05 , / 22-25-27 (,) / 33-24-20-12 / 16-23-18-43 , / 13-01-39-33 / 15-07-13-01-18 , / 22-37-42-25 / 07-24-40-35 / 02-26-36-40 / 27-25-38-01 (,) / 29-24-24-20-35 / 16-14-18 / 29-33-01 / 06-35-32-39-33 / 02-09-27-01 / 29-36-07-08 , / 29-08-13 / 29-45-07 , / 22-29-36-07-08 , / 27-34-23-25 / 07-18-35 / 07-45-07 , / 07-23-18-24 / 22-29-36-07-08 , / 09-30-39-18-07 / 02-06-35-23-07 / 29-34-23-25 / 45-07 ,

It's a big-league match—the biggest there is, for it's the ultimate Match of Wits. If you study this numerical text long enough, then you'll begin to see absolutely fascinating things going on here that will challenge your intellect like nothing in creation.

Keeping our analogy, let's say it's a big-league soccer match. Certain groupings of numbers often repeat themselves, like multiple players on the soccer field. Sometimes they recur in what one must acknowledge to be a key position, a "forward" or an "end." Other times they occupy wholly different positions. And then there are those numbers that occur only in exactly the same position even though their teammates in the very same field (between the "goals," the vertical field dividers) come and go.

Once you dedicate sufficient time to this exciting match, you sort of get the feeling that you're sitting in some twilight-zone grandstand able to pick out from among the jumble of activity on the field below precisely what players belong to what team—simply by where they are playing, in what direction they run, and with whom.

These repetitions and alternations—the actual "match" itself—are our first tangible evidence of the operation of a living language in the Phaistos Disk's inscription.

We'll now enhance these visible phenomena. We'll be clever and introduce special code markings that will help us perceive more easily what's going on. Let's do the right thing by our soccer players, in other words, and finally let them don some colorful uniforms.

First and most important, we'll see that each repeating number or grouping of numbers—each key player and squad in the team, if you like—will be marked as a "significant unit." These are the players and squads that stay intact when others in the same field between the goals come and go. We'll mark these constant key players and squads (the repeating numbers) simply by separating them from the wayfaring players (the non-repeating numbers) in the same field.

What can these significant units be? At this stage, with so little to go on, it's too difficult to tell, really.

In the past, most investigators have seen in them shared prefixes (*in*-action) and suffixes (action-*less*). For instance, with the English words "inaction" and "inharmony" and "ingratitude," we can clearly state that "in-" is a shared prefix. And with "actionless" and "motionless" and "timeless," we have a shared suffix, the "-less." However, these investigators have arrived at this conclusion by arbitrarily assuming that each individual field on the Phaistos Disk—that is, the glyph sequences between the vertical lines on both sides—comprises an autonomous and separate "word."

This assumption is untenable. If we make it, we're thinking modern, not prehistoric. We're sitting in Knossos's loggia judging Minos's boxers by the Rules of the Marquess of Queensbury.

For "words" really weren't known as such at the time of the manufacture of the Phaistos Disk, not in the grammatical sense that we appreciate today. (And even today's linguists cannot agree on a universal definition for "word." Is it the smallest unit of speech that has meaning when alone? Or is it a vocal sound or combination of vocal sounds used to express an idea? Or both of these? Or neither?) The later Mycenaean Greek Linear B script included between its own so-called word dividers the conjunctions ("and," "but") and adverbs ("here," "well," "newly") alongside the nouns (things) and verbs (actions). It sometimes put two nouns together, too. And the much later Linear C script of Cyprus insisted that the articles "a" and "the" (which are missing in Linear B's highly abridged accounting tablets) be yoked onto the nouns as well, yielding combinations inside the fields such as "theking," "agift," and "thetown."

Our ancient ancestors seemed instead to think—and therefore write—more in terms of "units of utterance" than in those carefully segregated parts of speech that we moderns learned about in grammar school.

Looking at it this way, in a script that might not indicate autonomous words, couldn't the examples mentioned above, "inaction" and "inharmony" and "ingratitude," just as easily be "in action" and "in harmony" and "in gratitude," as we also find these perfectly grammatical groupings in English? It's just that they are now separated orthographically and mean exactly the opposite.

You see what I'm getting at. Between the vertical field dividers on the Phaistos Disk, we have to be dealing with more than just single words. We must be prepared to encounter a vast array of linguistic possibilities: single words (like "Crete"), phrases ("in Crete"), and perhaps even entire sentences ("Abide in Crete"). All three possibilities might be functioning between the field dividers at the same time.

For this reason, it's more judicious to set apart for the moment these repeating numbers and groupings of numbers inside the Disk's individual fields and call them merely significant units, pending further evidence.

This initial isolation of significant units on the Phaistos Disk can be primary, the result of immediately contrasting pairs. Or it can be secondary, through transfer from the primary.

This means that if we find, for example, the textual readings 27-45-07 on Side A, field 6, and 29-45-07 on Side A, field 3, then primary isolation justifies restating the former as 27 45-07 and the latter as 29 45-07. This is because the numbers 45-07 seem to belong together as a significant unit. Because 27 and 29 are mutually exclusive alternations before this unit, we'll let them stand alone. Thus 27 and 29 become our key players, and 45-07 is the squad. And if later we find the number sequences 27-44-08 (Side A, field 7) and 29-33-01 (Side B, field 15), then through secondary isolation we are justified in suggesting— though no more than this—that 27 44-08 and 29 33-01 might also comprise independent significant units in these two fields. They, too, would be the same two key players, now functioning in front of two different squads.

Whether the glyphs 27 and 29 are indeed prefixes or are actually separate "words"—that is, whether they resemble in their function "inaction" or "in action"—we will have to determine through other, later methods, if possible.

There are further ways to break up the players in Retrieval Stage 1 into more easily visible key players and squads. We'll put all the multi-unit repetitions between brackets. And we'll mark the frequent unit 02-12 in **boldface.** All other repeating units will be underlined, including seemingly important end glyphs. (The overlining and double-underlining that I included in my scientific book are omitted here for easier reading.)

Our field boundaries will stay marked with a virgule /. And a period (.) will replace the scribal "thorn" that has been variously interpreted by scholars as a stanza separator, as a vowel-loss marker, and as a punctuation mark not unlike a modern period (or so Sir Arthur Evans).

And after marking Retrieval Stage 1 in this way, we suddenly discover that we have an edited numerical text.

Here's how it looks:

RETRIEVAL STAGE 2

Side A: **[02-12** [13-01] -18] . / 24 40-12 / [29 45-07] . / 29 29-34 (.) / **02-12** 04-40-33 / [27 45-07]-12 / 27 44-08 (.) / **02-12** 06-18-(-)(.) / 31-26-35 (.) / **02-12** 41-19-35 / 01-41 40-07 (.) / **02-12** 32 23-38 . / 39-11 / [02 27-25 10 23-18 / 28-01] . / **[02-12 31-26]** . / [[**02-12** 27] 27-35-37-21] / 33-23 (.) / **[02-12 31-26]** . / [02 27-25 10 23-18 / 28-01] . / **[02-12 31-26]** . / **[02-12** 27] 14-32-18-27 / 06-18 17-19 / 31-26-12 / **[02-12** 13-01] / 23-19-35 . / [10 03-38] / [[**02-12** 27] 27-35-37-21] / 13-01 / [10 03-38] °

Side B: **02-12** 22 40-07 / [27 45-07]-35 / 02 37-23-05 . / 22 25-27 (.) / 33-24 20-12 / 16 23-18-43 . / 13-01 39-33 / 15-07 [13-01-18] . / 22 37-42-25 / 07 24 40-35 / 02 26-36-40 / 27-25 38-01 (.) / 29 24-24 20-35 / 16 14-18 / 29 33-01 / 06-35 32 39-33 / 02 09 27-01 / [29 36-07-08] . / 29 08-13 / [29 45-07] . / [22 [29 36-07-08]] . / 27 34-23-25 / 07 18-35 / 07 45-07 . / 07 23-18-24 / [22 [29 36-07-08]] . / 09-30 39-18-07 / 02 06-35 23-07 / 29 34-23-25 / 45-07 .

What can we deduce from this new numerical text? Quite a bit, actually.

First of all, we can tell straight off that both sides of the Phaistos Disk must contain the same language. You really can't take this for granted. A Language X might be written on Side A, with a Language Y on Side B as its translation, for example.

But just look at the repetition of **02-12,** as well as the other frequent units 45-07 and 13-01 and so forth. And the initial key players 27 and 29. And the penults -40- and -23- and -39- that occur in second-to-last position. Not to mention the endings -01 and -18 and -12 and -07. All of these occur repeatedly on both sides of the artifact. This can mean only one thing.

That a single language is speaking to us on both sides of the Phaistos Disk.

Further revelations are legion in the frequency tables. These are long and detailed charts that one sets up and that show how each individual number and each grouping of numbers are related to all the others.

For example, addressing the prominent repetition of significant unit **02-12** in its alternating environments

02-12	13-01-18	**02-12**	27 14-32-18-27
02-12	04-40-33	**02-12**	13-01
02-12	06-18-(-)	**02-12**	22 40-07
02-12	41-19-35	**02-12**	32 23-38
02-12	31-26 (3x)	**02-12**	27 27-35-37-21 (2x)

shows us that **02-12**—with no apparent indication of inflection (that is, of changing its form to show its grammatical function)—is probably some sort of independent element within each of the 13 fields it occupies. It's perhaps a single word. It could be a two-syllable interjection or rhetorical phrase, like "Alas!" or "Heavens!" or "Praise be!" Or the name of the addressed person or deity. Or an imperative verb calling attention to or commanding something.

Similarly conspicuous is the significant unit 45-07:

29 <u>45-07</u>	29 <u>45-07</u>
27 <u>45-07</u> <u>-12</u>	07 <u>45-07</u>
27 <u>45-07</u> <u>-35</u>	<u>45-07</u>

This unit doesn't seem to involve inflection either. Yet, unlike unit 02-12, it's obviously functioning in several related environments as an integral member of the text, not as an isolate. If 02-12 is our "goalkeeper," then 45-07 is our "forward." One might infer that it is the name of a person or deity, lacking inflection. Or the subject of the Disk, repeated often. Or an adjective (descriptive word) qualifying something.

Because of their relationship to unit 45-07, it is only natural to turn to the endings -12 and -35. These are doubtless our "ends." They are utterly fascinating and caused me no end of hair-pulling for the longest time. Note in Retrieval Stage 2 how they alternate with each other in exactly the same terminal field positions. And note, too, that although they are mutually exclusive—that is, they never occur together—they appear to fulfill an identical function (in most but not all fields).

What could this shared function be?

The fact that they never changed their form in any of these positions suggested to me that they could belong to those parts of speech that are uninflectible. This means that the autonomous form of the word was never being modified in some way to show grammatical relationships; it always stayed the same. However, this possibility only obtained if I allowed that (as is the case with the Linear scripts B and C) the Phaistos Disk's field dividers, the vertical lines, corral more than just one so-called "word."

Such as accompanying articles, prepositions, or conjunctions.

With the "ends" -12 and -35, I suspected the latter.

Both end numbers seemed to be behaving suspiciously like conjunctions—words such as "and" that connect other words and clauses and sentences. That would explain why they were stuck here onto the end of so many different fields.

What had led me to this idea? Well, I had recalled how Michael Ventris, very early in his decipherment of Linear B, had identified Linear B glyph 78 as a conjunction. Though he still had no idea what Linear B's underlying language was, Ventris had observed 78's seemingly uninflected "word-final" position between dividers on many of the Mycenaean tablets from Knossos and Pylos, such as

36-14-12-41 / 70-27-04-27 / 51-80-04-**78**
11-02-70-27-04-27-**78** / 77-60-40-11-02-**78** / 61-39-58-70-**78**
/61-39-77-72-38-75-**78**
77-70 / 06-40-36 / 03-59-36-28-**78** / 38-44-41-**78** / 43-77-31-80

Ventris had suspected that the inscription was an accounting text. (Only much later was it identified as a list of weighed quantities of goods.) He had interpreted the text to read something like

> ... Alpha *and* Beta
> *and* Gamma *and* Delta *and* Epsilon
> *and* Zeta
> *and* Eta *and* Theta

with glyph 78 as the "and" in each instance.

In this way Linear B glyph 78 was really not an intrinsic part of some hypothesized "word-field" after all. Other words could also fit in between the so-called "word-dividers" (a dot or a virgule, as on the Disk). Glyph 78 was a wholly independent field-internal appendage. A separate part of speech.

Just like -12 and -35 on the Phaistos Disk, I finally concluded. A comparison to Linear B could be drawn from the way both -12 and -35 were similarly prominent on the field ends of the groupings

<u>31-26</u> -<u>35</u>	07 <u>24 40</u> -<u>35</u>	27 <u>45-07</u> -<u>35</u>
<u>31-26</u> -<u>12</u>	<u>24 40</u> -<u>12</u>	27 <u>45-07</u> -<u>12</u>
<u>31-26</u> (4x)		

Understanding this apparent autonomous function of -12 and -35 prompted a "corrected" reading for 24 40-12/-35. For these numbers I now suggested the coded form 24-40(-12/-35), with the final –12 and –35 representing possible conjunctions, as in Linear B.

With this new numerical text I hazarded a great number of other observations, too. Many of them later proved to be incorrect. This was because I was dealing with unfamiliar influences, not knowing the language these numbers were hiding.

I was "sailing to Hawai'i."

The expression jocularly recalls what had been an important life-lesson for me. It was the summer of 1968, and Taki and I had sailed our 21-foot sloop *Ta'aroa* over to Catalina Island, some 40 kilometers off the California coast, for the weekend. It was a sailor's dream.

Until our return trip.

Come dawn, a thick haze veiled the coastline. For just such an emergency I had brought my charts. And there was my compass, of course, secured just inside the transom right over the portable gas tank.

Hours passed. Not a whisper of a wind came up. The haze hung suspended like Poseidon's own curse. Still, on we putt-putted, closely minding the compass, confident that any minute now we'd lay eyes on the rusting hulk of the old *Dominator*, then a familiar landmark on the western tip of the Palos Verdes peninsula.

Suddenly a great white leviathan passed not a hundred meters in front of our bow—the Catalina Isthmus Ferry, heading for King Harbor, Redondo Beach, our own goal . . .

Ninety degrees to starboard!

Shocked numb, I eased the tiller hard to port and followed, tail between the legs, in the disappearing ferry's wake. And tried for the life of me to figure out what had played havoc with the compass. And then it dawned on me.

The gas tank.

A mass of magnetic metal. Just beneath its victim, not a meter away. *Of course.*

And it had thrown off the compass's reading so much that if we had putted along on our same innocent heading, then we could have dined the next day in the Santa Barbara Islands. If our fuel had lasted. Which it wouldn't have. And the next port of call?

... Hawai'i.

There's a lesson there. Take everything into consideration, certainly. But appreciate at the same time that even when life's detailed charts and expensive compasses are telling you one thing, something with greater priority in life's mad chase could actually have you "sailing to Hawai'i."

It's become a cherished family joke. Which means that Taki has never let me forget it. And it's good to be reminded now and again that the truth can lie in the deviation.

For this reason and a host of others, I was prepared to accept, then, that many of my conclusions in regard to these exhaustively detailed frequency charts derived from the Phaistos Disk might actually be false leads.

And they were.

A good deal had to be correct, too. Such is the irrefutable magic of numbers. There's a universal concord in the chaos and a pattern in the pandemonium. If only in numerical harmonics (for the moment), Crete's ancient past was being forced to speak. In only faintly audible bits of unknown tones, granted. But detectable tones all the same. They fell on my ears as an intimation of potential success with this internal analysis approach.

By the end of my internal analysis, I made bold to hazard certain statements about the Phaistos Disk's grammar. I pointed out possible examples of inflection and even suggested potential parts of speech with measured restraint.

Once all the data had been gathered and assessed, the conspicuous recurrence of the significant unit 02-12 and its contextual profile suggested to me, for one thing, a drastic differ-

ence in *structure* between Side A's text and Side B's. To all
appearances, Side A indeed warranted this designation of A by
being some sort of introductory "invocation" or "proclamation," I could state categorically. It repeated the unit 02-12
twelve times, probably to gain the attention of the addressed
deity or audience. And Side A seemed to forgo complete "sentences" in order perhaps to embrace instead much shorter
"phrases."

In striking contrast, Side B displayed fewer such numerical repetitions and fewer stops and fewer "phrase" recur-
rences. The inscrutable unit 02-12 initiated Side B but then
never occurred again. Most peculiar. Side B seemed to me,
then, to be the actual "message." It perhaps harbored full
"sentences."

The language of the Phaistos Disk had all the earmarks of
an inflectional language, too. This meant that it could very
well hail from the Indo-European family, whose constituents
are all inflectional. Of course, I didn't dare to guess which Indo-
European language this might be. It was still far too early.

What more could I adduce from this exhaustive internal
analysis? Nothing. To be sure, elaborate descriptions of fancied
"noun and verb classes" in the Phaistos Disk have been hazarded in the past on the basis of such internal studies of the
inscription. Yet the authors of these descriptions have, one and
all, implicitly based their findings on the arbitrary assumption
that each field of the Disk must, without exception, represent
one indivisible "word" in the modern sense.

This I reject, because there is no evidence for it. And the
history of writing strongly argues against it. Indeed, other
Aegean scripts display field-internal inclusions, belying the
hypothesis "one field = one word."

Thus in the end, my own internal analysis permitted,
besides everything mentioned above, merely a final "corrected" numerical transcription of the Phaistos Disk based on
the sum of these observed repetitions and alternations and
their interpretations:

RETRIEVAL STAGE 3

Side A: 02-12 13-01-18 . / 24-40(-12) / 29 45-07 . / 29 29-34 (.)
/ **02-12** 04-40-33 / 27 45-07(-12) / 27 44-08 (.) / **02-12** 06-18
(-) / 31-26(-35) / **02-12** 41-19(-35) / 01-41 40-07 (.) / **02-12** 32-
23-38 . / 39-11 / 02 27-25 10 23-18 / 28-01 . / **02-12** 31-26 . /
02-12 27 27-35-37-21 / 33-23 (.) / **02-12** 31-26 . / 02 27-25 10
23-18 / 28-01 . / **02-12** 31-26 . / **02-12** 27 14-32-18-27 / 06-18
17-19 / 31-26(-12) / **02-12** 13-01 / 23-19(-35) . / 10-03-38 (.) /
02-12 27 27-35-37-21 / 13-01 (.) / 10-03-38 °

Side B: 02-12 22 40-07 / 27 45-07(-35) / 02 37-23-05 (or: 02-37-
23-05) . / 22 25-27 / 33-24-20(-12) / 16 23-18-43 (or: 16-23-18-
43) . / 13-01 39-33 / 15-07 13-01-18 . / 22 37-42-25 / 07 24-40(-
35) / 02 26-36-40 (or: 02-26-36-40) / 27-25 38-01 (or:
27-25-38-01) / 29 24-24-20(-35) / 16 14-18 (or: 16-14-18) / 29
33-01 (or: 29-33-01) / 06-35-32 39-33 / 02 09 27-01 (or: 02-09-
27-01) / 29 36-07-08 (or: 29-36-07-08) . / 29 08-13 (or: 29-08-
13) / 29 45-07 . / 22 29 36-07-08 (or: 22 29-36-07-08) . / 27 34-
23-25 / 07-18(-35) (or: 07 18-35; or: 07 18 35) / 07 45-07 . / 07
23-18(-24) / 22 29 36-07-08 (or: 22 29-36-07-08). / 09-30-39-
18-07 / 02 06-35 23-07 / 29 34-23-25 / 45-07 .

I still felt like Theseus trapped in the Labyrinth.

That magical skein of Ariadne's was still wanting, though
the numbers had been a most productive way to draw out the
underlying structure of the message and also to suggest possible uses of grammar. The search for a pattern—the essential
procedure in any epigraphic work—had yielded a maze.

But no language.

During this time I had resolutely shunned the physical Disk
itself. Bizarre as this sounds, I had refused even to glance at my
replica or at any photograph of the object. I had to do this in order
to avoid mentally "sounding out" the glyphs' fancied syllables
and fabricating a language that wasn't really there. With my inter-

nal analysis—Retrieval Stage 3—I had wanted the cold fact of numbers and nothing more. I appreciated that the Phaistos Disk had to reproduce a "linguistic motor" with every valve, every piston of an inflection working with mathematical precision. Countless scholars had studied only the Disk's "paint job." For my part, I was determined to get "under the hood." All subjective speculation and guesswork had to defer to objective analysis.

Nothing substantial could yet be said about the "thorn," that virgule at the end of certain fields that resembled a modern comma or period.

But with my internal analysis now complete—particularly after I had isolated my field-internal "significant units"— I found the way clear to predict reliably which numbers in my numerical text might represent the pure vowels *a, e, i, o,* and *u.*

You see, in a syllabic script—and there can be no doubt that the Phaistos Disk is written in a syllabic script—those glyphs that are pure vowels appear with greater frequency at the beginning of a word than in the middle or at the end. This is because in the latter positions, they always are combined with a consonant.

For example, if we syllabically write the English words *e-co-no-my* and *e-co-lo-gy* and *e-lu-so-ry* (or, numerically, 01-02-03-04 and 01-02-05-06 and 01-07-08-09), then we can see right away how the inner vowels *-o* and *-u* as well as the three terminal *-y*'s in such a script are always "stuck" to their preceding consonant: *co, lu, my,* and so forth. Thus only one glyph bears the load for both functions: that of the consonant and that of the consonant's following vowel. In this way, we'd have a separate glyph for *co* and another for *no* and yet another for *lo.* And there's nothing to tell us what consonant or vowel is meant each time.

However, only one glyph would give us our initial *e-* too, because it is alone as a syllable. This occurs *exclusively* at the beginning of each word. Vowels can stand alone, then, as independent glyphs. Consonants can't, because in a syllabic script they are *always* paired with a following vowel.

This phenomenon is a statistical godsend for epigraphers. In an unknown syllabo-phonetic writing system, those glyphs that appear often at the beginning of a recognized "word" but seldom, if ever, in its middle or at its end might very well be the pure vowels *a, e, i, o,* and *u* standing alone without a consonant.

It's all a question of distribution.

So I did the same thing with the Phaistos Disk that Michael Ventris had done with the Linear B script. I set up a recurrence chart—in this instance, one that was based on Retrieval Stage 3 and that recorded all the initial-versus-internal occurrences of each number.

A dozen likely vowel candidates promptly stepped to the fore. Further analysis argued for the near-positive identification of glyph 02 as a pure vowel. It occurs exclusively at the beginning of nineteen separate fields and *not once* internally. (Only much later did I discover that earlier scholars had similarly "identified" 02 as a pure vowel according to its exclusively initial position.) I also suggested that glyphs 16, 28, 31, and 39 were the remaining vowels.

With just these numbers to work with, it happened that I wasn't far off. The final vowel retrieval later identified glyphs 02, 10, 16, 31, and 39 as the pure vowels of the Phaistos Disk's script.

Work Note, January 22, 1984: "The craving to put sound to number ... is worse than ever. But I must, like [Howard] Carter [the discoverer of Tutankhamun's tomb in Egypt], wait before I can open that tomb door...."

Once I had accomplished all I could alone with these numerical texts and their interpretation, I turned to the professionals. I was more than pleased when Herr Gerhard Eckstein of IBM told me, one snow-flurried morning after three hours of intensive language programming on IBM's most powerful computer in Nuremberg,

"*Herr Doktor,* with so little text to go by I must say no language programmer can begin to improve on these results you've come up with. I suppose this time human ingenuity has stalemated the almighty computer. *Ich gratuliere* ... My congratulations."

CHAPTER 4

THE SKEIN
OF ARIADNE

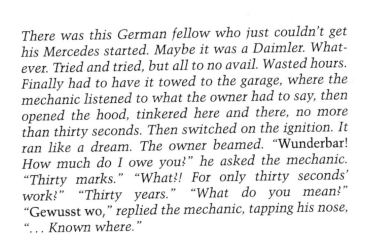

There was this German fellow who just couldn't get his Mercedes started. Maybe it was a Daimler. Whatever. Tried and tried, but all to no avail. Wasted hours. Finally had to have it towed to the garage, where the mechanic listened to what the owner had to say, then opened the hood, tinkered here and there, no more than thirty seconds. Then switched on the ignition. It ran like a dream. The owner beamed. "Wunderbar! How much do I owe you?" he asked the mechanic. "Thirty marks." "What?! For only thirty seconds' work?" "Thirty years." "What do you mean?" "Gewusst wo," replied the mechanic, tapping his nose, "... Known where."

In English we'd say "know-how." The mechanic knew just where to adjust the motor. The tennis champion knows just where to place the ball. And the scholar must know just where to go to find his information. It's what training is all about.

"Gewusst wo...."

It was UCLA's spring quarter of 1970, and I was a graduate student in the crowded bibliography course taught by the eminent chairman of the Department of Germanic Languages and Literature—then the largest in America—and former dean of the

Faculty of Arts, Professor Eli Sobel. And for all that anecdote's informality, Sobel's introductory lecture turned out to be one of the most important lessons of my entire eight-year university career. (Years later the short, quick-eyed professor with the old-fashioned bowtie was to become my own doctoral advisor and one of the closest confidants I have known. He died in 1987.)

Thus in 1983, once I had completed my internal analysis of Crete's ancient Phaistos Disk using numbers (as described here in Chapter 3), it didn't take long for me to tell where the motor needed tinkering in regard to continuation of the retrieval of the Disk's underlying language. For I had done my homework. I had put in my years of training. *Gewusst wo....*

It was that "point of reference" we talked about earlier as wanting in the work of Luigi Pernier and Sir Arthur Evans.

Some scholars claim that an internal analysis of the Phaistos Disk based on such numbers is *all* one will ever be able to achieve in retrieving the Disk's underlying language. These scholars can be found foremost among the opinion leaders of Linear B studies, who, since the mid-1950s, have had to construct a solid philological breakwater in order to define and protect the linguistic retrieval of an entire world—that of the Mycenaean Greeks. (The Mycenaean Greeks were the ones who wrote the Linear B tablets, as Michael Ventris's successful decipherment had proved in 1952.) This breakwater performed an admirable job up to the close of the twentieth century. However, nearly all classical scholars and historians throughout the world now fully understand and accept that the Linear B corpus of accounting tablets is written in a very early form of Greek. The philological breakwater, once indispensable, is now superfluous. It is also obstructive: It hinders voyages of exploration beyond the Mycenaean world.

Voyages into the earlier *Minoan* realm.

These few scholars who deny the Disk's solvability often cite Sir Arthur Evans, who, you may recall, maintained that there was no conclusive proof that the Phaistos Disk is even Minoan. Probably, these scholars say in seeming agreement with the long-deceased Sir Arthur, it's a foreign import. Perhaps the Disk comes from Anatolia, the area today called Turkey, they suggest. Moreover, such a useful invention as printing should have produced more texts on Minoan Crete than this one unique clay disk.

I disagree with these experts on all points. One can immediately remove the first stone in the superfluous breakwater by pointing out that Sir Arthur Evans's suspicion of the Disk's Minoan provenance was not beyond reproach. That is, Evans's statement that the object was perhaps imported from abroad is clearly contradicted by his numerous affirmations of the Minoan affinities of the Phaistos Disk's pictograms. It is possible that Sir Arthur was piqued by the Italian Luigi Pernier's "discovery of a century" on Evans's own Crete. And it is probable that had Sir Arthur himself, not Pernier, exhumed the Phaistos Disk in 1908, the fatuous controversy about the artifact's provenance would never have arisen in the first place.

And the second stone in these scholars' breakwater, that the Disk might have come from Anatolia? No artifact even faintly resembling the Phaistos Disk has ever been found in Anatolia. No script even faintly resembling that of the Phaistos Disk has ever appeared in Anatolia. The Phaistos Disk was found on Crete. In the ruins of an ancient Minoan palace-shrine. Alongside a clay tablet written in the Minoan Linear A script. And the Disk's script resembles the Minoan Linear A script as well as that adorning other contemporary Minoan artifacts.

Why weren't there more printed texts on Minoan Crete, then? the experts have countered, clutching the breakwater's third stone. To which I reply: There certainly had to be many more texts that were printed with the Phaistos Disk's glyphs. Printing is, after all, an eminently useful invention. But these other documents—palace accounts, correspondences, histories, perhaps even poems—were probably printed in cuttlefish ink on perishable papyrus or parchment. Or, if impressed in clay like the Phaistos Disk, they were not subjected to a disastrous fire such as the one at Phaistos's palace-shrine that baked and so miraculously preserved the Disk.

At which moment the nay-sayers' superannuated break-water, with these three critical stones removed, crumbles.

Despite those few voices that still echo Sir Arthur Evans's convenient "foreign provenance" hypothesis for the Phaistos Disk, for which there is no evidence at all, the consensus of opinion among today's archaeologists, historians, and epigraphers is that the Disk is of exclusively *Minoan* origin.

And for this there is overwhelming proof.

For example:

- Disk glyph 22 is clearly a Minoan handled jug. Today, at the Heraklion Museum on Crete, an identical jug from the same period is on display. Sir Arthur Evans himself did not hesitate to point out the glyph's resemblance to known Minoan jugs, noting that the cleaning of the Phaistos Disk in 1908–1909 had unfortunately effaced the glyph's handle—which Sir Arthur then restored in his own drawing (Figure 2.1).

- Disk glyph 24 shows the same palanquin, or chair, that is preserved in Minoan frescoes.

- Disk glyph 06 reproduces the typical Minoan female costume (of a priestess?—compare Crete's famous "Snake Priestess" statuette) of flounced skirt, apron, and low-cut bodice with bared breasts. In 1600 B.C. such a costume was worn only on Minoan Crete.

- Disk glyph 02's Mohican-like "crested warrior" was often, as by Sir Arthur Evans, advanced as "proof" of foreign provenance. That is, until 1963—when three similarly crested clay heads dating from 1950 to 1700 B.C. were discovered in the Traostalos Cave on Crete's east coast just north of the famous Minoan palace-shrine of Zakros.

- The Phaistos Disk's right-to-left script direction was also cited by critics as evidence for a non-Minoan origin. But then Linear A inscriptions were found on Crete that also read right to left. And Linear A was written exclusively by Minoans.

Additional proof of the Minoan provenance of the Phaistos Disk lies in the fact that numerous glyphs on the Disk correspond with those of the indigenous Cretan scripts. Sir Arthur Evans had to agree with Luigi Pernier on this point: "The general character of the hieroglyphic script [of the Phaistos Disk]," wrote Evans, "presents, in any case, a close parallel with the Minoan and *a certain proportion of the signs are identical.*" (My italics.)

And then there are the more general arguments, too, that favor a Minoan explanation.

Geographically speaking, only a seafaring people would reproduce the tunny (fish) of Disk glyph 33. The only maritime power in the Aegean in 1600 B.C. was the Minoans of Crete.

And artistically speaking—for any art historian will tell you that style alone can give voice to an entire world—Disk glyphs 01 and 31, as the eminent historian and philologist Professor Fritz Schachermeyr of Vienna once wrote, both reveal "typical Minoan portrayals of motion ... as are at this time to be expected only on Crete, and not in Asia Minor."

However, perhaps the most conclusive evidence for an exclusively Minoan provenance of the Phaistos Disk presented itself in the 1930s. Sixty years ago there was unearthed, in a cult cave at Arkalokhori in the geographical center of Crete, a bronze double-axe—dating from 1700 to 1550 B.C. and therefore contemporaneous with the Phaistos Disk—on whose haft are inscribed hieroglyphic characters "intimately related," so says Professor Schachermeyr, "to those of the Disk."

Later, a clay bar was discovered in the ruins of Mallia's palace-shrine on Crete's north coast just east of Knossos. It, too, bears a hieroglyphic script that could only be Minoan and that closely resembles the script of the Phaistos Disk.

It's no wonder, then, that in the 1980s one could read in the official tourist guide of Crete's Heraklion Museum, which was written by its erstwhile director Yannis A. Sakellarakis, associate professor of archaeology at the University of Athens and Crete's foremost archaeologist, "There can be no doubt that the script and unknown language of the Phaistos disc were the script and language of the Minoans of this period...."

The onus of proof of an alleged foreign provenance of the Phaistos Disk appears rather to be on those who would have us believe that the Minoan object was produced somewhere else than on Minoan Crete itself.

Personally, I always found it impossible to entertain the notion that the Disk could be anything but Minoan. Perhaps this was the result of my extensive research into Europe's first high civilization, research that had led me finally to begin writing my Minoan book in 1983. By this time, as with my earlier doctoral dissertation, I had collected several thousand notecards detailing everything from the temperature of eastern Zakros's bay to the hundred hues of western Khania's sunset. Like an Aegean dolphin, I had immersed myself in this wonderful sea world of passionate piety and reverent rage, typing all day long on my book and then investigating the Phaistos Disk each evening. This total immersion in the subject convinced me that one didn't really need to look for that official stamp on the Disk that those few nay-sayers seemed to demand: "Copyright Phaistos 1600 B.C." It was there already.

In the Minoan glyphs themselves.

What difference does it make, you might ask, whether we believe the Phaistos Disk to be Minoan or New Zealand Māori? It makes a great difference....

For here in Minoan provenance we have our point of reference.

Let's look at it logically. If we say that the Phaistos Disk is Minoan, then we are also claiming that it is written in the same language as that underlying Minoan Crete's Linear A script. Therefore, those insights that Linear A studies have furnished, especially in the 1960s and 1970s in the wake of Michael Ventris's successful decipherment of the related script of Mycenaean Greek Linear B, should be transferable to the language and script of the Phaistos Disk.

It's a bit like sorting out pottery shards from an archaeological dig. All those colorfully painted ones you've discovered from Section Alpha, Level Beta, certainly belong together with the unpainted ones from the same section and level. And that lovely painted vase you've found there, too—which shows exactly the same colors as the shards—isn't about to be classified as a "foreign import." It will be subject to the same stratum criteria as the shards, because the vase was obviously made by the same people. People who were doubtless working within the same cultural parameters ... and speaking the same language.

For the Phaistos Disk, this means that those *phonetic* (sound) parameters that various international scholars have conjectured for the Minoan Linear A script should apply to the Phaistos Disk's script as well. This is because both the Minoan Linear A tablets and the Minoan Phaistos Disk were manufactured at the same time and on the same island by the same people speaking the same language.

This is our point of reference.

And it allows us to put sound to sign at last.

What did Michael Ventris's decipherment of the Mycenaean Greek Linear B script teach us about the composition of the earlier Linear A script of the Minoans, from whom the Mycenaeans got their script in the first place?

For one thing, the Minoan Linear A script appears to accommodate the same five vowels (*a, e, i, o,* and *u*) as Mycenaean Greek Linear B. And Linear A probably shares a single series of glyphs for *r-* and *l-,* too. (This is a spelling convention that the Minoans might have borrowed from the Egyptians, with whom they carried on extensive trade.) Minoan Linear A—again like Mycenaean Greek Linear B—probably distinguishes between the *t-* and *d-* series, which means that three separate glyphs will show *ti ta to,* for example, and three different glyphs will represent *di da do.* But Linear A, again like the later Linear B, will perhaps not distinguish between the *p-* and *b-* and between the *k-* and *g-* (voicing isn't marked in the bilabial and palato-velar stops, a linguist would say). This means that the same three glyphs that signify *pi pa po* could also represent *bi ba bo* and that the three different glyphs that "spell out" *ki ka ko* also serve for *gi ga go*.

And with a few added details, this is what I postulated for Minoan Crete's Phaistos Disk script, too.

It was only logical. Weren't the people who manufactured the Phaistos Disk the same ones who wrote in Linear A? With ordered common sense, I reasoned that this contemporaneous Minoan inscription had to exhibit the same phonetic and orthographic parameters as the Minoan Linear A script.

Whereupon I set up my working syllabary (Figure 4.1). (I included in this working syllabary a *z-* series as well, but because no *z*-plus-vowel was ever forthcoming in the Phaistos Disk's inscription, this series was later dropped. We'll omit it here to keep things simpler.)

This working syllabary isn't the same as Michael Ventris's abstract "grid." It's simply a table showing which glyphs share

	A	E	I	O	U
J					
W					
R/L					
M					
N					
P					
T					
D					
K					
Q					
S					

FIGURE 4.1
The working syllabary of the Phaistos Disk.

the same vowel and consonant. It's a very handy decipherment tool that has been used by others in the past with other decipherments. When you retrieve a syllable—that is, a glyph that means *a* or *pu*, consisting of an autonomous vowel or of a consonant plus vowel—you simply insert this syllabic value in the proper slot in your working syllabary. The syllabary lets you know, then, how you're advancing, limits your choice of further possibilities, and allows easy transfers and adjustments later.

The working syllabary includes a further important consideration, too. None of the ancient Aegean scripts—not Minoan Linear A or Mycenaean Greek Linear B or the Cyprian Greek Linear C—demonstrates anything but the syllabic glyph structure V or CV: vowel (*a*) or consonant-vowel (*pu*). This we call an "open syllabic script." It means that you'll never find glyphs that hold the sound values VC (*at*) or VV (*aa*) or CC (*pp*) and so forth. Because I was convinced that the Phaistos Disk's script was also an ancient Aegean script, I was equally convinced that it had to share the same V or CV open syllabic structure of Linears A, B, and C. Indeed, the working syllabary is based on this fundamental conviction.

Might this V and CV structure tell us anything more substantial about the underlying Minoan language that this script reproduces? Something that might help us in the retrieval of sounds for the Phaistos Disk's glyphs? Not really, no. Most scholars are now in agreement that the Linear A script didn't have to approximate the Minoan language any better than the Linear B script approximated the Mycenaean Greek language. Consider the entry *pa-i-to* for "Phaistos"—a pre-Mycenaean place name that is found on both the Minoan Linear A and the Mycenaean Greek Linear B accounting tablets. This entry shows us immediately that even in Minoan Linear A, we are obviously dealing with an open syllabic script that uses spelling conventions that allow for closed syllables, too.

That is, *pa-i-to* was actually pronounced *p(h)a-i(s)-to(s)*. This demonstrates that though the Minoans had closed syllables in their language, they didn't show them in their various scripts. They kept the syllables open as V or CV. And later the Mycenaean Greeks simply borrowed this practice for their Linear B script, despite the fact that it was just as clumsy for the Greek language as it evidently had been for the Minoan.

From the 1950s to the 1970s, scholars claimed that the Mycenaeans of Greece's mainland were forced to "adapt" their foreign Greek tongue to Minoan Crete's "ill-fitting" Linear A script, resulting in Mycenaean Greek Linear B. By the 1980s, however, this idea had been discarded by most experts in ancient Aegean epigraphy. For it appears that both Minoan Linear A and Mycenaean Greek Linear B suffered exactly the same toothing problems, almost as though they were similar languages. Problems that one would expect from a writing system still in its infancy.

Like that of the Phaistos Disk.

I was aware that my working syllabary for the Disk would describe only gross phonetic values. It merely approximated the actual values of the underlying Minoan language, in other words. (In English, for example, the single letter *a* does service for *hat, all, date, pa, was,* and *an,* six different phonemes—distinguishing speech-sounds—represented by the single grapheme: *a.*) I would have in my working syllabary little more than the basic distinctive features of the Minoan language. All the same, hadn't past decipherers of other scripts shown that the majority of such postulated values for unknown inscriptions are, if not wholly, then at least *generally,* correct?

The skein of Ariadne led me further along. . . .

At last I dedicated myself to putting sound to number.

Remember those soccer players down on the field? First we gave them numbers. Then they got colorful uniforms. After that we figured out their respective positions on the team.

Now we'll ask them their Minoan names.

I knew that it was methodologically invalid merely to "identify" a glyph on the Phaistos Disk and then hazard an initial syllabic value for the object's name in ancient Luvian or

Lykian or Greek or even reconstructed Indo-European, that widest mother oak in the forest of world languages. Certainly, scholars in this field are in general agreement that the Aegean scripts derived from such an earlier "acrophonic" system of pictograms. This is a writing system in which the *in-di-vi-du-al* syllables constructing whole words would have originated from the initial syllables of the names of familiar objects.

For example, pictures of Athens's **A**cropolis, a **me**lon, a **ri**ckshaw, and a **ca**nary in this way would "spell" A-me-ri-ca. It's the most primitive system of writing there is.

And the Phaistos Disk was evidently written in just this way, as nearly all scholars agree.

Thus if in field A1 we can identify a "crested warrior," a "solid bossed wheel," a "cypress," a "walker," and a "plumb-square," then all we should have to do is to put these initial syllables together from the underlying language of the Phaistos Disk ... and read our inscription.

If only it were so simple.

Who can guarantee that these are indeed the abovementioned persons and objects? The "warrior" could be a priest, a clan leader, a guard, even a deity. The "wheel" could be a shield or something else. The "cypress" might be a small plant or even a unique cult item. And so forth. Even if we could correctly identify the persons and objects, who's to say what these were called in the Minoan language, which is still unknown? And even if the Minoan language were known, how could we possibly be sure what word was used for this object as far back as 1600 B.C.? There might have been several words used for the same thing, just as in English we could easily call Disk glyph 01 a "walker" or "stroller" or even "pedestrian." (On today's traffic signals from Munich to Tokyo, the identical symbol means "Walk!"—an imperative verb.)

You can't just arbitrarily appoint a language, and then a word from this language, and then declare an answer. This has been a favorite decipherment method of the dilettanti in the past, and it's wholly unscientific. It's to be strictly avoided ...

So long as the several Minoan scripts' underlying language remains unknown.

No, I knew I had to work *inductively*, from the parts to the whole, from the known to the unknown. I had to retrieve each Disk glyph's phonetic value—the *A* in *A-me-ri-ca*—not by arbitrarily "identifying" its underlying word (*A*cropolis) but rather by objectively transferring the known values of identical or similar glyphs (as Evans and others have acknowledged) in the related Aegean scripts of Linears A, B, and C.

In this I could profit from the work of four generations of scholars who have wrested sounds out of these various Mediterranean scripts that share signs with the Phaistos Disk.

At the same time, however, I still didn't dare assume that simply because they shared glyphs, there had to be some sort of language affiliation between the two Greek dialects of Linears B and C (Mycenaean and Cyprian, respectively) and the unknown Minoan language underlying Linear A and the Phaistos Disk. Linears B and C might very well have borrowed their scripts from the earlier Minoans without sharing the same tongue.

Look at English. We're writing our Germanic tongue in the Latin script.

At this stage I was willing to accept only what Evans and Cowley had suggested when they first investigated the apparent affinity of the Cyprian Greek Linear C script to the much earlier Mycenaean Linear B script, which was then still undeciphered. Evans and Cowley allowed the possibility that the glyphs these two scripts shared might convey the "same" sound values *regardless of actual language affiliation*.

Using this method, Cowley had even gone on to identify correctly the Linear B glyph values *ta* (*da* in B), *to*, *lo*, *pa*, and *se*, even though he never knew what language Linear B was written in. Copying Cowley's method of identifying glyph similarities to Cyprian Greek Linear C, Michael Ventris himself posited the glyph values *da*, *ti*, *to*, *pa*, *po*, *ro/lo*, *na*, *we*, and *se* for Mycenaean Linear B when its underlying Greek origin was still unknown to him, too.

The comparison of glyphs between *related* scripts constitutes, then, a valid decipherment method that boasts impressive precedents.

For this reason, I now addressed my working syllabary of
the Phaistos Disk (Figure 4.1) in the first instance with known
syllabic values for cognate (related by derivation) glyphs in the
Aegean scripts. Neither the language nor the content of the
Phaistos Disk was assumed at this point. The only assumption
was that the Disk possessed *a* language and *a* content.

In this way, there was no more a "Greek hypothesis" for
the ethnicity of the Minoan people of ancient Crete than there
was a "Māori hypothesis."

I began comparing glyphs. The sound values of the later Mycenaean Greek Linear B glyphs and of the much later Cyprian
Greek Linear C glyphs are well known by now. From these
known sound values, most of Minoan Linear A's glyph inventory—or at least a fair portion (it depends on what expert you
listen to)—has been reconstructed through formal glyph comparisons, statistical surveys, and structural analyses that have
occupied Linear A scholars for the past forty years.

All the same, it's a tricky business, this comparing signs of
one script with those of another. For one thing, you have to
make sure that the compared scripts are actually related. For
example, if you try comparing our English (Latin) alphabet A B
C with the Japanese syllabic *katakana* script アイウ (*a i u*) or its
companion *hiragana* script あいう (*a i u*), you might as well give
up. It's immediately obvious that these two Japanese writing
systems bear no genetic relationship to our own alphabet. But
if you know that the scripts are genetically related, as here
with the several Aegean scripts, then you can justify your comparison.

You can't just compare out of the blue, though. Outward
resemblance can often deceive even the most objective
observer. One must effect comparisons according to defined
formal criteria.

There are other difficulties, too. Like orientation. On the Phaistos Disk it doesn't seem to make any appreciable difference whether some glyphs stand on their ends (to conserve precious writing space), like glyph 25's "boat" and 33's "tunny" and 18's "plumb-square"; whether they are turned upside-down, like 28's "hoof-horn" and 40's "fig/testicles" and sometimes 27's "oxhide talent"; or whether they are even flipped any which way at the scribe's seeming whim, like 29's "cat's head in profile." Unlike a linear script, which by definition has to foot a line, a pictographic script such as the Phaistos Disk's prioritizes object identification, which can occur with the glyphs in any orientation.

Several of the glyph correspondences between the Phaistos Disk and Linears A, B, and C were so obvious that I was not surprised when I later found that other scholars had suggested them, too. Disk glyph 12 ☉ could only be Linear A ☉ and Linear B ☻, both of which have the sound value *qe* (or *kue*); because the Greek language later replaced the *q* sound, this glyph is missing in Cyprian Greek Linear C, a much later script. Disk glyph 35 ⚲ is obviously Linear A ⚲ and Linear B ‡ (Linear C's is not so transparent: ⟱), both of which harbor the sound value *te*. And Disk 19 Ⅴ has to be a reverse imprint of Linear A ⌐ and Linear B ⌐ and Linear C ⌐, all three of which claim the sound value *da* (Linear C: *ta*, because this script contains no *d-* series in its glyph inventory).

So far so good. These are the easy ones.

Other glyph correspondences aren't so manifest. The formal criteria are satisfied through more elaborate means. For example, take Disk glyph 34 ⚇. Most investigators see this sign as a "bee." Formally, it most assuredly corresponds to Linear A ⌂ *pi*, which some investigators have been so bold as to "identify" as a bee. Linear B's *pi* glyph is ⋔. Linear C's *pi* simply offers ⌄, which, I suppose, a person with laudable imagination might see as "two bees in flight"—for which there is no proof at all. Here one is allowed merely to suggest the Linear A value *pi* as the closest *formal* correspondent to Disk glyph 34 ... without presuming to identify the object itself.

A similar case obtains with Disk glyph 20 — the "Minoan handled vase," according to Sir Arthur Evans. The formal correspondents in Linears A and B would be and , respectively (Linear C shows the less transparent), which similarly have been "identified" by investigators as a *kissubion*—the handled pitcher or beaker of the ancient Aegean—a word of pre-Mycenaean origin. Because these linear glyphs all share the value *ki* for this object (it was suggested many years ago by another scholar that this value derives from the first syllable of the word **ki**ssubion), we'll provisionally award Disk glyph 20 the same value *ki*.

Then there is Disk glyph 29 , the "cat's head in profile"—perhaps indeed the *Felis domestica* that was bred in Egypt as early as 2000 B.C. Sir Arthur Evans and others have imagined in similar linear glyphs a "head of an animal of the feline genus." Michael Ventris found the sound value of Greek Linear B's formally similar glyph to be *ma*. This is the same sound value that most scholars have subsequently awarded to the glyph's various Minoan Linear A correspondents and so on, too. But on the Phaistos Disk, the same feline head—if this is what the glyph truly depicts—is not facing us but is in profile. Is it advisable to award to this glyph the same sound value *ma* that the similar feline heads in the linear scripts possess? I think so, because for a reader of a pictographic script, it is the object itself and not its orientation that is significant. For this reason, I was willing at least to test Disk glyph 29's feline head with the same phonetic value as that of the two linear glyphs' feline heads: *ma*.

Comparing in this way the glyphs of the Phaistos Disk with those of the Aegean linear scripts A, B, and C, I eventually arrived at eighteen tentative syllabic assignations (Figure 4.2). And I must stress the word *tentative*. It wasn't easy. There had to be later adjustments. But at the end of this particular stage of

Script: *Value:*

PD		L		LB		LC		Value
PD12	☉	L91		LB78		LC –		qe
PD35		L92		LB04		LC te		te
PD19		L30		LB01		LC ta		da
PD18		L78		LB37		LC ti		ti
PD38		L29		LB77		LC ka		ka
PD39		L100a		LB28		LC i		i
PD34		L41/56a		LB39		LC pi		pi
PD01		L99		LB53		LC ri		ri/li
PD37		L77		LB09		LC se		se
PD15		L21		LB11		LC po		po
PD36		L55		LB26		LC lu		ru/lu
PD24		L102a		LB45		LC –		de
PD20		L103		LB67		LC ki		ki
PD14		L66		LB72		LC pe		pe
PD26		L58		LB76		LC la		ra/la
PD29		L95		LB80		LC ma		ma
PD25		L19		LB24		LC ne		ne
PD22		L31		LB31		LC sa		sa (wa)

FIGURE 4.2
Formal glyph correspondences between the Phaistos Disk (PD)
and the scripts of Minoan Linear A (L), Mycenaean Greek
Linear B (LB), and Cyprian Greek Linear C (LC).

the decipherment, I could suggest the following preliminary
sound values for the Disk's glyphs:

01 *ri/li*, 12 *qe*, 14 *pe*, 15 *po*, 18 *ti*, 19 *da*, 20 *ki*, 22 *sa* (wa), 24 *de*, 25
ne, 26 *ra/la*, 29 *ma*, 34 *pi*, 35 *te*, 36 *ru/lu*, 37 *se*, 38 *ka*, and 39 *i*.

Disk glyph 22's suggested *sa* proved to be incorrect and a year later was corrected to the value *wa*. (Out of the Phaistos Disk's forty-five glyphs, only Disk glyph 22's value required correction after March 1984.)

Certainly one cannot pretend to have all the answers at once. A decipherment is like a new mechanical device. At first it clanks or wobbles or otherwise fails to perform as expected until all the parts are humming in relative harmony, each in its proper place.

Yes, but were we—Taki and I—in our proper place? I had to ask in these beginning months of 1984. After fifteen years of marriage, for the first time life wasn't easy for us, and the last thing we needed was to become obsessed with an esoteric project that brought us no income as it drained from each day an ever-increasing number of hours, precious time that we could ill afford in these lean years.

In 1980 we had moved to Germany from New Zealand to avail ourselves of the greater research potential there, having finally secured the services of a professional literary agent in New York who was predicting financial success for two historical books I had written. Six months after our arrival in Germany, however—when our savings of the previous ten years had at last been exhausted and what little we earned on the German economy hardly covered our monthly expenses—our agent quit his agency ... and us. Through a stroke of luck, I ultimately inspired enthusiasm in another literary agent in New York, one of the best in the business, who, he assured me, also saw promise in my literary works. A fortuitous commission to translate a technical work from German into English for Taki's firm brought an unexpected windfall that allowed us to fly down to Crete for two weeks, and I saw the Phaistos Disk for the first time. After two years in Germany things were finally looking up.

At which moment my prominent agent died of a heart attack.

After this Taki and I were forced to live extremely frugally, just getting by. Having both come from upper middle class families, we weren't at all used to this sudden penury, and it darkened each day like a black cloud. As I doggedly continued to research and write my Minoan book, despite the sad loss of my agent and my inability to find another, I would take the bus and then the subway into Nuremberg and fill my notecards there in the public library all day long without lunch, hungrily breathing in the heady aromas from the traditional Nuremberg sausage stands as I trekked back to the subway station late in the cold, windy afternoon. It was either lunch or my train ticket. There wasn't enough money for both.

At that time, our only luxury in life was the Sunday afternoon drive to a local castle or long walks in the woods holding hands and philosophizing about the Minoans and the meaning of life. The small things took on sudden importance, and we learned to appreciate these as never before. A favorite haunt of ours was the Ludwig Canal in the forest by Kornburg just one kilometer from our modest flat in the suburbs; we strolled along the canal for hours, enjoying the colorful wildflowers in summer and huddling together for warmth in the high snows of winter.

Like never before or since, my academic contacts then were minimal. I was wrestling with the Minoan world alone, though drawing inspiration from the writings of Sir Arthur Evans, Michael Ventris and John Chadwick, Maurice Pope of South Africa (later Oxford), Fritz Schachermeyr of Vienna, Paul Faure and Jacques Raison of France, Yves Duhoux of Belgium, Yannis Sakellarakis and Christos Doumas of Greece, Emmett Bennett, Jr., of America, and many others whose articles and books on the Minoan culture and scripts could be as frustrating as they were inspirational. With several of these scholars I commenced a profitable correspondence. What was probably of greatest importance to me at this time was my scholarly freedom: Independent of teaching duties, administrative responsibilities, and dogmatic superiors, I was free in my mid-thirties to pursue and discover.

I was also free to *challenge*.

"The greatest scientific achievements of the past decade," Barry Bishop told Taki and me as he chauffeured us to the prestigious Cosmos Club in Washington, DC, for a congratulatory reception just half a year after this period of hardship and struggle, "have all come from highly trained researchers working alone or in very small groups. They're the ones who've got the ability and the freedom to attain the impossible. Left alone they attain it." Barry would have known; then vice-chairman of the National Geographic Society's Committee for Research and Exploration, he had been the first American to stand atop Mount Everest. I've never forgotten Barry's subtle compliment; it gave me the courage to persevere against my disagreeable adversaries in the months that followed. Tragically, Barry Bishop was killed in a car crash in Idaho just months after his retirement ten years later, in 1994.

Decipherment is a lonely discipline. In stark contrast to the networks of communication and support that the natural sciences enjoy, no country in the world boasts an Institute of Decipherment where an epigrapher might associate with his academic peers and profit from their immediate wisdom and encouragement. There's no School of Decipherment, no Department of Decipherment, no Chair of Decipherment. There's not even a Seminar of Decipherment at a single university or a Congress of Decipherment that convenes at regular intervals. At the end of the twentieth century, the field of deciphering ancient scripts is still the domain of the lone linguist, philologist, or anthropologist who must hold a silent dialogue with his artifacts, photographs, and mountains of articles and books.

Month after month, year after year, wondering if the script can ever be read.

Now that we have our first phonetic values for the Phaistos Disk's glyphs, we can begin entering them into our hitherto blank working syllabary, as we see in Figure 4.3. (During the

	A	E	I	O	U
			PD 39		
J					
W	PD 22				
R/L	PD 26		PD 01		PD 36
M	PD 29				
N		PD 25			
P		PD 14	PD 34	PD 15	
T		PD 35	PD 18		
D	PD 19	PD 24			
K	PD 38		PD 20		
Q		PD 12			
S		PD 37			

FIGURE 4.3

The retrieved syllables PD (Phaistos Disk) 01 *ri/li*, 12 *qe*, 14 *pe*, 15 *po*, 18 *ti*, 19 *da*, 20 *ki*, 22 *sa* (*wa*), 24 *de*, 25 *ne*, 26 *ra/la*, 29 *ma*, 34 *pi*, 35 *te*, 36 *ru/lu*, 37 *se*, 38 *ka*, and 39 *i* have been entered into the working syllabary of the Phaistos Disk.

actual process of decipherment, I had entered these values one at a time to permit adjustments, replacements, and deletions.)

This enables us also to exchange the glyphs' corresponding numbers, as we read them in Retrieval Stage 3 (page 62), for these new sound values.

Whereupon we have a new phonetic-numerical text, Retrieval Stage 4—the beginning of a spoken text of the Phaistos Disk.

RETRIEVAL STAGE 4

Side A: 02-qe 13-ri-ti . / de-40(-qe) / ma 45-07 . / ma ma-pi (.) / **02-qe** 04-40-33 / 27 45-07(-qe) / 27 44-08 (.) / **02-qe** 06-ti(-) / 31-ra(-te) / **02-qe** 41-da(-te) / ri-41 40-07 (.) / **02-qe** 32-23-ka . / i-11 / 02 27-ne 10 23-ti / 28-ri . / **02-qe** 31-ra . / **02-qe** 27 27-te-se-21 / 33-23 (.) / **02-qe** 31-ra . / 02 27-ne 10 23-ti / 28-ri . / **02-qe** 31-ra . / **02-qe** 27 pe-32-ti-27 / 06-ti 17-da / 31-ra(-qe) / **02-qe** 13-ri / 23-da(-te) . / 10-03-ka (.) / **02-qe** 27 27-te-se-21 / 13-ri (.) / 10-03-ka °

Side B: 02-qe wa 40-07 / 27 45-07(-te) / 02 se-23-05 (or: 02-se-23-05) . / wa ne-27 / 33-de-ki(-qe) / 16 23-ti-43 (or: 16-23-ti-43). / 13-ri i-33 / po-07 13-ri-ti . / wa se-42-ne / 07 de-40(-te) / 02 ra-ru-40 (or: 02-ra-ru-40) / 27-ne ka-ri (or: 27-ne-ka-ri) / ma de-de-ki(-te) / 16 pe-ti (or: 16-pe-ti) / ma 33-ri (or: ma-33-ri) / 06-te-32 i-33 / 02 09 27-ri (or: 02-09-27-ri) / ma ru-07-08 (or: ma-ru-07-08) . / ma 08-13 (or: ma-08-13) / ma 45-07 . / wa ma ru-07-08 (or: wa ma-ru-07-08) . / 27 pi-23-ne / 07-ti(-te) (or: 07 ti-te; or: 07 ti te) / 07 45-07 . / 07 23-ti(-de) / wa ma ru-07-08 (or: wa ma-ru-07-08). / 09-30-i-ti-07 / 02 06-te 23-07 / ma pi-23-ne / 45-07 .

Can we tell what language it is? Is the Disk really speaking to us at last?

Asking myself the same questions in those first snowy days of 1984, I examined this phonetic-numerical text countless times. I paid particular attention to those structures that had been revealed in the earlier internal analysis—that is, all the curious underlined bits and the boldface **02-qe** and especially those field endings 12 *qe* and 35 *te* that had so engaged me earlier. I realized that if I dared to draw any firm conclusions at this early stage of the decipherment, then I'd be little different from Christopher Columbus, who described the glories of "India" after his first voyage to the New World. It was far too early for conclusions. The evidence allowed only speculation.

And speculation proves nothing but the investigator's imagination.

Field endings *qe* and *te* were fascinating, all the same. Hadn't both been identified in the internal analysis, using only numbers, as possible conjunctions functioning like "and"? Old Greek possesses a *te* that means "and." It derives from an earlier *qe* that also means "and," as found in Mycenaean Greek. This *qe* functions in the Mycenaean Greek Linear B tablets of ancient Crete and the Greek mainland just as it does here, linking things together.

But then that's the problem. Traditional etymology (word history) explains Old Greek *te* as the reflex (linguistic product) of the much earlier *qe*. The two words can't be contemporaneous. The *qe* came before the *te*. Or so says traditional etymology. For this reason—and because the Phaistos Disk was Minoan, not Greek—I had to accept at the beginning of 1984 that this was probably a false lead.

That a *qe* was functioning here as a conjunction (a linking word) could still mean, however, that the language of the Phaistos Disk might be of Indo-European origin. The word *qe* (as in Latin *Senatus Populus-que*, "Senate and People")—at the end of words, not appearing before them—was a common conjunction meaning "and" in ancient Indo-European languages. So maybe it was a conjunction here on the Phaistos Disk after all, just as the internal analysis had suggested. If this were true, then it would be the first tenuous indication of a possible Indo-European origin of the Minoan people of ancient Crete.

Disk glyph 24 in field B25, whose function I had earlier likened to that of a Greek *de* in the internal analysis when I was still using only numbers, turned out to have the very same sound value, too: *de*. This could only be linguistic coincidence, I told myself. Linguistic coincidence is common among the world's 6000-odd languages.

Then there was the complete "word" *de-de-ki*, if indeed it was an autonomous word. Didn't it look suspiciously like what linguists call reduplication—the significant repetition of a syllable or letter? This is a relatively common feature of the perfect tense of verbs (verbs of completed action) in Old Greek and a few other Indo-European languages.

Which brings us just about to the limit of what one could speculate about Retrieval Stage 4.

More sound values for the Disk's glyphs were needed, I realized, before any substantial conclusions about the artifact's underlying language could be tendered. And these sound values had to come from external sources. One couldn't distill them from imagination or wishful thinking.

I realized that at this juncture, the formal correspondences with the genetically related Mycenaean Greek Linear B script and the Cyprian Greek Linear C script were exhausted. I dared presume no further upon either. But there were still formal correspondences between the Phaistos Disk script and the indigenous Minoan Linear A script. And cogent correspondences between the Disk script and the Cretan hieroglyphic script existed, too.

It would well be worth positing possible sound values for the Disk's glyphs according to these two contemporaneous Minoan scripts, I felt, and then testing how these values function in a new and enhanced text.

Michael Ventris and John Chadwick, in the impressive tome they wrote on the Mycenaean documents in 1955–1956, had suggested thirty-one Minoan hieroglyphic correspondences with either Minoan Linear A glyphs or Mycenaean Greek Linear B glyphs or both. Of these, twenty-six corresponding Linear B sound values were already known at the time. (Several of these also figure in the above assignation of sound values: 12 *qe*, 18 *ti*, 24 *de*, 26 *ra/la*, 29 *ma*, 35 *te*, and 36 *ru/lu*.) Nevertheless, by 1973, only eleven years before my own work, Professor Paul Faure, then France's leading Minoan expert, was able to suggest an almost complete Minoan hieroglyphic syllabary based on similarities to the known sound values of the Linear A and Linear B glyphs (Figure 2.7).

Professor Faure's proposed Minoan hieroglyphic syllabary served as my basis of comparison for further Phaistos Disk correspondences. At the least, I reasoned, it might suggest possible sound values that are independent of any fancied textual distillations.

For example, Disk glyph 21 🕮 formally corresponds to the Minoan hieroglyphic signs ▤ ᗰ ᥩ , which, in turn, appear to reproduce the same object that Minoan Linear A ▤ depicts. The Mycenaean Greek Linear B derivative of this glyph is ▤ and its sound value is known to be *ja* (*ya*). For this reason, I proposed

Script:					*Value:*
PD21 🕮	L32 ▤	CH *ja*		ᥩ	*ja*
PD32 🐦	L54 Ψ	CH *re*		🐦	*re/le*
PD23 ᛉ	L86 ᗠ	CH *mo*		ǀ	*mo*
PD03 ᗡ	L26 ᵢ̄	CH *na*		⊗	*na*
PD08 ᛘ	L25 ⊢⊣	CH *nu*		ᛦ	*nu*
PD45 ⫴	L02 ‡	CH *pa*		‡	*pa*
PD28 ᛁ	L72 ⟩	CH —			*ke*
PD13 ◊	L36 ♀	CH *ku*		⬆	*ku*

FIGURE 4.4

Formal glyph correspondences among the Phaistos Disk (PD),
Minoan Linear A (L), and the Cretan hieroglyphs (CH).

that it would be worth testing Disk glyph 21 with the possible sound value *ja*.

Disk glyph 13 ⚊, with its upright shaft and bulbous bottom, appears to reproduce the varying Minoan hieroglyphic signs ⚊⚊⚊ to which Prof. Faure had tentatively awarded the sound value *ko/ku*. (More than a year later, I discovered that one German scholar in the 1920s had seen in Disk glyph 13 a "cypress," a word that begins with *ku-* in Greek and that the Greeks had borrowed from the pre-Mycenaean population of the Aegean.)

Though this approach was promisingly productive, using tentative values from Minoan Linear A and the Minoan hieroglyphs did not permit the retrieval of as many sound values as the philologically more secure comparison with Linears A, B, and C had afforded. Two of the sound values later required modification. In light of the Disk's emerging phonological (sound system) constraints, Professor Faure's suggested "birdlike" *ra* became instead the sound value *re*. And his *i* was discovered to be a *mo* on the Phaistos Disk.

Comparing the Phaistos Disk's glyphs with specifically the Minoan Linear A glyphs and the Minoan hieroglyphs had yielded eight more potential sound values: 03 *na*, 08 *nu*, 13 *ku*, 21 *ja* (*ya*), 23 *mo*, 28 *ke*, 32 *re/le*, and 45 *pa*.

These can now be inserted into our working syllabary (Figure 4.5).

As we did once before, we can now also replace the corresponding numbers in Retrieval Stage 4 with these eight new sound values.

Writing these into the text of Retrieval Stage 4 produces Retrieval Stage 5:

RETRIEVAL STAGE 5

Side A: 02-qe <u>ku-ri</u>-ti . / <u>de-40</u>(-qe) / ma <u>pa-07</u> . / ma ma-pi (.) / **02-qe** 04-40-33 / 27 <u>pa-07</u>(-qe) / 27 44-nu (.) / **02-qe** <u>06-ti</u>(-) / <u>31-ra</u>(-te) / **02-qe** 41-da(-te) / ri-41 <u>40-07</u> (.) / **02-qe** re-mo-ka . / i-11 / 02 <u>27-ne</u> 10 mo-ti / ke-ri . / **02-qe** <u>31-ra</u> . / **02-qe** 27 27-

	A	E	I	O	U
			PD 39		
J	PD 21				
W	PD 22				
R/L	PD 26	PD 32	PD 01		PD 36
M	PD 29			PD 23	
N	PD 03	PD 25			PD 08
P	PD 45	PD 14	PD 34	PD 15	
T		PD 35	PD 18		
D	PD 19	PD 24			
K	PD 38	PD 28	PD 20		PD 13
Q		PD 12			
S		PD 37			

FIGURE 4.5
The retrieved syllables PD (Phaistos Disk) 03 *na*, 08 *nu*,
13 *ku*, 21 *ja* (*ya*), 23 *mo*, 28 *ke*, 32 *re/le*, and 45 *pa*
have been entered into the working syllabary.

te-se-ja / 33-mo (.) / **02-qe** 31-ra . / 02 27-ne 10 mo-ti / ke-ri . /
02-qe 31-ra . / **02-qe** 27 pe-re-ti-27 / 06-ti 17-da / 31-ra(-qe) /
02-qe ku-ri / mo-da(-te) . / 10-na-ka (.) / **02-qe** 27 27-te-se-ja /
ku-ri (.) / 10-na-ka °

Side B: 02-qe wa 40-07 / 27 pa-07(-te) / 02 se-mo-05 (or: 02-se-
mo-05) . / wa ne-27 / 33-de-ki(-qe) / 16 mo-ti-43 (or: 16-mo-ti-
43). / ku-ri i-33 / po-07 ku-ri-ti . / wa se-42-ne / 07 de-40(-te) /
02 ra-ru-40 (or: 02-ra-ru-40) / 27-ne ka-ri (or: 27-ne-ka-ri) / ma
de-de-ki(-te) / 16 pe-ti (or: 16-pe-ti) / ma 33-ri (or: ma-33-ri) /
06-te-re i-33 / 02 09 27-ri (or: 02-09-27-ri) / ma ru-07-nu (or:
ma-ru-07-nu). / ma nu-ku (or: ma-nu-ku) / ma pa-07 . / wa ma
ru-07-nu (or: wa ma-ru-07-nu) . / 27 pi-mo-ne / 07-ti(-te) (or: 07
ti-te; or: 07 ti te) / 07 pa-07 . / 07 mo-ti(-de) / wa ma ru-07-nu
(or: wa ma-ru-07-nu). / 09-30-i-ti-07 / 02 06-te mo-07 / ma pi-
mo-ne / pa-07 .

Finally we have the beginnings of a real text. The numerical skeleton that had been so important for seeing the internal
structure of the inscription has taken on flesh. Entire words are
starting to appear. And this time I mean real *words*, not just
"significant units." This last stage of the ordered retrieval
process has produced an embryonic monument that in its own
way is no less extraordinary than Sir Arthur Evans's partial
reconstruction of the Knossos palace-shrine . . .

For the inscription on the Phaistos Disk shows every
appearance of being Indo-European!

Did the Minoans really belong to our own language family?

The evidence for this astounding possibility was mounting.

I postulated that the *ma* reproduced an Indo-European collective plural "my" and was able to "identify" an adjective
(descriptive word) and several nouns (things) as well, including
possible tribal names.

Most important, I concluded that the *qe* and *te* had to be conjunctions—linking words—after all, and that they both meant "and." Despite traditional etymological canon, the evidence for this in the solidifying text of the Phaistos Disk had to be acknowledged. Perhaps there had been two separate Indo-European origins for the later Greek *te* that meant "and," I dared to suggest, now convinced that the language of the Disk had to be an Indo-European tongue after all: the known *qe* as well as an already existent *te*. (Much later I discovered that one of the world's most respected scholars of the Greek language, studying *te* in ancient Greek, had hazarded the same heresy exactly fifty years earlier, in 1934.)

The soccer players down on the field weren't just getting names, it seemed.

They were starting to get passports.

CHAPTER 5

"HEAR YE, CRETANS AND GREEKS!"

Encouraged by these results—given that, all along, any stage of the ordered retrieval process might have collapsed like a house of cards—I was eager to advance the decipherment of the Phaistos Disk one critical stage further.

I decided to test the Indo-European solution *acrophonically.*

It hadn't been possible earlier. But there was finally enough evidence to justify using this controversial decipherment method. It's not valid for a linear script, of course, which isn't graphic enough for an investigator to identify the glyphs' objects. But acrophonic analysis is perfectly valid in the later stages of a pictographic script's decipherment.

And the Phaistos Disk's script was pictographic.

Remember *A-me-ri-ca,* wherein the initial **A-** was supposed to be indicated by the picture of Athens's **A**cropolis? That's the method I chose to implement at this point in the prioritized retrieval procedure. I would look for—and name—the "Acropolises" in the Disk's inscription.

Once there is sufficient evidence for identification of the underlying language family of an unknown acrophonic script, one is provisionally entitled to test *possible* (not absolute) initial values for a respective pictogram's word according to the consonant-vowel alternatives left in one's working syllabary. If one discerns an **A**cropolis being used as a glyph in a pictographic script, in other words, then one can call it by name and give the glyph the sound value **A-**, provided the *a* slot is still blank in the working syllabary.

Three-quarters of the total number of the Phaistos Disk's glyphs were now quite confidently associated with sound values that had been found through methods other than the acrophonic. The Disk's pictograms themselves had originated acrophonically, as many scholars in the past had affirmed.

The word "talent" was my first test case involving the acrophonic method with the Phaistos Disk. The talent was the contemporaneous Aegean denomination of weight—the currency of the ancient world—that even the Mycenaean Greeks of the second millennium B.C. had called a *talanton,* a word of venerable provenance. My test case was centered on Disk glyph 27 ☡, which I awarded the sound value *ta* that was still available in the working syllabary. (That is, the intersection of consonant *t-* and vowel *-a* remained blank, as Figure 4.5 shows.) The value *ta* derived from the corresponding *ta* of Minoan Linear A's ☡ and Mycenaean Greek Linear B's ☡ as well as from compelling external evidence, including Minoan and Egyptian frescoes and Mycenaean relics, that the depicted object perhaps represented an "oxhide talent."

But did the Minoans' name for the talent also begin with *ta-?*

In order to test this possibility, I inserted *ta* into the working syllabary, writing the numeral 27 in the corresponding blank slot (Figure 5.1). (The few remaining blank slots themselves now become effective controls for the final acrophonic assignations, because they significantly limit the number of remaining syllabic choices.) Then I exchanged each of the frequent 27s in Retrieval Stage 5 for the syllable *ta.*

This gave me Retrieval Stage 6:

	A	E	I	O	U
			PD 39		
J	PD 21				
W	PD 22				
R/L	PD 26	PD 32	PD 01		PD 36
M	PD 29			PD 23	
N	PD 03	PD 25			PD 08
P	PD 45	PD 14	PD 34	PD 15	
T	PD 27	PD 35	PD 18		
D	PD 19	PD 24			
K	PD 38	PD 28	PD 20		PD 13
Q		PD 12			
S		PD 37			

FIGURE 5.1
The retrieved syllable *ta* has been entered into the working syllabary.

RETRIEVAL STAGE 6

Side A: 02-qe <u>ku-ri</u>-ti . / <u>de-40</u>(-qe) / ma <u>pa-07</u> . / ma ma-pi (.) / **02-qe** 04-40-33 / ta <u>pa-07</u>(-qe) / ta 44-nu (.) / **02-qe** <u>06-ti</u>(-) / <u>31-ra</u>(-te) / **02-qe** 41-da(-te) / ri-41 <u>40-07</u> (.) / **02-qe** re-mo-ka . / i-11 / 02 <u>ta-ne</u> 10 <u>mo-ti</u> / <u>ke-ri</u> . / **02-qe** <u>31-ra</u> . / **02-qe** ta <u>ta-te-se-ja</u> / 33-mo (.) / **02-qe** <u>31-ra</u> . / 02 <u>ta-ne</u> 10 <u>mo-ti</u> / <u>ke-ri</u> . / **02-qe** <u>31-ra</u> . / **02-qe** ta pe-re-ti-ta / <u>06-ti</u> 17-da / <u>31-ra</u>(-qe) / **02-qe** <u>ku-ri</u> / mo-da(-te) . / <u>10-na-ka</u> (.) / **02-qe** ta <u>ta-te-se-ja</u> / <u>ku-ri</u> (.) / <u>10-na-ka</u> °

Side B: 02-qe wa <u>40-07</u> / ta <u>pa-07</u>(-te) / 02 se-mo-05 (or: 02-se-mo-05) . / wa ne-ta / 33-<u>de-ki</u>(-qe) / 16 <u>mo-ti</u>-43 (or: 16-<u>mo-ti</u>-43). / <u>ku-ri</u> i-33 / po-07 <u>ku-ri</u>-ti . / wa se-42-ne / 07 <u>de-40</u>(-te) / 02 ra-ru-40 (or: 02-ra-ru-40) / <u>ta-ne</u> ka-ri (or: ta-ne-ka-ri) / ma de-<u>de-ki</u>(-te) / 16 pe-ti (or: 16-pe-ti) / ma 33-ri (or: ma-33-ri) / <u>06-te</u>-re i-33 / 02 09 ta-ri (or: 02-09-ta-ri) / ma <u>ru-07</u>-nu (or: <u>ma-ru-07-nu</u>) . / ma nu-ku (or: ma-nu-ku) / ma <u>pa-07</u> . / wa ma <u>ru-07</u>-nu (or: wa <u>ma-ru-07-nu</u>) . / ta <u>pi-mo-ne</u> / 07-ti(-te) (or: 07 ti-te; or: 07 ti te) / 07 <u>pa-07</u> . / 07 <u>mo-ti</u>(-de) / wa ma <u>ru-07</u>-nu (or: wa <u>ma-ru-07-nu</u>). / 09-30-i-ti-07 / 02 <u>06-te</u> mo-07 / ma <u>pi-mo-ne</u> / <u>pa-07</u> .

The inscription's phonological face had taken on familiar expressions; unforeseen linguistic patterns were starting to emerge. If earlier I had suspected only a Proto Indo-European language, now with the surprising domain and linguistic functions that the syllable *ta* displayed in the inscription, the actual underlying language of the Phaistos Disk was becoming all too evident.

This is because the *ta*—which from these surprising distillations surely must represent the oxhide talent after all—was in many fields of the Phaistos Disk a pendant collective "the" or "those" in complementary distribution with the earlier identified *ma* that I had suspected meant "my" in a similar collective fashion. An inflected form of the *ta* appeared: *ta-ne.*

This permitted a field-internal word separation, resulting in the emergence of another form of an already proposed tribal name—*ka-ri*—which indicated a possible phonological rule (an internal regulation of the sound system) that somehow appeared to involve accent. I couldn't yet isolate this rule, however. More adjectives and nouns could be "identified."

The voiceless pictograms were indeed being forced to speak. And in a tongue that was "... if not Greek, at least an Indo-European language closely related to Greek," as Professor Faure had been quoted as saying about the language underlying the Minoan Linear A script in the early 1970s....

An extraordinary suggestion that most scholars of Aegean prehistory had chosen to ignore.

In order to make certain that I wasn't merely reading into the barely discernible text what I might be wishing to see or what my own pilot methodology might have falsely been steering me to see, I applied the same acrophonic method again. But this time I chose to use ancient words of acknowledged pre-Mycenaean provenance.

Hadn't Michael Ventris done something similar with the Linear B tablets before he knew them to be written in Mycenaean Greek? He had tested glyph values using "probable" pre-Mycenaean place names. With this method, Ventris had seen his *a-?-ni-?* become *a-mi-ni-so* for the Cretan town "Amnisos," his *? + o-no-so* become *ko-no-so* for "Knossos," and his *?-? + i-so* become *tu-ri-so* for "Tylissos."

Using a similar method based on recognized borrowings and modifications of known ancient words for the few remaining unassigned Disk glyphs that were left, I therefore tentatively awarded Disk glyph 40, the inverted "fig" or "testicles," the sound value *ni*. (Professor Schachermeyr of Vienna had earlier suggested that "the Minoan word for 'fig' apparently began with the syllable *ni-*.") Glyph 33, the "tunny," received the value *di* (for *dhinnus*, perhaps related to later Old Greek *thunnos*). The "slave" or "captive" depicted in Disk glyph 04 was taken to represent a word beginning with the syllable *do-* (possibly related to Mycenaean *do-e-ro*, "slave," a word of pre-Greek provenance). And the "traditional beehive" of the very frequent glyph 07 was tested with the value *si* after *simblos*, a pre-Greek word for the domed hive. Finally, this time on the basis of a known Mycenaean word, glyph 09's "helmet" was provisionally awarded the sound value *ko* (for *korus*, "helmet").

These values can now be entered into the working syllabary (Figure 5.2), whereupon we can replace the respective numbers in Retrieval Stage 6 with these new values.

Which gives us Retrieval Stage 7:

RETRIEVAL STAGE 7

Side A: 02-qe ku-ri-ti . / de-ni(-qe) / ma pa-si . / ma ma-pi (.) / **02-qe** do-ni-di / ta pa-si(-qe) / ta 44-nu (.) / **02-qe** 06-ti(-) / 31-ra(-te) / **02-qe** 41-da(-te) / ri-41 ni-si (.) / **02-qe** re-mo-ka . / i-11 / 02 ta-ne 10 mo-ti / ke-ri . / **02-qe** 31-ra . / **02-qe** ta ta-te-se-ja / di-mo (.) / **02-qe** 31-ra . / 02 ta-ne 10 mo-ti / ke-ri . / **02-qe** 31-ra . / **02-qe** ta pe-re-ti-ta / 06-ti 17-da / 31-ra(-qe) / **02-qe** ku-ri / mo-da(-te) . / 10-na-ka (.) / **02-qe** ta ta-te-se-ja / ku-ri (.) / 10-na-ka °

Side B: 02-qe wa ni-si / ta pa-si(-te) / 02 se-mo-05 (or: 02-se-mo-05) . / wa ne-ta / di-de-ki(-qe) / 16 mo-ti-43 (or: 16-mo-ti-43) . / ku-ri i-di / po-si ku-ri-ti . / wa se-42-ne / si de-ni(-te) / 02 ra-ru-ni (or: 02-ra-ru-ni) / ta-ne ka-ri (or: ta-ne-ka-ri) / ma de-de-ki(-te) / 16 pe-ti (or: 16-pe-ti) / ma di-ri (or: ma-di-ri) / 06-te-re i-di / 02 ko ta-ri (or: 02-ko-ta-ri) / ma ru-si-nu (or: ma-ru-si-nu) . / ma nu-ku (or: ma-nu-ku) / ma pa-si . / wa ma ru-si-nu (or: wa ma-ru-si-nu) . / ta pi-mo-ne / si-ti(-te) (or: si ti-te; or: si ti te) / si pa-si . / si mo-ti(-de) / wa ma ru-si-nu (or: wa ma-ru-si-nu). / ko-30-i-ti-si / 02 06-te mo-si / ma pi-mo-ne / pa-si .

By February 9, 1984, I had already attempted a cautious field-by-field transliteration—replacing the numbers with sound

	A	E	I	O	U
			PD 39		
J	PD 21				
W	PD 22				
R/L	PD 26	PD 32	PD 01		PD 36
M	PD 29			PD 23	
N	PD 03	PD 25	PD 40		PD 08
P	PD 45	PD 14	PD 34	PD 15	
T	PD 27	PD 35	PD 18		
D	PD 19	PD 24	PD 33	PD 04	
K	PD 38	PD 28	PD 20	PD 09	PD 13
Q		PD 12			
S		PD 37	PD 07		

FIGURE 5.2

The retrieved syllables PD 04 *do,* 07 *si,* 09 *ko,* 33 *di,* and 40 *ni* have been entered into the working syllabary.

values—based on my working syllabary as completed thus far (Figure 5.2). In the first eleven fields of Side A, I had provisionally assigned sound values to as many as nineteen separate glyphs. (Fourteen of these nineteen later proved to be correct.)

Work Note, same day: "Looking better than initial probes, but much too easy for [completed] reading. Doubt if as much as 20 percent accuracy at this stage."

I didn't realize I was right on the threshold.

By this time I had abandoned the writing of my Minoan book in order to dedicate myself full-time to decipherment of the Phaistos Disk.

It had transcended mere hobby: I was breathing, thinking, eating, and dreaming nothing but disk, *Disk*, DISK! It had become a three-dimensional chess game ... played with a partner who, though dead these 3600 years, never let me rest.

For the first time in my life I knew what obsession was.

While putting sound to number in this methodical series of phonetic retrieval steps, I was witnessing the seeming reincarnation of a Minoan text before my eyes. I wasn't reading into the inscription. My method of decipherment allowed the inscription to read *out* to me. I was beginning to read parts of words and complete words, and in some cases I could recognize entire phrases, though their meanings were still not wholly clear.

And then it happened.

The Phaistos Disk's code "broke."

I knew from my comprehensive study of the historic decipherments of the past that one of the most productive glyphbreaking methods in these decipherments had been the location and identification of personal, place, and tribal names in the investigated inscriptions. First suggested by the celebrated mathematician and philosopher Leibnitz back in 1714, this method had played a crucial role in the decipherments of the Egyptian and Hittite hieroglyphs, Persian cuneiforms, and Cyprian Linear C script. It had been an indispensable tool in Michael Ventris's decipherment of Mycenaean Greek Linear B, too, as we have already seen.

By this time, I had retrieved on the Phaistos Disk—as you've seen for yourself in the emerging text of the various Retrieval Stages—what appeared to be the three autonomous names *ku-ri-ti, de-ni,* and *do-ni-di* all within the first five fields of Side A. However, I still hesitated to accept these seeming "names" as irrefutable evidence for specific Aegean tribes. What proof did I have?

Yet *ku-ri-ti* did look like the Old Greek name for those enigmatic natives of ancient Crete, the Kourētes, whom the Greeks considered the source of all civilization. At least the consonants were a close match: *k-r-t-*. And the "name" *de-ni* suspiciously resembled the Danaans, Old Greek *Danaoi,* Homer's name for the ancient Greeks who fought at Troy in the second millennium B.C. and the name by which the Greeks were known to the ancient Egyptians—as the Tanaya—and others at the same time. (The Mycenaeans perhaps called themselves Danaoi, some scholars claim.) As for *do-ni-di,* it immediately brought to mind the mythical Danaïdes, the "fifty daughters of Danaus," whose name probably recalls a further prehistoric tribe of the Aegean.

The evidence continued to mount. I had just completed Retrieval Stage 7 and had deduced that the "word" *ni-si* found in Disk fields A11 and B1 might conceivably mean "immigrants"—*if* I could accept the growing conviction that the underlying language of the Phaistos Disk was indeed an extremely early Hellenic tongue.

I fully realized the heresy I was committing. I was allowing the possibility that the Minoans of ancient Crete—the source all civilization to the ancient Greeks—were prehistoric Hellenes related to the Mycenaeans. In other words, that the Minoans were Greeks themselves.

I wanted that final independent confirmation. The idea was just too heretical without it.

I simply couldn't trust my own eyes, despite the fact that these tribal names had been distilled objectively, independent of any willful manipulation. Nonetheless, I had here *ku-ri-ti, de-ni,* and *do-ni-di*. How to explain them? Perhaps the classical Greek names Kourētes, Danaoi, and Danaïdes originated long after the Phaistos Disk had been manufactured. Perhaps I subconsciously put together these imagined "Minoan names" myself, though I consciously believed that I was proceeding objectively. I might have been deceiving myself all along, in other words.

The problem was that I had no *bilingual* against which to test my emerging results objectively. A bilingual is a document or inscription that reproduces the same text in two separate languages or scripts. Jean-François Champollion's "Rosetta Stone," which in one of the finest hours of a glyphbreaker facilitated the brilliant young Frenchman's decipherment of the Egyptian hieroglyphic script in the early nineteenth century, is a "trilingual": One inscription appears in three separate scripts—in this case hieratic (priestly) hieroglyphics, demotic (plebeian) hieroglyphics, and the classical Greek script. (The Greek script let Champollion understand what the unknown Egyptian hieroglyphic text was saying.) But the Phaistos Disk, even though it may hold the "key" to prehistoric Europe's best-kept secret, is no Rosetta Stone.

The Disk holds only the one script consisting of these forty-five pictograms.

All the same, I couldn't forget what John Chadwick, Michael Ventris's colleague, had written about his first approaching the small, two-line, Mycenaean Greek Linear B tablet V 52 that, among others, he had used to test Ventris's new decipherment back in 1952. On this tablet, Chadwick had discovered the names of the goddess Athena and the gods Enualios, Apollo, and Poseidon. "Any one [deity] might have been an illusion," Chadwick wrote later, "but four in one list were too much for coincidence."

These were the things I was mulling over when I began addressing Disk fields A10 and A11.

One evening Taki came home from the office with an account of an amusing game she'd heard about that day that involved the correct spelling of the country Libya. (Most people put the *y* in the wrong place.) Curious, she wondered what the "Minoan" form of the word Libya might have been, at least according to what we had retrieved on the Phaistos Disk so far.

"Libya? Something like *Libu* or *Ripu*, I suppose," I replied. "The Minoan scribes didn't seem to distinguish between the *l*'s and *r*'s and *b*'s and *p*'s."

"Is Libya on the Disk?"

"Are you kidding? I wish. Anyway, if it were, then it would definitely have had to start with a *li-/ri-* pictogram, and I . . . I. . . ."

Momentarily stunned, I fell silent, thinking. Yes. *Of course.* The Minoans might very well have had close trading relations with the ancient Libyans. Hadn't Sir Arthur Evans devoted an entire chapter of his book *Palace of Minos* to this likelihood? Hadn't the Libyans been mentioned by the ancient Egyptians as the *Rbw* as early as 1300 B.C.? And later by the Hebrews, it's inferred, as the Lehabim?

However, if they were mentioned here in the inscription on the Phaistos Disk among my seeming list of tribal names on Side A, then this record would predate the earliest known mention of the Libyans by three hundred years. It would be the first mention of the Libyan people in history.

Yet even more important than this, I was recalling something else. Didn't I have in Disk field A11 in Retrieval Stage 7 the glyph sequence *ri-41 ni-si*? Wasn't this a possible "*li-*41 immigrants" with the significant unit *li-*41 already suggesting itself, from its position, to be yet another tribal name like those three—*ku-ri-ti*, *de-ni*, and *do-ni-di*—that had just preceded it in the inscription? If *li-*41, then, were indeed the Libyans . . .

Then here Disk glyph 41 would have to reproduce the sound value *-bu* (for *Libu*).

It just might work. At least it was worth testing.

And so I resolved to test Disk glyph 41 with the sound value *pu* (for *bu*, merging the two sounds *p-* and *b-* as in Linear B). This was a process that was both subjective and deductive, I admit.

Yet what followed was incontestable scientific confirmation.

For if Disk field A11's "*ri-41 ni-si*" really was "*Libu nīsoi*" or "Libyan immigrants," then the immediately preceding field A10's "*02-qe 41-da te*" would necessarily have to read, "*02-qe pu-da te.*" This is because glyph 41—the tested *pu*—occurs only one other time on the Disk: right in front of our *ri-pu ni-si*. The entire phrase, then, should read something like "*02-qe Puda* and Libyan immigrants." This retrieved *Puda* would also have to be a tribal name, in other words, so long as I was assuming the other four names to be correct.

But I'd never heard of an ancient tribe called the *Puda*.

Here was clearly an objective test case. *Libu* (*ri-pu*) might have been posited into the text as a working hypothesis, in search of the ancient Libyan people. But the independent emergence of the seeming name *Puda* in the Disk field just before the mooted (proposed) name Libya had been wholly beyond any wishful or subconscious manipulation. It had distilled itself. If there did exist such a tribe in the second millennium B.C., then this independent distillation of its name on the Phaistos Disk would have to be regarded as proof of the validity of my decipherment methodology so far.

And of my results, too, I told myself.

Reasoning that this *Puda* might have constituted some tribe neighboring the Libyans—if my conjectured *Libu* in Disk field A11 really was the Libyans—I reached for the new National Geographic *Peoples and Places of the Past*, a large historical atlas that had been published only a few months earlier.

I opened the atlas.

Taki watched at my side, as curious as I.

There it was. On page 43. *Putāya*, or the Land of the *Puta*. (It seemed to show that same *d/t* alternation that one sees with the Greek and Egyptian names for the ancient Greeks: Danaoi/Tanaya.) The Put of the Old Testament. The oldest designation for the North African coastline next to Libya . . .

And closest to Minoan Crete!

Both Taki and I realized at once what this confirmation signified. Our results were indeed correct so far. We had roused the Minoan language from its 3600-year slumber. And it was turning out to be a sister language of Mycenaean Greek.

The evidence for this—five historically attested tribal names within the first eleven fields of Side A of the Phaistos Disk—seemed, as John Chadwick had said about that list of four deities on the Mycenaean Greek Linear B tablet, "too much for coincidence."

However, what was this object that Disk glyph 41 depicted? It clearly began with the syllable *pu-* or *bu-*. But what was it?

"Fascinating.... You know, it must be the same word as the Greek *pugmē* and Latin *pugnus*," I later told Taki, who was sprawled out on the couch studying our Phaistos Disk replica. (She called it "fun.") "The same as our own English **pu**gilism."

"What's the pictogram then?"

"A boxing match!"

Sure enough, the sound value *pu* evidently comprised the first syllable of the ancient Minoans' word for boxing too: Disk glyph 41 depicts two overlapping fists and forearms in the moment of a hefty punch. And from Minoan frescoes and vase reliefs and statuettes and other illustrations, it has long been known that pugilism constituted one of the ancient Aegean's favorite sports ... second only to bull-springing.

The syllable *pu* was now entered into the working syllabary (Figure 5.3).

This allowed me to enter the two *pu*'s into the numerical text, replacing 41 with this retrieved sound value.

Whereupon I could posit Retrieval Stage 8:

RETRIEVAL STAGE 8

Side A: 02-qe <u>ku-ri</u>-ti . / <u>de-ni</u>(-qe) / ma <u>pa-si</u> . / ma ma-pi (.) / **02-qe** do-ni-di / ta <u>pa-si</u>(-qe) / ta 44-nu (.) / **02-qe** <u>06-ti</u>(-) / <u>31-ra</u>(-te) / **02-qe** pu-da(-te) / ri-pu <u>ni-si</u> (.) / **02-qe** re-mo-ka . / i-11 / 02 <u>ta-ne</u> 10 <u>mo-ti</u> / <u>ke-ri</u> . / **02-qe** <u>31-ra</u> . / **02-qe** ta <u>ta-te-se-ja</u> / di-mo

	A	E	I	O	U
			PD 39		
J	PD 21				
W	PD 22				
R/L	PD 26	PD 32	PD 01		PD 36
M	PD 29			PD 23	
N	PD 03	PD 25	PD 40		PD 08
P	PD 45	PD 14	PD 34	PD 15	PD 41
T	PD 27	PD 35	PD 18		
D	PD 19	PD 24	PD 33	PD 04	
K	PD 38	PD 28	PD 20	PD 09	PD 13
Q		PD 12			
S		PD 37	PD 07		

FIGURE 5.3
The retrieved syllable PD 41 *pu*
has been entered into the working syllabary.

(.) / **02-qe** <u>31-ra</u> . / 02 <u>ta-ne</u> 10 <u>mo-ti</u> / <u>ke-ri</u> . / **02-qe** <u>31-ra</u> . / **02-qe** ta pe-re-ti-ta / <u>06-ti</u> 17-da / <u>31-ra</u>(-qe) / **02-qe** <u>ku-ri</u> / mo-da(-te) . / <u>10-na-ka</u> (.) / **02-qe** ta <u>ta-te-se-ja</u> / <u>ku-ri</u> (.) / <u>10-na-ka</u> °

Side B: 02-qe wa <u>ni-si</u> / ta <u>pa-si</u>(-te) / 02 se-mo-05 (or: 02-se-mo-05) . / wa ne-ta / di-<u>de-ki</u>(-qe) / 16 <u>mo-ti</u>-43 (or: 16-<u>mo-ti</u>-43) . / <u>ku-ri</u> <u>i-di</u> / po-si <u>ku-ri</u>-ti . / wa se-42-ne / si <u>de-ni</u>(-te) / 02 ra-ru-ni (or: 02-ra-ru-ni) / <u>ta-ne</u> ka-ri (or: ta-ne-ka-ri) / ma de-<u>de-ki</u>(-te) / 16 pe-ti (or: 16-pe-ti) / ma di-ri (or: ma-di-ri) / <u>06-te</u>-re <u>i-di</u> / 02 ko ta-ri (or: 02-ko-ta-ri) / ma <u>ru-si-nu</u> (or: <u>ma-ru-si-nu</u>) . / ma nu-ku (or: ma-nu-ku) / ma <u>pa-si</u> . / wa ma <u>ru-si-nu</u> (or: wa <u>ma-ru-si-nu</u>) . / ta <u>pi-mo-ne</u> / si-ti(-te) (or: si ti-te; or: si ti te) / si <u>pa-si</u> . / si <u>mo-ti</u>(-de) / wa ma <u>ru-si-nu</u> (or: wa <u>ma-ru-si-nu</u>). / ko-30-i-ti-si / 02 <u>06-te</u> mo-si / ma <u>pi-mo-ne</u> / <u>pa-si</u> .

Work Note, February 26, 1984: "Tremendous advances made while suffering from cold. . . . I made up trial transliteration and translation, never got to translation, so excited about transliteration.—Believe I can see text for first time. Thrilling. And sobering."

"War. . . ."

"Was seue nē sin Deneis ... *Strike ye out with the Danaans and smite the Carians, mine enemy, and succor my stricken. Safeguard me, Idaians: I am sore afraid. . . .*"

It was all tumbling into place now. Hypotheses had been formulated and put to the test. Many had been rejected, but those few that had passed muster had gradually grown in number to organize themselves into ever larger shards of soundness that, when finally glued together with ordered common sense, began to resemble an identifiable shape.

And at this moment I discovered the linguistic key that unlocked the door to the Minoan language.

You see, the pioneering linguists of the early nineteenth century—Rask and Grimm and Bopp, as well as the later Neogrammarians, among others—taught us to appreciate not only that languages change over the centuries but also that they do so according to describable patterns of what is traditionally called "sound change."

This explains why so many words that the related Indo-European languages share, though they mean the same thing, sound so different from one language to the other.

The Germanic tribes, for example, took an original Indo-European *māter* and turned it into *mōthar*, which, altered by a sub-tribe, became Old English *mōdor* and eventually our Modern English "mother." A cousin sub-tribe pronounced it *muotar*, which is why, with still later changes, the Germans say *Mutter* today. In Latin, the Romans said *māter*, which in time became Italian and Spanish *madre* but French *mère*. Old Greek *mētēr* was supplanted by Modern Greek *mitéra*. Old Irish *māthir* is now pronounced in Dublin *máthair*. And whereas medieval Muscovites said *mati*, their modern descendants say *matj*. And so on—all from the same alma *māter*.

However, one of the most modern theories of linguistics, called "transformational generative grammar" and developed by the American linguist Noam Chomsky back in the 1950s and 1960s, tells us that as related languages evolve away from one another in this way, it is not really sounds that change—*e a o* will always sound like *e a o*—but *grammars*. A new "rule" is added to the grammar of a language dictating, say, that in each unstressed syllable the pure vowels *e a o* (that is, AY, AH, OH) are replaced with *i e u* (EE, AY, OO) respectively, their next-higher vowel level.

And this is exactly the rule that I now suspected had been added to the grammar of the underlying language of the Phaistos Disk.

I was by now utterly convinced that these retrieved names in the first few fields of Side A of the Disk were indeed the known tribal names I had suspected. And weren't "Minoan" *ku-ri-ti*, *de-ni*, and *do-ni-di* differing from historical Greek Kourētes, Danaoi, and Danaïdes according to describable patterns? Several phonological rules were obviously at work here,

I reasoned, one of which evidently compelled the speakers of Minoan to replace each of the three vowels *e a o* in an unstressed syllable with its next-higher neighbor *i e u*—a rule missing in all other Hellenic languages.

Curious, turning to other retrieved words on the Phaistos Disk, I noted that *all* (with a few minor exceptions) were apparently affected by this same grammatical rule. Simply by suspending this rule—that is, by reverting these surface forms *i e u* into their sub-surface pre-rule forms *e a o*—I could readily identify the words' earlier Hellenic etyma (parent words). Many of these etyma were similar or even identical to later Greek words. And they immediately made contextual and historical sense in the Phaistos Disk's solidifying message.

With the direct application of the modern linguistic theory of transformational generative grammar to the Phaistos Disk's decipherment, I could observe two separate stages of the ancient Aegean language operating at the same time. It was sort of like straddling the fence and watching our soccer players play in two games simultaneously.

I was discerning the Minoan language for the first time, I realized. With this linguistic insight, I had identified the ancient tongue's quintessential rule. It gave me the means to achieve word separation in run-together phrases within the fields of the Phaistos Disk.

Another phonological rule soon became evident: In front of an *s* or *n* in stressed syllables, an original *a* was replaced by *o* and an original *o* was replaced by *a* (a so-called "flip-flop rule," a known linguistic phenomenon). Also in stressed syllables, the *u* appeared to be replaced with an *i* in front of an *n*, and the *e* was an *a* before *n* and *s*. As a seeming throwback, the Minoans hadn't replaced their inherited *dh* with a *th* as the Hellenes on the mainland had done sometime in the second millennium B.C.

And then there were the unusual spelling conventions of the Phaistos Disk. (These I had first assumed, wrongly as it turned out, to be grammatical rules.) Later I identified these spelling conventions as usually the same as or similar to phenomena that one finds in the Mycenaean Greek Linear B script.

That is, every *s* and *n* in the script was being elided, or dropped, in front of a consonant (*p, t, k,* and so forth) and at the end of a word; the *s* and *n* were in the spoken language, but they just weren't being written in these positions in the script. Every diphthong in *-i* (*ai ei oi ui*) gave only the *-i*. Every *-l-* between opposing vowel levels was seemingly written as a *t* as though it were a palatal "click." (This phenomenon is similar to the known *d/l* alternation we find in such ancient synonyms as Odysseus/Ulysses.) And the sound *w* after a consonant was not shown, only its following vowel.

Essentially, any word that could be pronounced as one syllable (*rheus, ans*) was also written as one syllable in the form CV (consonant plus vowel, *re* for *rheus*) or simply V (vowel, *a* for *ans*).

During the earlier internal analysis, as you might recall, five vowels (*a e i o u*) had provisionally been "identified" using only numbers according to their functional positions in each field of the Phaistos Disk. The correct vowels were now isolated. Other sound values emerged—from the very few possibilities left in the nearly complete working syllabary—through further acrophonic identifications, grammatical constraints, and contextual transparencies.

These latter are a particularly fascinating linguistic phenomenon.

When you hear in English, for example, the phrase "Thank you very ..." or "Well I'll ...!" doesn't your mind automatically fill in the missing words? And with Honolu- and Mississip- the missing syllables?

The combined methods described above made it possible to posit the final sound values of the Phaistos Disk: 02 *e*, 05 *wi*, 06 *me*, 10 *a*, 11 *to*, 16 *u*, 17 *ro/lo*, 30 *tu*, 31 *o*, 42 *we*, 43 *mi*, and 44 *wo*.

These values could then be entered into the working syllabary, which was now complete (Figure 5.4).

	A	**E**	**I**	**O**	**U**
	PD 10	PD 02	PD 39	PD 31	PD 16
J	PD 21	–	–	–	–
W	PD 22	PD 42	PD 05	PD 44	–
R/L	PD 26	PD 32	PD 01	PD 17	PD 36
M	PD 29	PD 06	PD 43	PD 23	–
N	PD 03	PD 25	PD 40	–	PD 08
P	PD 45	PD 14	PD 34	PD 15	PD 41
T	PD 27	PD 35	PD 18	PD 11	PD 30
D	PD 19	PD 24	PD 33	PD 04	–
K	PD 38	PD 28	PD 20	PD 09	PD 13
Q	–	PD 12	–	–	–
S	–	PD 37	PD 07	–	–

FIGURE 5.4

The retrieved syllables PD 02 *e*, 05 *wi*, 06 *me*, 10 *a*, 11 *to*, 16 *u*, 17 *ro/lo*, 30 *tu*, 31 *o*, 42 *we*, 43 *mi*, and 44 *wo* have been entered, completing the working syllabary of the Phaistos Disk.

I exchanged the final numbers in Retrieval Stage 8 for these newest sound values, also completing the phonetic text of the Phaistos Disk.

This is Retrieval Stage 9:

RETRIEVAL STAGE 9—FINAL PHONETIC TEXT

Side A: e-qe ku-ri-ti . / de-ni(-qe) / ma pa-si . / ma ma-pi (.) / **e-qe** do-ni-di / ta pa-si(-qe) / ta wo-nu (.) / **e-qe** me-ti(-) / o-ra(-te) / e-qe pu-da(-te) / ri-pu ni-si (.) / **e-qe** re-mo-ka . / i-to / e ta-ne a mo-ti / ke-ri . / **e-qe** o-ra . / **e-qe** ta ta-te-se-ja / di-mo (.) / **e-qe** o-ra . / e ta-ne a mo-ti / ke-ri . / **e-qe** o-ra . / **e-qe** ta pe-re-ti-ta / me-ti ro-da / o-ra(-qe) / **e-qe** ku-ri / mo-da(-te) . / a-na-ka (.) / **e-qe** ta ta-te-se-ja / ku-ri (.) / a-na-ka °

Side B: e-qe wa ni-si / ta pa-si(-te) / e se-mo-wi (or: e-se-mo-wi). / wa ne-ta / di-de-ki(-qe) / u mo-ti-mi (or: u-mo-ti-mi) . / ku-ri i-di / po-si ku-ri-ti . / wa se-we-ne / si de-ni(-te) / e ra-ru-ni (or: e-ra-ru-ni) / ta-ne ka-ri (or: ta-ne-ka-ri) / ma de-de-ki(-te) / u pe-ti (or: u-pe-ti) / ma di-ri (or: ma-di-ri) / me-te-re i-di / e ko ta-ri (or: e-ko-ta-ri) / ma ru-si-nu (or: ma-ru-si-nu) . / ma nu-ku (or: ma-nu-ku) / ma pa-si . / wa ma ru-si-nu (or: wa ma-ru-si-nu) . / ta pi-mo-ne / si-ti(-te) (or: si ti-te; or: si ti te) / si pa-si . / si mo-ti(-de) / wa ma ru-si-nu (or: wa ma-ru-si-nu). / ko-tu-i-ti-si / e me-te mo-si / ma pi-mo-ne / pa-si .

Work Note, March 2, 1984: "So excited by solving Disk—stayed up virtually all night working on it.... Very little left of complication."

I suppose every achievement has its price. At times I had felt as though I were thrashing for my life in Homer's "wine-dark sea" for want of some hard linguistic flotsam. I'd been working up to twenty hours a day, with a never-before-experienced intensity. My right hand began uncontrollably shaking at times. It's a nervous palsy that I still suffer from, twelve years later. My doctor diagnosed it as an "action tremor." I have to drink my tea with both hands now.

A decipherment only hoists the sail. It takes an interpretation to fill it.

Here I had the Phaistos Disk's text only in its "raw," unedited form, with many possible reading variants. Now I had to fill its sail with meaning, the obligatory summation of any decipherment—and one that theoretically can take years, even decades, to perfect.

Approaching each word of the text through its Indo-European root, I compared it with some twenty other sister languages, and bit by bit, like soft clay slapped onto the murmuring potter's wheel, the entire terrible message of the Phaistos Disk took shape.

Remember "significant unit" 02-12? It had been the most conspicuous pairing in those early days of numerical analysis. Now it was doubtless the most important single word retrieval of this final stage. Glyph comparison with Linears A and B had quite early shown Disk glyph 12 to be a word starting with the sound *qe*. And now 02, predicted even earlier than this through internal analysis to be a vowel, revealed its actual value to be *e*. This made out of 02-12 the Minoan word *e-qe* or *ekue*, which, if we revert to the sub-surface form (before the Minoan Sound Rule, that is), should have been an *akue* on the Greek mainland. And *akue* is just the word—in its classical Greek form *akoue*—that the famous Greek orator Demosthenes used in his speeches 1250 years later to gain the attention of his audiences in Athens's Agora. Old Greek *akoue* means "listen!" or, more archaically, "hear ye!"

And the "thorn" that terminates several fields on both sides of the Disk? It turned out to be a punctuation mark acting, not unlike a modern comma or period, to mark the slowing of speech or a pause. This is just what Sir Arthur Evans, back in 1909, had speculated it might be.

A final syllabic text, incorporating all the recognized elements (but maintaining significant repetitions), was now possible. Here is Retrieval Stage 10:

RETRIEVAL STAGE 10—FINAL SYLLABIC TEXT

Side A: e-qe <u>ku-ri-ti</u> , / <u>de-ni</u> qe, / ma <u>pa-si</u> , / ma ma-pi . / **e-qe** do-ni-di / ta <u>pa-si</u> qe / ta wo-nu . / **e-qe** <u>me-ti</u> / <u>o-ra</u> te / **e-qe** pu-da te / ri-pu <u>ni-si</u> . / **e-qe** re mo ka . / i-to / <u>e-ta-ne</u> <u>a</u> <u>mo-ti</u> / <u>ke-ri</u>. / **e-qe** <u>o-ra</u> . / **e-qe** ta <u>ta-te-se-ja</u> / di mo / **e-qe** <u>o-ra</u> . / <u>e-ta-ne</u> <u>a</u> <u>mo-ti</u> / <u>ke-ri</u> . / **e-qe** <u>o-ra</u> . / **e-qe** ta pe-re-ti-ta / <u>me-ti</u> ro-da / <u>o-ra</u> qe . / **e-qe** <u>ku-ri</u> / mo da-te . / <u>a</u> <u>na-ka</u> . / **e-qe** ta <u>ta-te-se-ja</u> / <u>ku-ri</u> . / <u>a</u> <u>na-ka</u> .

Side B: e-qe wa <u>ni-si</u> / ta <u>pa-si</u> te / e-se-mo-wi . / wa ne-ta / di-de-ki qe / u-mo-ti-mi . / <u>ku-ri</u> <u>i-di</u> / po-si <u>ku-ri-ti</u> . / wa se-we ne / si <u>de-ni</u> te / e-ra-ru-ni / ta-ne ka-ri / ma de-de-ki te / u-pe-ti / ma di-ri . / me te-re <u>i-di</u> . / e-ko ta-ri . / <u>ma</u> <u>ru-si</u> <u>nu</u> . / ma nu-ku / ma <u>pa-si</u> . / wa <u>ma</u> <u>ru-si</u> <u>nu</u> . / ta <u>pi-mo-ne</u> / si ti te / si <u>pa-si</u> , / si <u>mo-ti</u> de . / wa <u>ma</u> <u>ru-si</u> <u>nu</u> . / ko-tu i-ti si . / e me te-mo-si / ma <u>pi-mo-ne</u> / <u>pa-si</u> .

This stage at last made possible an edited text incorporating those elements that the spelling conventions omitted. I cannot stress strongly enough that this edited text, which reflects the state of scholarship at the time of this book's publication, is interpretative and provisional. To single out one example, the word *ku-ri-ti* might represent an actual *Kurwītis, Kurwītai, Kurītis, Kurītai,* or something else. Also, it is a moot point at this juncture whether the Minoan *i* truly represents later Greek *ai, ei,* and *oi.* For example, the *de-ni* that suggests a provisional *Deneoi*—the classical Greek form for this is *Danaoi,* meaning "Danaans"—might instead have been a Minoan *Denei.* In the following provisional edited text, I have suggested forms that are closer to the classical Greek, however, for better comprehension and control.

RETRIEVAL STAGE 11—PROVISIONAL EDITED TEXT OF THE PHAISTOS DISK

Side A: "Ekue, Kurwītis Deneoi-que: ma pasīs, ma mapoi! Ekue, Donaïdis: ta pasīs-que, ta wosnu! Ekue, melai holwa, te ekue, Puda te Libu nīsoi! Ekue, rheus mōn gā: Hillos entā nē an mōlois Kēriūn. Ekue holwa! Ekue, ta thaleseiān Dhioi, mōn ekue holwa: entā nē an mōlois Kēriūn. Ekue holwa! Ekue, ta plēthita melai lōdha holwa-que! Ekue, kūrioi, mōn dhātes: ans Nax! Ekue, ta thaleseiān kūrioi: ans Nax!"

Side B: "Ekue, was nīsoi, ta pasīs te esēmowoi; was nestās dideskoi-que ūmotimoi; kūrioi Idaioi; ponsis Kurwītis: was seue nē sīn Deneis te erarunai tans Kārīs, ma dedwekoi, te ūphelīn ma dweiloi. Me tēre, Idaioi: ekhō tarweis. Man lūsai nū. Mā nux, mā pasī: was man lūsai nū. Ta pīmone sis toioi te sis pasīs, sis mōloi dē: was man lūsai nū. Kotu-ithi sis! Ē, me temosai ma pīmone pasīs!"

On the basis of Retrieval Stage 11, it is now possible to attempt a provisional free translation of the Phaistos Disk's inscription that, it is to be hoped, captures the archaic mood of the ancient original.

RETRIEVAL STAGE 12—PROVISIONAL FREE TRANSLATION OF THE PHAISTOS DISK

Side A: "Hear ye, Cretans and Greeks: my great, my quick! Hear ye, Danaïdans, the great, the worthy! Hear ye, all blacks, and hear ye, Pudaan and Libyan immigrants! Hear ye, waters, yea earth: Hellas faces battle with the Carians. Hear ye all! Hear ye, Gods of the Fleet, aye hear ye all: faces battle with the Carians. Hear ye all! Hear ye, the multitudes of black people and all! Hear ye, lords, yea freemen: To Naxos! Hear ye, Lords of the Fleet: To Naxos!"

Side B: "Hear ye, ye immigrants, the great and the small; ye countrymen skilled, most stalwart; lords Idaian; all Cretans: Strike ye out with the Greeks and smite the Carians, mine enemy, and succor my stricken. Safeguard me, Idaians: I am sore afraid. Loose me now. My night, my great: Ye loose me now. These afflictions so terrible and so great, verily so molestful: Ye loose me now.

Down to the sea, everyone! Yea, deliver me of my great afflictions!"

I must confess that I was not a little surprised at what the message on the Phaistos Disk had revealed itself to be. Many scholars had been expecting and arguing for a religious hymn in the inscription. Yet here was clearly a call to arms—a "Mobilization Proclamation"—announcing a horrible invasion that threatened to destroy not only the Minoans' sea world but the Danaans', the mainland Mycenaean Greeks', coastal realm as well.

And it was an extremely powerful prose, heralded at the same time that the last horseshoe of bluestones was being erected at Stonehenge in far-away England.

I documented the work that had been done up to April 1984 in a copyrighted 108-page working monograph titled "Observations on the Phaistos Disc and the Nature of the Minoan Language." In this working monograph I also approached several Minoan Linear A inscriptions, using my knowledge of the grammatical rules of the Phaistos Disk as they were then understood. I even returned to each individual Disk glyph and attempted to identify each object by name using a variety of Indo-European evidence. This I could not, and would not, do earlier, before the proof had become available that Minoan was indeed a very early Hellenic language. "Observations" was written to share my working principles, methods, and results with fellow scholars in order to elicit comment and critique and perhaps even support.

I mailed off the numerous copies to select experts and institutions in Europe and America and then simply waited, wondering who, if anyone, would reply. . . .

Saturday morning, June 23, 1984, and the doorbell rang.

"*Herr Doktor Fischer?—ein Telegramm.*"

"*Dankeschön.*"

I walked back into the living room and opened the envelope, not having a clue who would be sending me a telegram.

"Who's it from?" asked Taki. "It's the Disk, isn't it?"

"Listen to this," I said, breaking into a smile.

Dear Dr. Fischer: Our congratulations on a splendid piece of work.... I would be amazed if scholarship does not applaud you unanimously, for it certainly looks like a duck, walks like a duck, and quacks like a duck, and a duck it must be....

Signed: Joseph Judge. National Geographic Society. Washington, DC

Side A of Crete's ancient Phaistos Disk (ca. 1600 BC). Its diameter averages 16 cm, its thickness 2.1 cm. (Photo courtesy of the Heraklion Museum, Heraklion, Crete)

Side B of the Phaistos Disk. (Photo courtesy of the
Heraklion Museum, Heraklion, Crete)

The Easter Island *rongorongo* tablet "Tahua" (RR 1), now deposited in
the Archives of the Congregation of the Sacred Hearts in Rome,
is incised on the blade of a European or American oar.
(Photo by S. R. Fischer)

The *rongorongo* tablet "Mamari" (RR 2), measuring 29 × 19.5 × 2.5 cm,
is also in Rome. (Photo courtesy of the Congregation of the
Sacred Hearts, Rome)

The *rongorongo* tablet "Aruku Kurenga" (RR 4), measuring 41 × 15.2 × 2.3 cm, is deposited in the Archives of the Congregation of the Sacred Hearts in Rome. (Photo by S. R. Fischer)

CHAPTER 6

THE BATTLE
OF NAXOS

During that exciting fortnight that followed in Washington, DC, in 1984, Taki and I enjoyed spirited and never-to-be-forgotten discussions with many prominent epigraphers and journalists. All waxed enthusiastic about what the decipherment of the Phaistos Disk had revealed:

■ Crete's celebrated Phaistos Disk comprises Europe's oldest documented literature.

■ The Disk contains the first mention in history of the Greeks and Libyans, two Mediterranean peoples who still play major roles in international affairs nearly 4000 years later.

■ "Pre-Greek" in the ancient Aegean now had to mean "pre-Minoan Greek," making prehistory history and extending the Hellenic threshold back into the third millennium B.C.

They also took special notice of the linguistic insights this decipherment gave us:

■ The Minoan language of ancient Crete is the oldest documented language not only of Europe but also of the entire Indo-European language family.

■ The Minoan language was a Hellenic tongue, sister to Mycenaean Greek. (Henceforth it's to be called Minoan Greek.)

■ The various rules that had been identified in Minoan Greek indicate that this tongue differed from mainland Mycenaean Greek to roughly the same degree that Swiss German today differs from High German. In other words, the correspondence between Minoan Greek and Mycenaean Greek—about 70 percent—lies on the border between dialect and autonomous language.

■ The Minoan Greek text that adorns the Phaistos Disk was evidently reproduced many times and read aloud, perhaps by a royal herald, to Minoans and other resident ethnic groups at the various centers of ancient Crete. Though this text was short, it was read, not memorized; this indicates a preference for the written word on ancient Crete. (It also suggests widespread literacy.) Perhaps the Phaistos Disk and other such conjectured "proclamation disks" served as visible proof of royal authority on Minoan Crete.

■ The Hellenes were the first in the Aegean—indeed in Europe—to use writing, the syllabo-pictographic script, an invention apparently borrowed from their wealthy trading partners in the Levant. The pre-Greeks of the Aegean had no writing.

More fascinating for those we met and talked with in Washington, DC, were the historical revelations:

■ Someone wielding great power is speaking on the Phaistos Disk. Judging by later accounts, the "author" might very well have been the Minos himself, the mythical King of Crete in the second millennium B.C. whose name probably recalls an ancient Aegean title. If this is true, then the Phaistos Disk was probably mass-produced at the northern capital of Knossos and later read out by a royal herald at the southern palace-shrine of Phaistos, where this one proclamation disk remained and was miraculously preserved by a conflagration.

■ The numerous ethnic communities this speaker addresses on the Phaistos Disk reveal the Cretan "melting-pot" of about 1600 B.C. The ethnic rulers of Crete at that time were evidently the Cretans—the *Kurwītis* or Kourētes—who were Minoan Greeks. But also living on Crete were Danaans or mainland Greeks, Danaïdans (perhaps western Cretans), black people (known from Minoan art), Pudaans and Libyans of North Africa, and Idaians (probably the central and southern Cretans of Mt. Ida and Phaistos).

■ These names of these ethnic communities evidently appear on the Phaistos Disk in order of their importance in Minoan society. First mentioned are the Minoans and then, immediately thereafter, the Danaans, as though the twain enjoyed some sort of affiliation or were otherwise of equal social status. The speaker addresses both using the word "my." Then come the Danaïdans, whom the speaker addresses using the word "the" or "those" as if they somehow eluded Knossos's royal dominance or affiliation. Next the "black people"—one can assume the words signify Egyptians or Nubians from the Upper Nile—are addressed; they were a significant part of the Minoan palace guard in the middle of the second millennium B.C. Least important of the ethnic contributors appear to be the Pudaan and Libyan immigrants from North Africa. The Idaians, mentioned twice on Side B, perhaps constitute the audience this particular clay disk immediately addressed, the Cretan residents of Phaistos. Identical "proclamation disks" might have here addressed other regional communities by name.

■ That the speaker addresses the Minoans and Danaans together using the word "my" may even suggest some kind of political bonding that extended beyond Crete's shores at this time. The possibility of a Greco-Minoan Confederation about the year 1600 B.C. cannot be entirely dismissed, especially in light of the Phaistos Disk's clear injunction: "Strike ye out with the Greeks...." There is no reason, however, to assume a Minoan hegemony over mainland Greece.

■ The name *Hillos*, or Hellas as used here on the Phaistos Disk—the first mention in history of the Greek nation as a geographical entity—transcends the boundaries of the Hellas mentioned in Homer's *Iliad*, that is to say, some geographical location lying west of the island of Naxos. (Also mentioned for the first time here on the Phaistos Disk is Naxos, the largest island of the Cyclades, which lies exactly midway between Asia Minor and the Greek mainland.) In the Disk's inscription, Hellas seems to indicate a much larger geographical territory occupied by all indigenous Hellenes: the mainland Greeks (Danaans), the Minoan

Greeks (*Kurwītis*/Kourētes), and the assumed Hellenic inhabitants of the island colonies of the Cyclades just north of Crete who are described here by the speaker as "my stricken (ones)." The name Hellas as used here would, then, appear to encompass roughly the area claimed by the southern half of today's Hellenic Republic. The name Hellas is probably ethnic, rather than political.

Of paramount importance, everyone in Washington, DC, agreed, was the Phaistos Disk's message:

- The Disk announces a major invasion by Carians near the island of Naxos in the Cyclades. Inhabiting southwest Asia Minor (today Turkey) in the second millennium B.C., the Carians were known as the "pirates of the Aegean."

- The royal authority on Minoan Crete—perhaps the Minos or King of Crete—is here calling on the various ethnic communities to sail out, together with the mainland Greeks, and repel these invading Carians.

- If this combined Greco-Minoan flotilla did join battle against invading Carians, then the "Battle of Naxos" would have constituted one of the greatest historical events of prehistoric Europe, the "Trafalgar of the Ancient World." It would have rescued the region for continued Hellenic occupation, which made possible the evolution of the later classical world that gave birth to our own Western civilization.

- One can easily deduce that this inferred Battle of Naxos was won: Only the victor would have kept the Phaistos Disk that announced the battle in his own indigenous Minoan Greek language.

- The historical feasibility of such a joint campaign is evidenced by two famous scenes from that same time and place. Both the famous "Expedition Fresco" dated about 1630 B.C. at the ruins of Akrotiri on the island of Thera (Santorin) just north of Crete and the relief on a celebrated silver rhyton dated about 1560 B.C. from one of the shaft graves at Mycenae on Greece's mainland display what some scholars have interpreted to be a combined sea and land force of Greeks and Minoans battling a common foe. The Mycenaean Greeks are known to have amassed sudden inexplicable wealth after about 1600 B.C. They and the Minoans both thrived, until the Minoan island empire was gradually taken over by the mainland Mycenaean Greeks several centuries later.

■ Writing in the fifth century B.C., the Greek historian Thucydides claimed that Minos of Crete had driven the Carians out of the Cyclades. This tale was evidently so important to Hellenic prehistory that it was passed from grandfather to grandson for over a thousand years....

This last fact—that Thucydides claimed Crete's Minos had driven the Carians out of the islands of the Cyclades—was fortuitously discovered by Taki as we stood in the history section of Foyle's bookshop in London on our way home from Washington, DC. Neither of us had known this before. As she read it aloud to me over the din of the customers and musak, we looked at each other and shook our heads in amazement. For the only other time we had heard this was when we were exhuming the text of that 3600-year-old clay disk from Crete! It was pleasantly surprising—and personally gratifying—to discover a confirmation like this halfway between hither and yon. It made us feel that everything was falling into place, perhaps better than we could ever have imagined....

It was only the quiet before the storm.

There's a holy relic in London, one I always make sure to honor with a pilgrimage whenever I am passing through the familiar megalopolis. The first time I entered its sanctum I was only three months shy of 18 years of age, back in 1965. Then came many memorable visits when I was in my early twenties. In 1984, on the way back to Germany from Washington, DC, I just had to pay homage to the holy relic again, drawn like a believer to the sacred spring to commune in silent awe and gather strength.

It's the "Rosetta Stone" in the British Museum.

This black basalt tablet, which bears an inscription in two Egyptian hieroglyphic scripts (demotic and hieratic) and in Greek, was found near Rosetta, lower Egypt, by Napoleon's troops in 1799. It enabled the young Frenchman Jean-François Champollion to commence his ultimately successful decipherment of the literature of the ancient Egyptians. Today, the term "Rosetta Stone" is often used metaphorically to signify any potential or real "key" to an undeciphered script. For a dedicated epigrapher like myself, this imposing monolith constitutes much more than white markings on black stone. It's the petrified wonder of human genius—the genius of both those who inscribed it and the rare man who used it to unlock the incredibly rich secrets of the Egyptian world.

I stood there, as always, in quiet veneration. Then I left the relic, as I had done so many times before, like a special friend I knew I'd see again one day, though many years might pass.

A visit of a different sort also stood on the agenda in England.

Taki and I had arranged an appointment with John Chadwick at the University of Cambridge, and on a sunny August morning we took the train from Liverpool Street Station up to the famous university town north of London to meet the distinguished classical scholar at his office in Downing College. You will recall that John Chadwick had been Michael Ventris's helpful colleague in the decipherment of Mycenaean Greek Linear B back in the early 1950s. This summer of 1984 he was retiring from lecturing at Cambridge, and he was in the process of removing all personal effects from his office.

"Dr. Steven Fischer, I presume?" he asked as he came up the stone steps in the dark passageway and extended his hand. I introduced Taki.

We entered the old-fashioned room that looked down onto a grassy quadrangle and took our seats. Whereupon we exchanged pleasantries about this and that, about the National Geographic's endorsement of my decipherment of the Phaistos Disk, and about various aspects of deciphering scripts in general. The atmosphere was civil. However, Taki and I were very much "donned to" by the senior scholar as though we were still young graduate students. (I was 37 in 1984, having acquired my Ph.D. eleven years earlier.) If I had secretly been hoping for John Chadwick's support of the Phaistos Disk's decipherment, then I was to be disappointed. All his life, Chadwick had been constructing and defending a Linear B fence that had defined and protected the enclosed world of Mycenaean Greek. And essential to the structural integrity of this fence for Chadwick was the posture that Crete's Phaistos Disk was a foreign import that had nothing to do with the Minoan people of ancient Crete.

Yet here I was, the American-born New Zealander from Germany, threatening that same fence by saying that the Minoans not only had manufactured the Phaistos Disk but had spoken Greek as well, as the Mycenaeans had done. Indeed, the Minos was a Greek, I was telling John Chadwick.

This was apparently too much for the distinguished senior scholar, who, tempered by his era, still held this fence to be sacrosanct.

In the end we parted in a civil but irreconcilable understanding of each other's positions.

That same evening, Taki and I found consolation in a superb performance by 83-year-old Claudette Colbert and Rex Harrison on the stage of the Theatre Royal Haymarket in Lonsdale's tried and true comedy "Aren't We All?" This splendid rendition by a brilliant cast did wonders to dispel the dark clouds of Cambridge.

Until the first critiques arrived.

The celebrated German scientist Max Planck, winner of the 1918 Nobel Prize for Physics, was once asked how he had changed the minds of those who doubted the new physics he had helped to found. He hadn't changed their minds, he replied.

"They died."

Upon my return to Germany from Washington, DC, and London, I feared the decipherment of the Phaistos Disk might meet a similarly enthusiastic welcome. Naturally, I hadn't been expecting champagne and fireworks from my fellow linguists and philologists. I was only too mindful of the fierce opposition that Michael Ventris had met thirty years earlier when he revealed—through successful decipherment of the Linear B script—that the Mycenaeans had spoken Greek.

New ideas are never universally accepted. They are a path slashed into the wilderness. Of course, there will always be those select pioneers who recognize the promise and at once follow the path. However, most people only gradually, if ever, see that the way into the wilderness is there. This inertia is inherent in every human endeavor and is as old as humankind itself. Yet despite it, we now tread where our primitive ancestors thought only gods ranged.

In short, I never expected instant endorsement of my discovery. But I recognized to my chagrin, in the second half of 1984, that my working monograph "Observations on the Phaistos Disc and the Nature of the Minoan Language" was being read by classicists and epigraphers in a way that I hadn't intended it to be read. It was being misinterpreted and misunderstood. This caused me no end of disappointment, and I actively sought to discover what it was in my description of the decipherment that these critics failed to comprehend. The new path was there, but they apparently were still unable to see it.

What were these critics saying?

Some were calumnious, alleging that I had "concocted" my retrieval steps on the basis of a foregone conclusion that the Minoans had been speaking a Hellenic tongue. This allegation was too odious to reply to. Calumny has no place in a scholar's toolkit.

Other critics had got the impression from the working monograph "Observations" that my *entire* retrieval method had consisted of subjectively identifying the depicted objects in the glyphs and then giving them their purported "Greek" names. I suppose these critics believed this because in "Observations," at the end of the decipherment process, I had returned to each underlying word and had suggested possible root words for each glyph based on Indo-European sister languages. The critics failed to understand that I had done this work only *after* the decipherment had been successfully completed through more objective retrieval steps.

Others complained that "Observations" had not been presented in a formal scientific fashion and said that for this reason they were loath to accept the working monograph's results as proof.

Others suggested tentative solutions of their own, which defied common sense and betrayed a superficial acquaintance with the Phaistos Disk and with the internal analysis of its glyph distribution.

Still others maintained that no matter what solution *anyone* might come up with for the Phaistos Disk—even if it were the correct one—no one would ever be able to prove anything because the Disk's text is simply too short. Those who took this stance were invariably the same scholars who denied the Minoan provenance of the Phaistos Disk and its kinship to the other ancient Cretan scripts.

One eminent linguist from Berkeley, California, wrote that because the Disk was an inscription in spiral form, he would expect it to be a curse.

And then there was the leading Greek archaeologist who proclaimed that only a Greek could solve the riddle of the Phaistos Disk.

All this came like a rude slap in the face. To be sure, there were those scholars and epigraphers who endorsed the decipherment. But at this stage, theirs was like a voice in the wilderness. The first reaction of the Establishment had been to attack the intruder. This is because my decipherment—at least as it had been presented in my working monograph "Observations," which had never been intended as a formal scientific essay in the first place—was very much regarded by the high priests of Aegean epigraphy as a disruptive virus.

Something had to be done to show that this discovery was no intruder, but rather a colleague and a friend. If anything, it was the ultimate confirmation of the "Mycenaean Greek hypothesis" of the 1950s.

I had to describe the actual process of deciphering the Phaistos Disk step by step (much as I have done here for the lay reader, in Chapters 3 to 5). A scholarly book had to be written. A wholly new, formal study had to be completed. For this I would have to conduct intensive research in order to document my results better and put them in their correct linguistic and historical context. And then I would have to find a reputable academic publishing house that would make the book available worldwide.

This was the only way, I realized, to deal with my vociferous—and at times even contumelious and irrational—critics. If I had one consolation at the end of 1984 and the beginning of 1985, it was this very furor that my successful decipherment of the Phaistos Disk had immediately provoked.

Silence would have been fatal.

There was one promising way to encourage among international scholars an acknowledgement of the success of the decipherment of the Phaistos Disk. This was to demonstrate— beyond any reasonable doubt—that by identifying the Disk's underlying language, I had simultaneously identified the language underlying the Linear A script.

Most (though certainly not all) scholars of the ancient Aegean are in agreement that the language of the Minoan Phaistos Disk is the same as that of the contemporary Minoan Linear A script. As a logical corollary to this, the linguistic and orthographic rules that I had discovered for the Minoan Greek language of the Phaistos Disk should also apply to the Minoan Greek language of the Linear A script. In other words, if you use these same discovered rules to bring out the language of the latter (the Minoan Linear A script), then you'll have successfully proved the decipherment of the former (the Minoan Phaistos Disk).

There was a famous test case among scholars for just this eventuality.

John Chadwick had once written, "The meaning of one [Minoan] Linear A word is certain: *ku-ro* is the word which introduces totals, and must mean something like 'total' or 'so much'.... If we could find such a word in a known language, the problem of Linear A might be solved; but unfortunately no decipherment has so far passed this test convincingly." I now addressed this challenge, applying to Minoan Linear A *ku-ro* the linguistic and orthographic rules that I had identified in the Minoan Greek language of the Phaistos Disk.

By this means I could show that Linear A *ku-ro* would represent Minoan Greek *krōs*, which would have derived from an earlier Proto-Hellenic *krās*. Classical Greek *krās*—which is attested in the earliest Greek texts—is interchangeable with epic Greek *karā* and *kar* and with poetic Greek *krāta*, which all mean "head, limit, extremity, outer point, summit or peak." These words are related to Classical Greek *karānos* "head, chieftain," *karēnon* "head, extremity, summit," *kranos* "helmet", *krānion* "cranium, skull," and *koruphē* "uppermost part, top, summit, head, crown." In light of this, Minoan Linear A *ku-ro* would have to mean "total," just as John Chadwick had declared: Minoan Greek *krōs* "sum, total" would have derived from *krās* "head, extremity" in much the same way that later Classical Greek *kephalaiōma* "sum, total" had derived from *kephalē* "head, extremity."

One mustn't underestimate the importance of this single test case. It clearly demonstrates the Hellenic provenance of the Minoan Linear A script—and in so doing confirms the validity of the linguistic and orthographic rules identified through the successful decipherment of the Phaistos Disk.

There's further proof linked with *ku-ro*, too. Twice on the Minoan Linear A tablets the word *ku-ro* is preceded by the word *po-to*, forming the Minoan phrase *po-to ku-ro*. Scholars have tentatively awarded *po-to* the meaning "total" because of its suspected descriptive function; hence the entire phrase should signify something like "total sum." According to the linguistic and orthographic rules identified on the Phaistos Disk, *po-to* would have to be Minoan Greek *phthōs* that would have derived from a Proto-Hellenic *phthās*. (Classical Greek *phthās* or *phthamenos* means "first" or "initial.") In this way, we can now appreciate that Linear A *po-to ku-ro* is in actual fact a Minoan Greek *phthōs krōs* that meant "first total" or "initial sum." (The contemporary mainland Greek form of this would have been *phthās krās*.)

In both cases, with *ku-ro* and with *po-to ku-ro,* applying the linguistic and orthographic rules identified in the Minoan Greek language of the Phaistos Disk has led to verifiable identication of Minoan Linear A words whose basic meanings have already been suggested by other classical scholars.

But there was further, more sensational evidence to come.

Evidence that would point to the prehistoric Minoan pantheon of gods.

On three Minoan stone libation tables, a silver hairpin, and a lustral scoop there is engraved in the Linear A script the Minoan "word" *a-sa-sa-ra,* with variants *a-sa-sa-ra-me / ja-sa-sa-ra / ja-sa-sa-ra-me / ja-sa-sa-ra-ma (-na).* Because of its prominence, scholars have long assumed that the "word" must identify an important but unknown Minoan deity. However, they have been unable to solve this "word's" further reading. Now, the same linguistic and orthographic rules identified through the successful decipherment of the Phaistos Disk that made possible the correct reading of Linear A *po-to ku-ro* as Minoan Greek *phthōs krōs* "initial sum," as described above, similarly suggested a possible identification of this Minoan "word" *a-sa-sa-ra.*

Actually, *a-sa-sa-ra* and its variants could just as validly have been the two separate Minoan words *a-sa* and *sa-ra.* The *-me/-ma* of *a-sa-sa-ra-me / ja-sa-sa-ra-ma (-na)* probably represents an *-m* ending whose graphic reproduction was optional for the Minoan scribe. Thus *a-sa-sa-ra* might actually have been a "more correct" *a-sa sa-ram.* The form *ja-sa-sa-ra* suggests an initial *h-* sound whose graphic reproduction was similarly optional: In Mycenaean Greek Linear B, as John Chadwick wrote back in the 1950s, *a/ja* alternations of this kind probably indicate the presence of an initial *h-.* Here, the initial *h-* would then give the indicated phonetic statement *ha-sa sa-ram.* The *-sa* of *ha-sa,* because it hasn't risen to *-se* as the Minoan Sound Rule would demand in an unstressed syllable, would suggest a "silent vowel," here one that falls between the two *s*'s. Accordingly, if one incorporates the optional elements, the original form of the two words initially transcribed by epigraphers as *a-sa-sa-ra* might actually have been *has saram*. Minoan Greek *hās* was evidently a preposition meaning "to"; this would have derived from the same Proto-Hellenic word that provided later Classical Greek *hōs*, which means "to" whenever a person is the object. The original Minoan phrase underlying the engraved forms *a-sa-sa-ra* / *a-sa-sa-ra-me* / *ja-sa-sa-ra* / *ja-sa-sa-ra-me* / *ja-sa-sa-ra-ma* *(-na)* would therefore probably have been *hās Sārām*, or "to Sārā" (the *-m* ending is an ancient feminine accusative inflection).

If the foregoing is correct, then "Sārā" would have been the name of that important deity who was the frequent recipient of Minoan libations on ancient Crete.

The fact that the final unstressed *-ā* of *Sārā* hadn't been replaced with an *-ē* as the Minoan Sound Rule dictates might mean that this name entered the Minoan language *after* the Sound Rule had been implemented. If this is what happened, then the Minoan Greeks would have borrowed the name *Sārā* at a relatively late date from some other ethnic group.

Who was *Sārā*? To judge by the surprising number of artifacts dedicated to her among the sparse legacy of the Minoan civilization, she was apparently the paramount deity of the Minoan people, their goddess, their Divine Mother. What is even more surprising is that her name gives every indication of being the source of the later Greek goddess Hera (*Hērā*, also Ionian *Hērē*).

Hera was the eldest daughter of Cronos and Rhea, sister and wife to Zeus, and principal female on sacred Olympus.

The linguistic evidence linking Minoan *Sārā* to later Greek Hera is persuasive. There is a further sound rule in early Greek—one that the Mycenaeans were using after the Minoans had been assimilated—that sees each initial *s-* in the language replaced with an *h-*. In this way, an earlier *Sārā*, perhaps a form that the earliest Mycenaeans themselves had known, would have become a later Mycenaean *Hārā*, which, in turn, after the Mycenaean era, would have been Classical Greek

Hērā and Hērē. (Classical Greek replaced each inherited long *ā* with long *ē*.) In this way the Minoan Divine Mother Sārā would eventually have become the Classical Greek supreme goddess Hera.

Where did this name come from, then, given that it appears to have been borrowed from some language foreign to the Hellas of the Greeks?

Sārā might have been Semitic. Perhaps the Minoans borrowed both her name and veneration of her during the course of their extensive trade with the wealthier and more advanced Levant. About 1800 B.C., the principal deity of Umma—whence the Biblical Abraham hailed—was Sara. This documented Sara might well be related to the goddess Ashērah of Ugarit and to 'Asērā of the ancient Hebrews and to the later Hittites' Ishas-Sara, the "Divine Mistress." The Canaanite mother goddess 'Asērah was venerated as the principal female deity throughout the Levant at the time of the manufacture of the Phaistos Disk. 'Asērah was also known as Tannit or Consort of Tan. This is reminiscent of the later classical Hera being alleged by some early Greek writers once to have been the consort of her brother Poseidon—the etymology of whose name, again following the linguistic rules from the Phaistos Disk, argues for a Minoan Greek *Pasi Dān* or "Great Dan, Lord Dan."

Perhaps a Semitic Sārā and Dān were already the ruling female and male deities of the Minoan Greeks in much the same way that their later (conjectured) manifestations Hera and Poseidon ruled the first classical Greeks—that is, until the Cretan Zeus banished his brother Poseidon into the sea and took his sister Hera to wife and queen.

This can never be proved, of course. The story belongs to the realm of prehistoric myth. Nevertheless, the defensible isolation of the name Sārā that is inscribed on several Minoan Linear A libation tables and other artifacts signals a potential breakthrough in our understanding of the ancient Hellenic culture of Minoan Crete.

Before I could begin writing this formal documentation of the successful decipherment of the Phaistos Disk—in order to demonstrate my methodology and confirm its results—Taki and I clearly had to move. We'd been living outside of Nuremberg for five years. I now needed access to a university library offering open book stacks (most German research libraries have closed stacks, a situation that seriously encumbers the scholarship of professionals). I was also desperate to find a locale that was free of hayfever-causing grass pollens.

And so, in the summer of 1985, we moved southwest to Meersburg on Lake Constance, population 5000. Meersburg is one of Germany's—indeed Europe's—most picturesque small towns, boasting an Upper Town and a Lower Town with a celebrated medieval castle looming between them. The gleeming façades of this historical ensemble illuminate the vineyard-strewn shore of Germany's largest lake at the foot of the majestic Alps, sharing borders with Austria in the south and Switzerland in the west. Here, immediately above the Meersburg castle and the lake, Taki and I lived for the next nine years, the longest I have lived in any one spot in my life.

Daily availing myself of the marvelous opportunity to ferry only twenty minutes across the lake to the research library at the University of Konstanz (Constance), I plunged into linguistic and historical studies in order to present my formal description of the successful decipherment of the Phaistos Disk.

The result of this was the scholarly book *Evidence for Hellenic Dialect in the Phaistos Disk.*

It was still not too late for discovery. One senior colleague at UCLA had taken exception to my sound value *sa* for Disk glyph 22. The sound value did not "fit," he said, in the pronominal ("you") position it obviously occupied five times on Side B of the Disk: One should "expect" an Indo-European *wes* or *wos*, meaning "you," he wrote. Reasoning that either *wes* or *wos*, again according to the identified rules of Minoan Greek, would have to be a *was* in the text, I tested the sound value *wa* for Disk glyph 22. (The *wa* value had until then remained a blank in the working syllabary, because I had initially identified Disk glyph 22 to be a *sa*.) But what was the object that the glyph depicted, then, if it was supposed to start with the syllable *wa-*? The value *wa* in the other Aegean scripts—Minoan hieroglyphic 𐃏, Minoan Linear A 𐙇, Mycenaean Linear B 𐃏, and Cyprian Linear C 𐙼—appeared to depict some object standing on four, three, or just two legs. This couldn't be the hearth, I mused. No, the Proto-Hellenic word for the hearth would have started with *wes-* (compare Classical Greek *hestia* "hearth"), not *was-*. Then I remembered. *Of course.* The Minoan sound rules again! A Proto-Hellenic *westia* for "hearth" would have been a Minoan Greek *wastie* (to go strictly by the identified rules). So the object—in the collective Aegean scripts, which were all based on the original Minoan sound values—represented the ancient hearth after all, the Minoan *wastie*. That was why the glyph had been given the sound value *wa-*, not *we-*. And the word this initial syllable *wa-* represented in the inscription on the Phaistos Disk? It was indeed "you" after all. The Minoan word for "you" was evidently *was*, from an earlier Proto Indo-European *wes* or *wos* (like Latin *vōs* "you").

I was also in a position now to distinguish orthographic practices on the Disk that earlier I had wrongly assumed to be phonological innovations of the Minoan language. Further, I showed in the book *Evidence* that the Minoan language was a Hellenic dialect, and I demonstrated how the decipherment provided sensible answers in the three different spheres of *grammatology* (the grammar of the identified language), *philology* (historical and comparative linguistics), and *contextual probability* (historical likelihood of the retrieved message). *Evidence* required consulting hundreds of research books and articles and was exhaustively documented in copious footnotes. In the end, a distinguished Swiss academic publishing house agreed to publish the book and see to its international distribution.

By 1988 *Evidence* was available to the scholarly community.

At the end of 1986 I had to get away from my Aegean studies; I couldn't sustain the psychic battle. Every day, in all my waking hours, my mind would run, over and over again, through the Minoan Greek text of the Phaistos Disk, searching for possible grammatical inconsistencies. Then it would put each individual word of the inscription to the test in light of twenty-odd Indo-European languages. And then survey the etymologies of the word of which each glyph constituted only the first syllable. I just couldn't escape the cerebral whirlpool.

I felt like the final victim of the Battle of Naxos.

Though the move to Meersburg had helped tremendously, I felt trapped. The long strolls along the shore and through the vineyards had calmed my nerves, but they failed to calm my mind.

The Phaistos Disk was literally driving me mad.

"What about doing that other decipherment now?" suggested Taki, returning to a subject we had discussed in recent weeks. Already at the National Geographic headquarters in Washington, DC, then assistant editor Howard Paine, the Geographic's "resident genius," had asked me if I might be interested in addressing the decipherment of a fascinating script to be found halfway round the globe from the Aegean Sea. His query had startled both Taki and me, for we had already recognized the personal challenge in the same script.

"I'm not ready," I now told Taki.

"When will you be ready?"

"I don't know."

She didn't seem happy with the answer. I could tell she was worried about me.

Over two years were to pass. In the meantime, I had to find some work therapy that might enable my mind to turn away at last from the Phaistos Disk in particular and from epigraphy in general. Even the Disk facsimile that we had bought at Kritsá on Crete had to be stored away in the closet. I couldn't look at it. I never spoke of the Disk, and Taki dared not mention it to me. One word, one question about the Disk would have set the entire machinery of the glyphs and their intricate, clock-like linguistic statement and word-histories into smoking high gear in my mind.

It wasn't a healthy situation.

And so, for solace and comfort, I returned to my academic womb. I turned tiller and hove into the lee of a scholarly isle that was as familiar to me as Mom's apple pie—that of musty old manuscripts and medieval archives. In quiet contemplation, and with relaxed enjoyment, I began researching the earliest chronicles of my chosen home, Meersburg on Lake Constance, with the idea of publishing its first professionally documented history. In time, the thousands of faded parchments in a variety of medieval hands let me range farther and farther from the Sea of Minos. It was a difficult weening. But the selected subject of my work therapy was something I was not only used to but enamored of. Having collected thousands of notecards filled with medieval citations, I finally began writing the first draft of the historical book at the end of 1987. By the summer of 1988—for the occasion of the One-Thousandth Anniversary of the first documented mention of Meersburg (the German government issued a special stamp for the event)—my treatise *Meersburg im Mittelalter (Medieval Meersburg)* was in the bookstores.

The book was a critical and financial success. More important for me personally, however, it allowed my mind to find at last that long-sought respite. I had truly delighted in delving into the fascinatingly refreshing world of medieval Lake Constance. I had discovered a Meersburg that none had suspected, and I had been able to share this new vision of the old town with countless others who loved and admired beautiful Meersburg and her rich history as much as I.

By the end of 1988 I felt it was time. *Meersburg im Mittelalter* had been merely an interlude, conscious therapeutics, a homecoming to the philological sanctum I had known and cherished at UCLA so many years earlier. It had been a means, not an end. And it had worked. Now I was ready for the long-term commitment.

"I'm going over to the campus tomorrow morning," I told Taki.

At first she didn't understand. But then she noticed that the facsimile of the Phaistos Disk had mysteriously reappeared on the mantlepiece. She grinned.

And so, the very first week of 1989, I ferried over to Staad on the west side of the lake and then briskly walked the twenty minutes through residential streets and snow-laced orchard to the University of Konstanz. In its research library I finally looked up the long article from the 1930s that I had seen over two years earlier but had wisely set aside until my mind was clear and my spirit revived. An article about an enigmatic Polynesian writing system that was soon to change my life forever....

Rongorongo.

CHAPTER 7

RAPANUI

It was the twentieth day of November in the Year of Our Lord 1770. On the barren flank of the island's volcano, brightly uniformed Spanish marines hefted ponderous muskets up to firing position. Behind them, a Christian cross crowned each of three small secondary volcanic cones. "Viva el Rey!" roared over a hundred Spaniards, at which moment the marines discharged an ear-splitting salvo. Several hundred naked islanders who had gathered nearby suddenly cried out for sheer terror, many still able to recall the murders that attended the first visit to their island by outsiders exactly forty-eight years earlier—after more than a millennium and a half of mind-numbing isolation. This was now only the second visit. For each cross the Spaniards shouted "Viva" three times. And the marines marked each bellow with a resounding fussilade. Down in the broad green bay below, two Spanish vessels—the *San Lorenzo* and the *Santa Rosalia*—responded with 21-cannon salutes that boomed like thunder. Then the marines paraded, their colorful flags fluttering, while resonant drums thumped out a martial cadence and pipesmen began celebrating the Spanish king.

The dazzling and deafening display glorified the taking possession of Earth's most isolated inhabited island—"in the name of the King and of Spain, our Lord and Master Don Carlos the Third." The Spaniards now renamed the island "San Carlos" after their holy liege in Madrid on the other side of the globe.

Just one day earlier, Don Felipe González de Haedo, commander of the Viceroy of Peru's South Pacific Expedition, had instructed his second-in-command to "cause the Paymasters to furnish you with a declaration of all that is done, to which you will procure the attestations of the recognized Chiefs or Caciques of the islanders, rubricated in the form of their characters...."

For this reason Paymaster Don Antonio Romero was now carefully recording, at a large oaken table that had been brought ashore especially for the historic event, the entire ceremony in fine ink flourishes on a white foolscap. Romero then instructed the Spanish officers who were standing alongside to sign the official deed of cession. Whereupon, as Romero later wrote, "to better corroborate this so solemn act some of the Indios autographed or signed at the same time, writing down on the document to be witnessed certain characters according to their style."

What Don Antonio's statement actually means is that those islanders who looked like "chiefs" were handed the paymaster's ink-dipped plume and, through sign language, were bidden to make their marks on the very piece of paper that was meant to steal their ancestral homeland from right under their noses.

Certainly understanding neither what the bright and boisterous ceremony was about nor what this process of writing was or meant, several elderly islanders stepped cautiously to the table to make queer marks on the flat white leaf as they had seen the colorful aliens do. Most simply copied the Spaniards' elaborate flourishes. One islander made an oblong mark that represented the vulva, the island's most common petroglyph sign. Another drew a large bird figure, the second most important symbol in the inventory of the local rock art (see Figure 7.1).

FIGURE 7.1
The marks of attestation that several Rapanui men were invited
to make in pen and ink on the Spanish deed of cession
on November 20, 1770. (From the *Journal of the
Royal Anthropological Institute,* 1874: 528, plate 27)

Their demonstration of utter superiority successfully completed, the contented Spanish officers, relieved to have experienced no violence at the hands of these wild savages, peaceably led their men in disciplined files back to the two ships.

And the dumbstruck islanders watched with a fascination bordering on disbelief as these brilliantly plumed beings unfurled sails larger than the largest house on the island and then slowly glided off toward the horizon as though they were departing gods.

Spain never enforced its claim. The name "San Carlos" was soon forgotten.

Yet the wonder of writing had arrived on Rapanui.

Rapanui—as Easter Island has preferentially been called by its Polynesian inhabitants since 1864—lies in almost unimaginable isolation 3600 kilometers west of Chile's coast and 2110 kilometers east-southeast of the Polynesian–British island of *Bounty* fame, Pitcairn, Rapanui's closest inhabited neighbor. Constituting over 160 square kilometers of rough black lava strewn with intermittent scrub, the triangular land mass of Rapanui is formed by the eroded remnants of three small overlapping shield volcanos. There are no permanent rivers or streams. Until very recently, the island was all but devoid of larger trees.

The one-and-only settlers of Easter Island probably arrived here nearly two thousand years ago, Polynesian immigrants from the Marquesas Islands in the distant northwest—almost as far away from Rapanui as Hawai'i is from Los Angeles. The approximately seventy courageous men and women found in their new island home a luxurious, subtropical paradise covered with high, thick palms that bulged in the middle; adorned with some familiar and many unfamiliar plants of various uses; and laced with many freshwater courses. Together with their own imported plants, chickens, dogs, and pigs, here the Marquesan settlers not merely survived but thrived, wholly undisturbed by intruders over the next 1500 years—eventually to number some seven thousand Rapanui who elaborated in their unparalleled isolation one of the most fascinating neolithic cultures on Earth.

During the early first millennium after the birth of Christ, the settlers had probably occupied the island's western coast, eventually spreading out to establish new settlements on the northeastern coast of the island only about the year 1000. They had split into two separate tribes by this time: the western Tu'u and the eastern 'Otu 'Iti. After a further four hundred years had passed, the settlement of Rapanui's south coast would have completed the last stage of the island's human occupation.

The settlers had brought with them from their Marquesan homeland their East Polynesian gods, too. Most important among these was the terrifying warrior god Tu'u. But they also venerated, among others, the god of the ocean Tangaroa, the god of light Tāne, the god of agriculture Rongo, and the moon goddess Hina. The Rapanui carved statues of these deities and of their own ancestors out of the plentiful wood, which they then erected on intricately masoned, raised ceremonial platforms called *ahu*. The *ahu* dignified each village, and the long rows of what ultimately became exclusively ancestor images atop them nearly always faced inland toward each small village—for protection and bountiful crops and plentiful catches of fish. Already by the medieval period, about A.D. 1000, gifted Rapanui sculptors were using the island's ubiquitous lava for these statues, too, carving them out of sheer rock walls by hand with only stone tools. The ancestor images, called *moai*, eventually numbered over a thousand and often stood more than 11 meters in height and weighed over 100 tons (one reclining *moai* measures over 20 meters and weighs up to 270 tons).

Nothing on Earth could compare to the *moai* of ancient Easter Island.

Moving the monoliths from the quarry to the *ahu* demanded entire forests of palm trunks. The island's forests had already been dangerously thinned, however, by the accidentally or intentionally imported Polynesian rats. Over the centuries, the rats had proliferated by feeding on the palm's plentiful nuts, inhibiting regrowth. Chopping down what forests remained in order to move the increasing number of giant stone ancestors now proved to be an ecological time bomb. By the end of the seventeenth century, about the year 1680, most of Easter Island had been reduced to near-barren wasteland. Once no more statues could be transported on palm-trunk rollers, all *moai* carving was abandoned almost overnight. By this time, most freshwater courses had already dried up. Social pressures over land and water and fishing rights led to violent warfare between the western Tu'u and eastern 'Otu 'Iti.

At which point Rapanui society imploded.

In 1722 three sailing ships of the Dutch West India Company chanced upon this hitherto unknown fleck of volcanic rock in the middle of nowhere—perhaps the first humans to sight the island in over fifteen hundred years. Because he had "discovered" it on Easter Sunday, Dutch fleet commander Jacob Roggeveen named the island "Easter Island." Roggeveen found the land to be well populated with a vigorous, healthy, and outwardly friendly people—some dark, others as light-skinned as the lightest Europeans. During their visit, the Dutch shot one Rapanui by mistake and later musketed a dozen others when an attempted theft led to an altercation.

It was only the first of many atrocities perpetrated by visitors from abroad.

This inaugural visit to the island by outsiders left an indelible impression on the isolated Polynesian society. It also altered this society beyond redemption. The Dutch had marveled at the hundreds of high, pouting *moai* that stood erect on their monumental *ahu*. Within a century after the Dutch visit, the Rapanui people had violently toppled them all. From the late eighteenth to the middle of the nineteenth century, every visitor to the island recorded a people caught in the throes of social disintegration. What exactly was transpiring on Easter Island in these decades of repeated alien intrusion and internal restructuring of the ancient society is still imperfectly understood today. However, one thing is clear: The Rapanui people had chosen to turn away from their past ...

And confront the outside world they now knew existed.

The further history of Easter Island is a frenzied chronicle of accelerating ruin: the many visits by South Sea whalers and naval vessels in the first half of the nineteenth century, bringing confusion, contamination, disease, and death; the Peruvian slave raids of late 1862 and early 1863, whereby as many as one-third of the Rapanui people were forcibly removed to households and plantations in Peru; the return of only 12 of these captives in 1863, one of whom introduced a smallpox epidemic that abruptly reduced the island population to some 800 suffering souls surrounded by the unburied corpses of their loved ones; the arrival three years later of Catholic missionaries, who attempted as best they could to arrest the crash and mitigate the misery; the escape of hundreds of Rapanui, together with these same missionaries, to Mangareva and to harsh indenture on a Tahitian plantation in 1871 when a power-crazed Frenchman claimed Easter Island for himself; the reduction of the remaining island population to only 111 by 1877; the transformation of Rapanui into a private sheep farm ruled from Tahiti; the island's forced annexation by Chile in 1888; its exploitation by a Chilean–Scots company as a sheep station; the withholding from the Rapanui people of citizenship and civil rights by the government of Chile until 1966; the modern commercialization and exploitation by mass tourism in the 1990s, with an island population of some 3000—over half of these being continental Chileans.

Today, Earth's most isolated inhabited island is yet another troubled barrio of the global village.

However, historical Easter Island boasted not only the spectacular *moai* for which it is today best known throughout the world. Unique among the thousands of islands of Oceania before the twentieth century, it also possessed its own indigenous writing system ... a fact that wasn't recognized until as late as 1864.

Easter Island's first documented non-Rapanui resident was the Frenchman Joseph-Eugène Eyraud (1820–1868). Bolivian mining interests had made Eyraud moderately well-to-do. Emulating his missionary brother Father Jean Eyraud of China in wishing to dedicate his fortune and talents to the Paris-based Catholic missionary order of the Congregation of the Sacred Hearts (SSCC), Eyraud eventually sailed on his own recognizance—legally independent of the SSCC—to Easter Island to

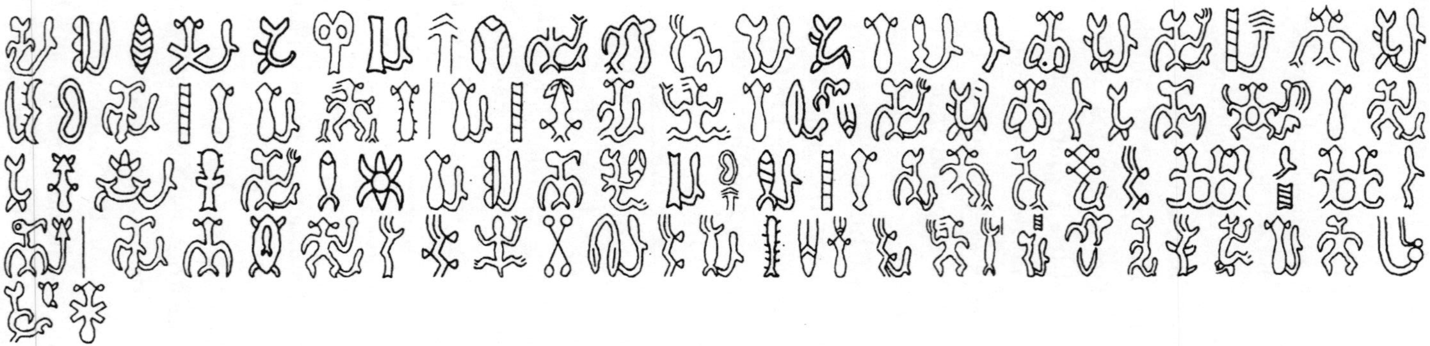

FIGURE 7.2
The *rongorongo* script of Easter Island. Shown here is the transcription of the first line of the famous "Santiago Staff" (RR 10) from the Museo Nacional de Historia Natural, Santiago, Chile.

reside from January until October of 1864. Here he wished to test the feasibility of an authorized Catholic mission to the island.

Once back at the SSCC's Chilean mission at Valparaíso, Eyraud penned a detailed report dated December 1864 to his Secretary General in Paris, in which he observed,

> There is another matter about which I shan't be more explicit. One finds in all the houses [of Easter Island] wooden tablets or staffs covered with sorts of hieroglyphic characters. These are figures of animals unknown on the island, which the natives trace by means of sharp stones. What significance do they attach to these characters? It is likely they are not too knowledgeable of it. Each figure, without doubt, has its name. But the little they make of these tablets persuades me to think that these characters, probably a script in origin, are for them now just simply a custom that they preserve without attempting to account for it.

This extraordinary custom is what later came to be celebrated as the *rongorongo* script of Easter Island (see Figure 7.2).

Eyraud's observations are revealing:

- Incised wooden tablets or staffs were to be found "in all the houses" of Rapanui in 1864. No previous visitor to Easter Island had mentioned this.

- Eyraud identified the incisions on these artifacts to be "hieroglyphic characters"—that is, a form of writing.

- He characterized the glyphs as those of "animals unknown on the island," the first non-Rapanui attempt at a sign identification.

- Eyraud appears to have witnessed the Rapanui tracing the glyphs "by means of sharp stones" (obsidian flakes), which proves that the Rapanui were still manufacturing the inscriptions as late as 1864.

- He queried the Rapanui people about the glyphs' significance, this being the first recorded attempt at an informant "reading."

- Eyraud's "little they make of these tablets" indicates a neglect of the writing custom by most of the surviving population in 1864, the result of the horrific smallpox epidemic of the year before. Nevertheless, Eyraud specified that it is still "a custom that they preserve."

■ Eyraud thought the glyphs were "probably a script in origin."

The Frenchman did not undertake a methodical study of the curious Easter Island script. The exigencies of his precarious situation on the island in 1864 hardly permitted this. Although Eyraud suspected here a form of writing in origin, he was convinced at the same time that the surviving Rapanui had "no idea either of reading or of writing." Though Eyraud's letter was immediately published in a missionary journal in France and in a popular geographical magazine in Germany, no one apparently took notice.

The incredible announcement of the existence of an indigenous writing system in Oceania was simply ignored.

In the months that followed in the first half of 1989, I ferried each day across the blue placid waters of Lake Constance to the research library of the University of Konstanz to learn more about this unique writing system from Easter Island called *rongorongo,* ordering hundreds of obscure books and articles that documented the fascinating tale. Unhappily, the mountain of reports—in Spanish, French, German, Russian, and only sometimes English—were often garbled and contradictory. Obviously, very little genuine archival work had ever been accomplished on the subject. Much about the script was still unknown. And astonishingly, no one seemed ever to have effected a complete documentation of Oceania's only indigenous script. One solitary scholar, Thomas Barthel of Tübingen in southwestern Germany, had published in the 1950s a book on *rongorongo* that scientifically described the script for the first time and offered almost complete line drawings of the small *rongorongo* corpus of inscriptions. But the true story of the script itself had never been told. Its history was still unsung, its traditions hardly investigated, its texts incompletely published.

For these reasons I resolved back in 1989 to write this documentation myself. I had the philological training. I knew the languages necessary to do it. And above all, I felt the personal challenge. Only by becoming immersed in a mystery could one perhaps begin to solve it, I told myself. Little did I know then that this documentation would demand my full-time dedication for the next seven years and utterly exhaust all of Taki and my financial resources.

Nor could I have divined with this decision that—evidently for the first time in the history of epigraphy—the one documenting an undeciphered writing system was also simultaneously going to be its glyphbreaker.

For the moment, I merely concentrated my efforts on gathering everything that had been written on Easter Island's *rongorongo* script. The investigation eventually gemmated some 14,000 handwritten notecards as it led Taki and me from St. Petersburg, Russia, to Honolulu, Hawai'i; from London, England, to Vienna, Austria; from Rome, Italy, to Santiago, Chile; and ultimately to exotic Easter Island itself. It acquainted us for the first time with this beautiful and mysterious script, letting us appreciate that here lay not only the apogee of the Polynesian woodcarver's skill but perhaps the finest graphic elaboration to be found anywhere in the world.

It's a story of sheer superlatives.

Only 25 authentic *rongorongo*-inscribed artifacts survive in museums and institutions dispersed over the entire globe. One is in private hands. Easter Island itself possesses none. Nearly all of these artifacts are flat or slightly warped wooden boards, usually of rare driftwood, that most often are referred to in the literature as "tablets." However, *rongorongo* glyphs also adorn a 2-kilogram wooden staff that measures 126 cm by 6.5 cm and, with some 2300 individual glyphs, comprises the longest single *rongorongo* inscription that survives. (This "Santiago Staff," as it is called, ultimately proved to be the "Rosetta Stone" that unlocked the secret of the *rongorongo* script.) *Rongorongo* glyphs are also to be found on two wooden gorgets for hanging about the neck; on a "Birdman" statuette 33 cm high that is half man and half bird; and on a small, six-sided, wooden snuffbox cannibalized from an erstwhile tablet by an early nineteenth-century European sailor. There are no authentic *rongorongo* inscriptions on stone.

Eventually I was able to inventory the surviving genuine *rongorongo* pieces and establish their whereabouts at the end of the twentieth century:

"Tahua" (RR 1): SSCC, Rome.

"Mamari" (RR 2): SSCC, Rome.

"Échancrée" (RR 3): Museum of Tahiti at Punaauia, Tahiti.

"Aruku" (RR 4): SSCC, Rome.

"Paris Snuffbox" (RR 5): Musée de l'Homme, Paris.

"Keiti" (RR 6): Destroyed by Germans in the siege of Louvain, Belgium, in 1914, this artifact survives only in photographs.

"Chauvet Fragment" (RR 7): In private hands in New York City.

"Small Santiago" (RR 8): National Museum of Natural History, Santiago, Chile.

"Large Santiago" (RR 9): National Museum of Natural History, Santiago, Chile.

"Santiago Staff" (RR 10): National Museum of Natural History, Santiago, Chile.

"Honolulu 3629" (RR 11): Bishop Museum, Honolulu, Hawai'i.

"Honolulu 3623" (RR 12): Bishop Museum, Honolulu, Hawai'i.

"Honolulu 3622" (RR 13): Bishop Museum, Honolulu, Hawai'i.

"Honolulu 445" (RR 14): Bishop Museum, Honolulu, Hawai'i.

"Small Washington" (RR 15): Smithsonian Institution, Washington, DC.

"Large Washington" (RR 16): Smithsonian Institution, Washington, DC.

"Small St. Petersburg" (RR 17): Museum of Anthropology and Ethnology, St. Petersburg, Russia.

"Large St. Petersburg" (RR 18): Museum of Anthropology and Ethnology, St. Petersburg, Russia.

"**London Tablet**" (**RR 19**): Museum of Mankind, London.

"**London *rei miro* 6847**" (**RR 20**): Museum of Mankind, London.

"**London *rei miro* 9295**" (**RR 21**): Museum of Mankind, London.

"**Berlin Tablet**" (**RR 22**): Museum für Völkerkunde, Berlin.

"**Small Vienna**" (**RR 23**): Museum für Völkerkunde, Vienna.

"**Large Vienna**" (**RR 24**): Museum für Völkerkunde, Vienna.

"**New York Birdman**" (**RR 25**): American Museum of Natural History, New York.

In the years that followed, I was fortunate enough to be the first person to work with all but four of these surviving *rongorongo* inscriptions.

The Rapanui master scribes had first lightly etched on each artifact hundreds—in rare cases even thousands—of glyphs in outline contours using sharp flakes of obsidian. Then they deeply incised these shapes with a dull shark's tooth (as experiments at the end of the twentieth century have proved). The 14,000 total glyphs that survive today—depicting birds, fishes, turtles, stylized standing and sitting humans, flora, and geometric figures—are invariably arranged in lines running from left to right. This reading direction is known from Rapanui informants in the nineteenth and early twentieth centuries, as well as from studies in the 1950s showing that a given series of glyphs that appears on one line of one artifact can also be repeated on two lines of another, "breaking" over the artifact's right end (never over its left end). Every other line of a *rongorongo* inscription is upside down. This would have ensured one continuous and uninterrupted reading from left to right and from one line to the next. The writing covers both sides of the wooden tablets. Over half of the tablets show traces of burning, and many are so damaged by fire and/or rot (from having lain hidden in lava caves for several years) that today their inscriptions are barely legible.

Slowly scaling this mountain of literature about the *rongorongo* script, I met at every twist and turn the same three questions:

- Where did the Easter Island script come from?
- How old was it?
- What did the *rongorongo* inscriptions say?

Yet all three questions invariably had no satisfactory answer.

CHAPTER 8

TALKING BOARDS OF THE PACIFIC

Joseph-Eugène Eyraud returned to Easter Island as a conse-crated lay brother in 1866 in the company of an ordained priest of the Congregation of the Sacred Hearts (SSCC). Several months later, another priest and lay brother joined them, and for the next few years the four Catholic missionaries evange-lized on ravaged, tuberculosis-gripped Rapanui. In 1868 Eyraud himself died of TB on the island, curiously enough without having informed his three colleagues of the remarkable "hiero-glyphics" he had witnessed there four years earlier.

Not one *rongorongo* inscription was visible in 1868, those that Eyraud had observed having in the meantime been burned, hidden, cannibalized, or otherwise disposed of by the Rapanui themselves. It was as though the wooden tablets and staffs that once sanctified all the houses of Easter Island had never existed.

In 1869 one of Rapanui's two Catholic priests paid a rare visit to his superior Bishop Tepano Jaussen of Tahiti, bringing as a gift from the bishop's new Rapanui converts a jet-black skein of human hair that was wrapped around a small fragment of a wooden board. Imagine the priest's surprise when his bishop unwrapped the hair to discover that the board was covered with many curious little figures ... "in lines and well drawn." The Bishop of Tahiti seemed even more surprised. Indeed, the unexpected discovery altered the bishop's life forever: He thereafter devoted a considerable portion of his remaining days to solving the mystery of the Easter Island script.

Florentin Étienne Jaussen (1815–1891), who had been named by Papal Bull the first Catholic bishop of a diocese that included all the Pacific islands between 100° and 155° West and 0° and 40° South, was a personality of historic proportions. "Bishop Tepano"—Tahitian for Étienne—always strove to understand and be a part of the island world he loved so well. This was a period of great political turmoil and human misery in East Polynesia. While the Polynesians were dying in large numbers from various foreign contagions, the French government was politically battling both the English and the Vatican for absolute control of the area. Bishop Jaussen always fought to enrich his islanders' power base in order to counteract what he believed was a virulent European exploitation. In the process, he also became an expert in the Tahitian language—even authoring a Tahitian grammar, dictionary, and catechism—hoping thereby to save the language from impending extinction.

Because of such heroic efforts as Jaussen's, the Tahitian language thrives today.

When he unwrapped that black skein of human hair to reveal the lines of Easter Island writing hidden beneath, Bishop Jaussen was 54 years of age and at the height of his ecclesiastical and mental powers. He was to become the most formidable figure in *rongorongo* research in the nineteenth century.

Bishop Jaussen immediately instructed the priest to find out all he could about this mysterious writing from Easter Island, what Jaussen himself called the "talking boards." He suspected that in these talking boards of the Pacific lay the key to the origins of the Polynesian people.

On his return to Rapanui, the priest and his colleagues scoured the island for more tablets for their bishop, and they eventually were able to send several of the incised artifacts to Tahiti. Meanwhile, a Chilean naval vessel had called at Easter Island. Once its officers had been informed by the priests of the extraordinary script's existence, they managed to secure for Chile—which at this time still had no political affiliation with Easter Island—three magnificent inscriptions, one of them the unique "Santiago Staff."

The Berlin-born Director of Chile's new National Museum of Natural History in the capital Santiago, Dr. Rudolf Philippi, soon spread the word throughout Europe about the existence of the inscribed tablets of Easter Island. And in 1870 the celebrated Russian naturalist Nikolai Nikolaevich Miklukho-Maklai, on his way to New Guinea for an historic two-year expedition, before leaving Europe consulted leading scientists in Berlin and London about the Easter Island writing; he later studied the original tablets in Santiago's National Museum. He subsequently visited Easter Island—leaving after only two hours, however, when he found that most islanders and both surviving priests had fled only weeks earlier—and then sailed on to Mangareva in the wake of the refugees to gather information about the script. Here on Mangareva, the Russian was told that the tablets were called *rongorongo*, a Mangarevan word that meant "professional chanter." (Until then, the Rapanui people had simply called the inscriptions *tā* "writing" or *kouhau* "staffs.") Miklukho-Maklai continued on to Tahiti to pay a cordial visit to Bishop Jaussen and inspect his unique collection of Easter Island tablets, informing the Catholic bishop at this time of the name *rongorongo*, of Europe's tremendous excitement about Oceania's only indigenous writing, and of its possible historic implications.

Because of the young Russian's visit, Bishop Jaussen grew even more fascinated with the Easter Island script. Two years later, in 1873, the bishop was able to spend a fortnight eliciting more information about it from a young Rapanui named Metoro Tau'a Ure, who was one of those refugees who had been indentured to a Tahitian plantation. Jaussen's own Rapanui house staff claimed that Metoro had once received rudimentary training in one of the *rongorongo* "schools" that had existed on Easter Island before the slave raids of 1862–1863. Once put to the test, however, Metoro only pretended to sing in the style of the ancient masters of the *rongorongo* script, regarding the tablet he was holding in both hands and arbitrarily putting a name to each glyph as he merrily singsonged along. More often than not, Metoro used different words and phrases for the same recurring glyph. Much of the vocabulary of his pretended "chants" wasn't even in Rapanui, but Tahitian.

Undeterred when he detected this contradiction and similar inconsistencies, Bishop Jaussen wrote down each "reading" that Metoro had tendered. After this the bishop spent two full months at the Catholic mission on the nearby island of Mo'orea, cutting out pictures of each glyph and pasting them onto sheets of paper in their proper sequence according to the four tablets that had been used, afterward writing below each glyph the "readings" that Metoro had given him. Once this was done, Jaussen compiled his "*rongorongo* dictionary"—a long list showing the separate glyphs in one column on the left and their "identifications" according to Metoro in a second column on the right.

This so-called "Jaussen List" of *rongorongo* signs, eventually published posthumously in 1893, came to serve generations of scholars as the basis for countless attempts to decipher the *rongorongo* script of Easter Island. The list is still enthusiastically cited by amateur epigraphers at the end of the twentieth century.

Unhappily, it proves only the wealth of Metoro's imagination and the poverty of the good bishop's prudence ... at least where *rongorongo* was concerned.

About three months after Bishop Jaussen's fortnight with Metoro Tau'a Ure, a resident American on Tahiti worked with an unidentified Rapanui informant in the same manner. However, after only three Sunday sessions, the American angrily tossed the Rapanui into the street, accusing him of willful deception. This is because these three sessions had yielded three wholly different "readings" for the same *rongorongo* inscription! His informant might have been Metoro.

Because they had no Rapanui informants to work with, scholars in Europe in the 1870s were taking a different approach to the solution of *rongorongo*. One young Englishman read the plaster *rongorongo* facsimiles—now available in Europe's leading capitals—from right to left (that is, backwards), skipping every other line of text and interpreting the script pictorially—as though each glyph were the frame of a continuous cartoon story. When he presented his paper about this bizarre method at the Royal Anthropological Institute in London in 1875, the famous British scholar Edward Burnett Tylor (1832–1917), who virtually invented modern anthropology in the mid-Victorian age, rose to voice his differing opinion that the number of *rongorongo* inscriptions that had now been gathered "would justify the investigation being carried into the second stage—that of tabulating the various pictures or symbols employed, to ascertain how often and in what connection they occurred." Tylor went on to draw the audience's attention to a number of signs in particular that "had ceased to be pictorial, and had passed into regular symbolic characters, repeated from time to time with variations." Tylor had offered a brilliant insight that put the young speaker to shame.

Some French scholars of the time suspected ancient Egyptian connections, thinking the hieroglyphs of the Nile had inspired the Easter Island signs. Others, including Bishop Jaussen, wondered whether the origin of *rongorongo* was to be found instead in Malaysia.

A German naval vessel that called at Rapanui in 1882 learned from the remaining islanders that *rongorongo* was used for genealogies. The commander of the vessel speculated that the tablets appeared to record male and female couplings in conjunction with the season of each birth. According to him, then, the artifacts were indeed genealogies, as the Rapanui had claimed.

Albert Étienne Jean Baptiste Terrien de Lahaymounais Peixotte de Poncil, Baron de Lacouperie (1845–1894), mercifully also referred to as Terrien de Lacouperie, Professor of Chinese Philology at University College, Cambridge, England, and a naturalized Briton, proposed his own "decipherment" of *rongorongo*. This was before a general meeting of the prestigious Royal Asiatic Society the following year, in 1883. Closely examining the *rongorongo* glyphs, Terrien de Lacouperie found the "forked heads" of some glyphs to be similar to the Vengi-Châlukya inscriptions of Southern India. On the basis of this supposed genetic relationship, he effected an analysis by "comparing the small differences (vocalic notation) existing between several of [the signs]," the details of which he—unfortunately or fortunately—does not provide. From this analysis, the illustrious Professor became convinced that the "Vaïhu characters" (as he called the Easter Island script)

> ... are nothing else than a decayed form of the ... writing of Southern India returning to the hieroglyphical stage. With this clue, the inscriptions of Easter Island are no more a sealed text. They can easily be read after a little training.

Terrien de Lacouperie related the Harappa script of the Indus Valley to Southern India's Açoka script and linked the latter to Rapanui's *rongorongo* with a surprisingly cavalier disregard for time and space.

While these and similar musings were proliferating, other European scholars, in particular the professional epigraphers, exercised both sobriety and precision in their assessment of the Easter Island script. They could appreciate that *rongorongo* was indeed a form of writing and that it ran from left to right and employed a very small inventory of glyphs that could alter their shape in significant ways. Perhaps most important of all, *rongorongo* appeared to be of very recent date. Every indication was, they concluded, that the script was entirely the product of the Rapanui people themselves, not the descendant of an ancient foreign tradition.

However, these professional scholars were few and far apart, and their voices were not heard by those amateurs and journalists who, for a variety of reasons, chose to favor the more exciting "mystery" over the rational explanation.

The most important scientific visit to Rapanui in the nineteenth century was that paid by the American crew of the USS *Mohican* in 1886. During their thirteen days on Easter Island, the Americans amassed the single most substantial collection of information about the island's archaeological patrimony and traditional culture. They were also expressly instructed to gather what information they could about the island's puzzling *rongorongo* script and, if possible, to acquire original tablets bearing this same writing.

The Americans succeeded on both points. Two authentic *rongorongo* tablets—the last to be acquired on the island—and a large collection of traditional artifacts were purchased for the then exorbitant price of $200. In addition to this, the last Rapanui to harbor knowledge of the original *rongorongo* traditions and songs was found to be still alive!

Back in the 1850s, Daniel Ure Va'e Iko had been the royal steward of Easter Island's last *'ariki mau*, or "paramount chief." Ure—literally, "Penis," then a common Rapanui name—had heard the *rongorongo* tablets chanted daily by the many script experts, he still knew their songs by heart, and he still honored the *rongorongo* practice intimately ... and feared its mighty *tapu* (sacred prohibition). Always in the past he had avoided questions from the priests about the *rongorongo* inscriptions, "fearing for his Christian soul" as he would claim. But on this one stormy night in December 1886, there in his tiny hut on the slope of the volcano that overlooked Easter Island's single settlement of Hangaroa, the patriarch Ure yielded to the brash Americans—and their felicitous bottle of powerful firewater—as they urged him like old comrades, hour after hour, to sing the *rongorongo* chants for them, trying to slide into his hands the two original script tablets they had purchased.

Ure refused even to look at the tablets, fearing their *tapu*. But he did look at the several photographs of Bishop Jaussen's tablets that the Americans had taken just the month before at Tahiti. Ure had never seen photographs before. He was captivated. And he appreciated that these holy *rongorongo* artifacts that the photos showed in smaller black and white exemplars were the personal possession of the revered Bishop of Tahiti. "Bishop Tepano" was a hero to all Rapanui. Singing to Bishop Tepano's tablets wouldn't bring damnation.

So, in the late hours of the night, old Ure began to sing to the photographs. The Americans listened. Their important interpreter, the Tahitian Jew Alexander Salmon, co-owner of the island's sheep station and the leading personality on Easter Island in those troubled years, lay sprawled out on the dirt floor writing down the Rapanui words as best he could, Rapanui being a sister language to Tahitian. Through the entire rain-lashed night Ure chanted, as he held each photograph of his bishop's *rongorongo* tablets in both hands and rocked back and forth in the traditional Rapanui rhythm for chanting.

Some of Ure's songs were contemporary creations: a popular love tune or a melody about a departing child off to the mangos and money of Tahiti. But two of the chants were real paydirt, genuinely ancient songs from premissionary Rapanui. And one reproduced the authentic structure of nearly all original *rongorongo* inscriptions; indeed, it furnished the key to unlock at last the secret to the *rongorongo* script.

But this was not to be recognized until the 1990s.

Over a hundred years later.

The litany of balderdash about Easter Island's *rongorongo* script persisted in Australia, America, and Europe. To furnish here only one notorious example, "Dr. Allen Carroll"—the assumed name of ostensibly the illegitimate son of the thirteenth Duke of Norfolk—of the Anthropological Society of Australasia in Sydney, Australia, published from 1892 to 1908 a series of hobbyhorse articles about *rongorongo* that the physician Carroll proudly pranced from frivolity to absurdity.

Offering no proof and few examples, in these articles Carroll declared that the Easter Island script was not Polynesian at all but was written in a South American tongue using "words and phrases from the Toltcan, Queché, Aztecan, Tschimu, Carañ, Quito, Bacatan, Quichua, Muiscan, Collan, and others." Carroll's proffered "translations" of the *rongorongo* inscriptions (he never identifies which inscription he is reading or what language it's supposed to be) are obvious Victorian self-indulgences:

> To those who are our Guardians, oh give ear to us in your temple. You are our protectors. You are the good spirits of our ancestors. I, and we, know you as the Chiefs who are the powerful protectors to these sons of the Sun-chiefs. Ye gods....

Ye gods indeed. Fortunately, no one seemed to take Carroll seriously, and the good doctor was soon forgotten.

In another vein, Paul Gauguin, the famous French impressionist painter who lived in Tahiti, was enthralled by the Easter Island writing. He used *rongorongo* glyphs on three separate occasions to achieve a uniquely Polynesian statement redolent of mystery and antiquity. In his well-known painting from 1893 called "Merahi Metua no Tehamana"—literally, "Parental Angels of Tehamana"—in which 43-year-old Gauguin portrays his 13-year-old Tongan mistress Teha'amana, Gauguin fills the background with *rongorongo* glyphs. He also included similar glyphs on a later wooden carving of a Polynesian crucifixion of Christ and on its negative print in black and white. Gauguin had arbitrarily selected these glyphs from Bishop Jaussen's posthumous publication on *rongorongo* that also appeared in 1893.

The *rongorongo* script helped inspire the celebrated expedition to Easter Island in 1914–1915 by the well-to-do British husband-and-wife team of Scoresby Routledge and Katherine Pease Routledge. Both were trained anthropologists who had already spent two years among the Kikuyu of Kenya. Katherine's copious notes on the premissionary *rongorongo* customs of Easter

Island lay forgotten for decades and would not be assessed until my own work in the early 1990s. It was these unseen notes that, more than anything else, prompted my acknowledgement of Daniel Ure Va'e Iko's importance for *rongorongo* research.

Rongorongo was also the primary *raison d'être* of the Franco-Belgian Expedition to Easter Island in 1934–1935. An emigré Hungarian scholar in Paris had detected many remarkable correspondences between the *rongorongo* glyphs and the signs of the script of the Indus Valley civilization of 2000 B.C. Alleging a relationship between this script of the ancient Indians and that of the prehistoric society of Easter Island, he created an international furor that eventually led the governments of France and Belgium to sponsor an important expedition to Easter Island to investigate the veracity of his unusual claim. The leader of this expedition, Swiss anthropologist Alfred Métraux, who was to become the leading authority on early Rapanui ethnology, soon disproved the Hungarian's allegation to the scientific world's satisfaction by establishing the exclusively Polynesian and, more specifically, Marquesan origin of the ancient Easter Island society. Métraux himself studied the *rongorongo* script in considerable depth right up to the end of the 1930s, revealing much of substance.

However, such scientific integrity was rare among *rongorongo* investigators. Now that they had come firmly to believe that no information of value was to be had from the Rapanui people themselves, the search for the assumed foreign origin of the *rongorongo* script was on in earnest. The rationale for this search lay in the conviction that known sign values of a known script might be able to furnish the unknown sign values of the unknown but related *rongorongo* script of Easter Island. Accordingly, it was proposed in all seriousness that the answer to *rongorongo* lay in Sumatran sail patterns or in the Chinese ideographs or in the Egyptian or Maya hieroglyphs or in the pre-Inca writing of Peru or in Panama's picture-writing.

Later, in the 1960s and thereafter, the enthusiastic dilettantes would also claim that the origin for Easter Island's *ron-*

gorongo probably lay in the scripts of the ancient Semites, Phoenicians, Greeks, early Germans, Norwegian Vikings, the lost continent of Lemuria, and—what was to become especially popular—those visiting extraterrestrials who had also carved the standing *moai* using prehistoric laser beams.

However, by the 1950s a new movement was under way. Reputable science had also discovered *rongorongo*. It was finally accepted by most trained professionals that no Rapanui was alive who could tell us what the inscriptions really said and that no other script in the world really shared any genetic trait with the Easter Island script. So the answer to *rongorongo*—if there was ever going to be an answer to *rongorongo*—had to come from within the *rongorongo* script itself. That is, it would reveal itself through an internal analysis of the sequences of glyphs and their recognized repeating patterns.

You may recall that this is just what Alice Kober had concluded about the Linear B script of ancient Greece only a few years earlier than this in the 1940s. The new approach reflected the epigraphic mood of the era.

Already there had been several attempts along similar lines in the first half of the twentieth century. However, these attempts had led to dead ends. Their authors had professed an ignorance of the Old Rapanui language that the inscriptions had doubtless been written in. And most had wrongly assumed that Bishop Jaussen's "*rongorongo* dictionary" held something of substance.

The first scholar to approach *rongorongo* using modern epigraphic techniques was the German ethnologist Thomas S. Barthel. Then attached to the University of Hamburg, on his thirtieth birthday in 1953 Barthel began collating the *rongorongo* inscriptions and studying the patterns of glyph distributions. He also identified and described all the variable elements each glyph could display. Barthel gave each glyph its own number and then wrote the *rongorongo* inscriptions using only these numbers so as to be able to study the glyphs' distribution and frequency independent of their pictures. He published Metoro Tau'a Ure's "readings" of 1873 for the first time in their entirety, personally believing at the time that these readings held the key to the script's decipherment. He also identified a segment of one tablet as containing a calendar text of some kind because of its significant repetition of crescent moons. His book on the subject, *Grundlagen zur Entzifferung der Osterinselschrift (Rudiments Toward the Decipherment of the Easter Island Script)*, published in 1958, because of its solid methodology clearly established *rongorongo* research as an autonomous member of epigraphic science.

For the next thirty-five years, Barthel continued his *rongorongo* investigations as Professor of Ethnology at the University of Tübingen in southwestern Germany. His interpretations of the *rongorongo* inscriptions, initially hailed by journalists in the mid-1950s as the "decipherment" of the Easter Island script, unfortunately failed to convince the academic community. However, Barthel's rudiments of *rongorongo* research—especially his line drawings of nearly every inscription, his glyph location-finding tables, and his analyses of important glyph patterns and repetitions—were still serving *rongorongo* scholars well at the end of the twentieth century.

The Soviets had not been idle during these darkest days of the Cold War. At the same time that Thomas Barthel was carrying out similar investigations in Hamburg, two Russian epigraphers in Leningrad (St. Petersburg), Yuri Knorozov—who was simultaneously solving the syllabic key to the hieroglyphic Maya script of Central America—and Nikolai Butinov, pointed out near-identical passages of glyphs that were repeated on different *rongorongo* inscriptions. This was a significant breakthrough that had been accomplished by a young Russian epigrapher who had died during the horrendous German siege of Leningrad in World War II. These parallel passages of *rongorongo* glyphs Knorozov and Butinov then explained as possible Rapanui genealogies.

Another Soviet investigator working closely with Knorozov and Butinov at the Museum of Anthropology and Ethnology in St. Petersburg was Irina Fedorova. In the early 1960s, Fedorova approached *rongorongo* through the structure of its underlying language. Comparing the frequency and distribution of certain glyphs with those of syllabic and word structures in the Rapanui language, she suggested possible linguistic correspondences. This was a formal attempt to isolate individual words on the Easter Island tablets.

Both Barthel and Fedorova suggested sound values for the *rongorongo* glyphs on the basis either of Metoro's whimsical "identifications" for Bishop Jaussen or of subjective interpretations of outward shapes. However, a scientifically verifiable reading of the *rongorongo* inscriptions was still not possible by the end of the 1980s, though both Barthel and Fedorova were still suggesting possible "translations" of various passages in academic articles published in Germany and Russia.

Unbeknownst to me by Christmas of 1989, I would soon meet Yuri Knorozov and Nikolai Butinov in St. Petersburg. I would also come to know Thomas Barthel and Irina Fedorova well and eventually to count these two rare individuals among my closest personal friends ...

While I discovered for the first time in the 130-year history of *rongorongo* investigation the key that cracked the *rongorongo* code.

CHAPTER 9

ATOP
TERE VAKA

"Smile," shouted Taki over the blustering wind. "You finally made it. You're here!"

I smiled the smile of the victorious and she snapped the photograph. Then we embraced and held each other tightly, marveling at one of the most stupendous panoramas this planet can offer.

It was February 1993 and we were exulting atop Tere Vaka (TEH-REH VAH-KAH), the highest peak of Earth's most isolated inhabited island ... Easter Island. As far as the eye could see—in 360° of soul-numbing isolation—there was only horizon. Ten kilometers to the southwest, directly in front of us this windy and sunny summer's day, rose gently the volcano Rano Kau, at its foot Rapanui's only village, Hangaroa. Ten kilometers to the east, on our left, sloped the island's third volcano, the Poike peninsula. Just before it and to the right bulged the famous quarry and lake Rano Raraku, where the many monolith *moai* still stood rooted in the earth after three centuries of stony silence. It was eerily deserted here at Tere Vaka's summit, visited only by the blasting wind of the limitless South Pacific. Yes, I had finally made it. I was here at last. And I was

surveying more than inimitable, barren Easter Island in its ecological indigence and archaeological awesomeness.

My view finally encompassed the island's unrivaled story,
too.

Since 1989 I had made myself one of the world's experts in
the old Rapanui language and culture. I had met most of the
international scholars who, like me, had dedicated their lives
to the search for the truth behind Easter Island's rich and bru-
tal patrimony. Country after country Taki and I had already
visited by this time, from one end of the globe to the other. We
had seen the original *rongorongo* inscriptions for ourselves and
written down their texts and documented their individual
fates. Not only had I become an active member of the professional organizations devoted to Easter Island and the Pacific; I
was by now one the leading figures in these organizations—
with concomitant responsibilities. I had even founded the first
scholarly journal dedicated exclusively to Polynesian languages and literature, with worldwide distribution.

During this peripatetic engagement of the previous four
years, from 1989 to 1993, the same three questions followed
me wherever I went to investigate the arcane script of Easter
Island: Where did the *rongorongo* inscriptions come from? How
old are they? And what do they say?

To answer these questions properly, I knew I had to approach
rongorongo altogether differently than I had approached the
Phaistos Disk of ancient Crete. You see, with the Disk, understanding the other Aegean scripts made it possible to apply a
methodology that closely resembled the decipherment of these
other scripts. This is because all the Aegean scripts—including
that of the Phaistos Disk—are related. There existed in the
ancient Aegean a shared mindset, a collective uniformity in the
particular way that human speech was set to sign and in the various scripts' general outward appearance and statement. But
Easter Island's *rongorongo* script claims no relatives. *Rongorongo*
is an epigraphic orphan. To find out just who this orphan was, I

had to get into the Polynesian mind. Only this way, I realized, could I begin to understand the essence of Oceania's only indigenous script.

I should add that I wasn't exactly a neophyte in the Polynesian world. In 1965 I had taught myself Hawaiian and Samoan, with a view at that time to "touring Polynesia and compiling Polynesian dictionaries"—or so I had explained to one of my professors at the University of California at Santa Barbara when he had asked me about my future career plans. After immigrating to New Zealand in 1975, I had learned the Māori language of Aotearoa (New Zealand) and over the next five years had thoroughly acquainted myself with Polynesian customs and history.

By the time I first approached *rongorongo* at the beginning of 1989—while I was still living in Meersburg on Lake Constance, in Germany—I could already tally some twenty-four years of Polynesian studies.

This experience was to prove indispensable for the task that lay ahead.

All of the *rongorongo* complex was utterly contrary to that of the Phaistos Disk, I soon discovered to my dismay in 1989. It wasn't just a different world. It was a different universe. The Phaistos Disk and Minoan culture had been exhaustively and soberly documented by others. Easter Island's *rongorongo* inscriptions, in distracting contrast, enjoyed few treatments of merit, and the true story of ancient Rapanui society had been wildly distorted by decades of journalistic extravagances concentrating on ineffable "mysteries." The Phaistos Disk was a single artifact; I had seen this artifact for myself in the Heraklion Museum on Crete and had been inspired by this encounter to undertake its decipherment. Rapanui's *rongorongo* inscriptions adorned no fewer than 25 artifacts, dispersed in museums and institutions throughout the world. Initially I had seen only a handful of them, and these only in photographs, once my interest in the script had been awakened through literature and

Howard Paine of the National Geographic. (It took two full years to collect usable photographs of all the surviving *rongorongo* inscriptions.)

But I needed to see the original *rongorongo* artifacts. I had to measure, transcribe, and document each one of these for myself, too.

And therein lay the rub.

Perhaps the greatest difficulty posed by Easter Island's *rongorongo* script, compared with the Phaistos Disk, was the logistic and financial challenge. Working with each inscription directly, which was indispensable for a proper scientific assessment, meant expensive flights to the farthest corners of the globe. To cover these awesome costs, I applied—as a qualified scientist who had ceased gainful employment in order to carry out this research full-time—for the relevant fellowships and grants in Germany (where I had been living and paying taxes for ten years), the United States, and New Zealand. Each application was unsuccessful. (It did smart to find out later that the successful applicants for these fellowships and grants already held lucrative university positions.) I also applied for travel grants to conferences to which I had been formally invited in order to present a scientific paper; I intended stopovers on the way to these conferences so as to include *rongorongo* research at the relevant institutes. But these applications, too, were unsuccessful. In one unforgettable case, it was poignantly ironic that a German government DFG travel grant for scholars who had been invited to present formal papers—a grant that I had earlier applied for, too, in vain—had been awarded to a wealthy colleague who was then building a house for over one million German marks.

In the end, Taki and I had no recourse but to pay for everything out of our own pockets. For each longer international flight to see a *rongorongo* tablet, we had to take out a bank loan, at 15 percent interest. With this began a renewed saga of debt and financial worry, only four years after we had at last overcome the penury that our move to Germany had caused.

The new struggle was this time to last seven long years. There was to be no more dining out. No more movies. No more birthday celebrations or purchases or weekend trips. It was to our benefit that we had no children. And because we had been without a telephone since 1977, we were able to save that expense too. (Friends never understood this, and we hesitated to explain the reason why.) Every penny we made went to travel and research expenses.

This we did in order to document Easter Island's *rongorongo* inscriptions for the first time.

Unless one has experienced something similar, one cannot appreciate how difficult life can be in such a financial situation. It's a gut-wrenching anxiety, this "scraping along" day after worrisome day. Even posting a simple letter becomes a momentous decision, and our postage bill in some months— especially with the growing list of international colleagues in Pacific studies with whom I began an active correspondence— equaled our grocery bill. Sometimes we even had to dispense with the essentials. A computer would have cost us Fort Knox, so my 1950s Adler typewriter did overtime in these bread-and-butter days. Privation is hardly conducive to happy scholarship. But Taki and I both felt the need to complete this task and agreed wholeheartedly to the sacrifices required.

It was the dedication of conviction.

The only problem was that I wasn't at all certain that deciphering Easter Island's *rongorongo* script was even possible, and this was, of course, our ultimate goal. For the longest time I harbored serious doubts ... which Taki simply refused to accept.

"I know you can do it," she would tell me.

And for the next seven years, our again-humble lives focused on documenting the story of *rongorongo;* on collecting usable photographs of each side or line of each inscription; on compiling thousands of notecards detailing every conceivable aspect of ancient Easter Island society; on seeking out original *rongorongo* inscriptions, from St. Petersburg to Santiago; and

on writing—over a period of several years—the scholarly monograph that told *rongorongo*'s complete story and reproduced all
its known texts for the first time.

We lived only for this.

Rongorongo became our adoptive child.

One of the first things that had to be scientifically clari-
fied, I realized as a professional linguist, was the underlying
language of the *rongorongo* inscriptions. Some scholars had
declared that this language was West Polynesian (though Easter
Island lies in East Polynesia) or even a vestige of some other
ethnic community, from pre-Inca Peruvian to ancient Chinese.
The Russian Irina Fedorova had asserted that the language of
the *rongorongo* inscriptions, though Polynesian, was so ancient
that it would no longer be understandable to us today. The
cumulative weight of evidence eventually suggested to me,
however, that these inscriptions could only have been written
in Old Rapanui.

Old Rapanui was the language of those Easter Islanders
who were alive in the first half of the nineteenth century when
these artifacts were still being incised with the *rongorongo*
glyphs and when the elaborate customs surrounding the writing still flourished. But of what did Old Rapanui consist linguistically? Could we still understand this tongue after so
many years? Or had it been replaced completely by the
Rapanui–Tahitian hybrid idiom that was now spoken on Easter
Island? I devoted years to this question. Eventually I was able
to show that Old Rapanui was indeed still comprehensible,
though it differed significantly from Modern Rapanui.

It appears that the *rongorongo* inscriptions are all written
in the Rapanui language that had evolved from the Proto East
Polynesian language spoken in the Marquesas Islands about the
time of Christ. Old Rapanui's vocabulary is retrievable through
comparison with such East Polynesian sister languages as
Hawaiian, Māori, Tahitian, and especially Marquesan and
Mangarevan. The informants of the British ethnologist Katherine Routledge who were alive at the beginning of the twentieth

century still knew and spoke this Old Rapanui language, though in an already contaminated idiom. This means that we also possess songs and stories in Old Rapanui. It allows us to understand better the language that underlies the *rongorongo* inscriptions themselves.

I spent so much time on this particular subject because I understood that any decipherment must be predicated on the known. If a known script describes an unknown language—the situation one finds with the undeciphered Etruscan script, for example, which uses the known Greek script to express the unknown Etruscan language—then the script must be expected to assist in the identification or reconstruction of the unknown tongue. But if an unknown script describes a known language—the challenge that was offered by Easter Island's *rongorongo*—then the language will have to explain for us the script.

I realized that the Old Rapanui language had to underpin any method used to decipher the *rongorongo* script. Indeed, the Old Rapanui language—in conjunction with properly conducted internal analyses of the script (that is, determining the frequency and distribution of individual glyphs and repeated segments of texts)—had to be the only truly reliable key to unlock *rongorongo*'s secrets.

The Rapanui language is an autonomous language belonging to the East Polynesian subgroup of languages. These in turn are part of the larger Polynesian group of languages within the greater Austronesian family of languages. Austronesian is the largest language family in the world; it includes some 1200 languages, or one-fifth of all the world's known tongues. Austronesian begins at African Madagascar and ends at Rapanui 15,000 kilometers to the east. Rapanui is in fact the apogee of Austronesian's eastward expansion.

The language of Easter Island—displaying as it does many features that the other East Polynesian languages have lost or replaced, and failing to display many features that these languages share—constitutes a special East Polynesian isolate.

This indicates an extremely early divergence from the East Polynesian proto-language that was evidently spoken in the Marquesas Islands some two millennia ago. Indeed, Rapanui apparently constituted East Polynesia's first such divergence. Because Hawaiian—which shares with the other East Polynesian languages those innovations that Rapanui missed—might have diverged as early as A.D. 300, it is theoretically conceivable, as my own investigations revealed, that the Rapanui colonists quit their Marquesan home island as early as the first century A.D. Rapanui's subsequent period of isolation (until 1722) evidences in its linguistic profile neither a "non-Polynesian substrate" (such as an earlier South American occupation, as Thor Heyerdahl always alleged) nor a "second Polynesian wave of settlers." That is, once the Marquesan colonists arrived at uninhabited Rapanui nearly two thousand years ago, they remained there in complete isolation and were not visited again until European intrusion over a millennium and a half later.

Easter Island may actually represent the greatest example of isolation, both geographically and temporally, known to humankind.

I was ultimately able to suggest tentatively to my linguistic colleagues various stages of the Rapanui language. There's Proto-Rapanui, which must be reconstructed from the East Polynesian proto-tongue. Then there's Old Rapanui, the premissionary language of the early 1800s that is still preserved—if corrupted and contaminated—in the earliest accounts from the island. And finally we have Modern Rapanui, a blanket designation for the continually changing late-nineteenth- and twentieth-century stages of the language that finds itself in an ever-accelerating process of contamination and, more ominously, disuse. (Spanish is now preferred by the modern-day Rapanui people, who are citizens of Chile).

I knew I had to make myself an expert in this Old Rapanui language ... one that gave voice to the *rongorongo* writings and one that today's Rapanui people themselves could no longer speak.

This task alone took over two years.

One of the more fortuitous events during the first year of research in 1989 was the animated correspondence—and later the intimate friendship—of the American archaeologist Georgia Lee of Los Osos, California. Born in 1926, Lee had been the dynamic initiator and leader of the University of California's Archaeological Field Project to Easter Island that during the 1980s documented Oceania's greatest open library of rock art. Her book on the subject, *The Rock Art of Easter Island*, is a modern classic. At the end of the 1980s, she founded the quarterly *Rapa Nui Journal*, which has since become the world's foremost periodical on Easter Island, its science, and its history. She was also a founding member of the Easter Island Foundation, an international non-profit organization devoted to the investigation and preservation of Rapanui's physical and human heritage. (I was later to become regional editor of the *Rapa Nui Journal* and a vice-president of the Easter Island Foundation.) Georgia Lee was my mentor and guide during the struggling years of the Rapanui saga. Her sage counsel was always specie in the hand.

Over the next four years I was able to work directly with all of the *rongorongo* inscriptions but four. Taki and I beheld our first original tablets from Easter Island in August 1989. This was at the Senckenberg Museum in Frankfurt, Germany, to which we drove for four hours from Meersburg on a long day trip. Between the months of April and September 1989, the Senckenberg was presenting a special exhibition dedicated to Easter Island and its ancient past. What a thrill it was to see at last the same tablets that I had known only from photographs. There was a feeling of awe, too. These were holy objects, imbued not only with history but also with the veneration of generations of Rapanui ... and with the magic of a message still to be deciphered. I left them reluctantly in their dimly lit showcases, certain I would see them again in the not-too-distant future.

The *Wiedersehen* came sooner than I had anticipated.

A colleague in Kronberg near Frankfurt wrote in March 1990 to invite Taki and me to accompany a small group of Easter Island experts for two days to the Easter Island exhibition at the Cinquantenaire—the National Museum of Natural History in Brussels, Belgium. It was a wholly new presentation of Frankfurt's Senckenberg exhibition. We readily accepted, and the evening before the bus was to depart, we drove up to the colleague's house in Kronberg for a special dinner gathering . . .

Where we met Thomas and Maria Barthel for the first time.

Thomas Barthel, then Emeritus Professor of Ethnology at the University of Tübingen and the world's senior scholar of Rapanui's *rongorongo* script, knew only too well of my earlier Phaistos Disk work and was acquainted with my book *Evidence for Hellenic Dialect in the Phaistos Disk,* which he had even recommended to others, he told me. That evening at Kronberg we chatted superficially about *rongorongo* and decipherment in general—the first of many such discussions over the next few years, as the strength of my Easter Island research and production grew and as our relationship with Thomas and Maria Barthel deepened to mutual respect and affection.

The next day we boarded the chartered bus to Brussels, which lies several hours away; the Barthels followed by train. And here in the majestic Cinquantenaire, whose entrance had been decorated with several large imitation *moai,* Taki and I revisited the same tablets we had first beheld at the Senckenberg Museum in Frankfurt only seven months earlier. A special treat was the inclusion of the tiny "Paris Snuffbox" made of six pieces of a cannibalized *rongorongo* tablet; this had not been featured at the Senckenberg exhibition, and Thomas Barthel and I inspected it together closely. The lighting here in the Cinquantenaire was not merely subdued: It was downright dark—ostensibly to accentuate the dread "mystery of Easter Island." And the hundreds of Belgian and foreign visitors pushed and jostled in this tenebrous cavern of an exhibition, making it something more than unpleasant to attempt a proper transcription of each *rongorongo* artifact with pencil in jittery hand.

In October of 1990, I was able to perform this task at leisure with three of these same tablets in Rome. Taki and I had boarded a local German bus company's special four-day Rome excursion that had us transversing the Swiss Alps for the twelve-hour drive down to Europe's ancient capital. While Taki toured magnificent Rome and wandered in fascination through the Colosseum, the Forum (her favorite), and the Vatican Museum, I spent two days with the goodhearted Fathers of the Congregation of the Sacred Hearts. At their general headquarters just one kilometer west of the Vatican, I huddled over three of the original tablets that had once belonged to Bishop Tepano Jaussen of Tahiti, who had been of the same Catholic order.

It was the first time I had held in my hands original *rongorongo* tablets. I experienced a feeling of reverent joy, imagining those Rapanui scribes whose names I had resurrected in the world's archives: how they had incised these very same inscriptions while squatting in front of their thatched huts on premissionary Rapanui; how they had also chanted them incessantly, rocking back and forth to the chant's rhythmic cadence. I held each precious artifact as though it were gold. Only in the National Museum in Santiago, Chile, are there gathered as many choice *rongorongo* inscriptions as here with the Fathers of the Sacred Hearts in Rome. Our tight schedule allowed only a quick visit to the Colosseum with Taki, a stroll through St. Peter's while Pope John Paul II was conducting a special Synod, and a sunset walk over the Tiber to the square of St. Peter's communing with the first stars, the milling well-dressed crowds, and the transcendent antiquity that is Rome. This was a rich and educational and emotive visit that neither of us will ever forget.

The following year, 1991, I founded the scholarly journal *Rongorongo Studies: A Forum for Polynesian Philology.* I was—and still am—both its publisher and its editor. This is the world's first journal dedicated exclusively to Polynesian languages and literature, and the world's leading experts in these two fields have not failed since to supply me, year after year, with high-quality contributions treating everything from onomatopoeia in Hawaiian song to an ancient chant from tiny Manahiki in the Cook Islands. In 1994 *Rongorongo Studies* also began sponsoring the Polynesian Literary Competition, presenting a certificate of award and a cash prize to the winning poem or short story in the Polynesian language of each year's theme area (Samoa 1994, Hawai'i 1995, Cook Islands 1996, Niue 1997). This annual competition is meant to promote and preserve the use of the indigenous languages of Polynesia—almost all of them currently under threat of imminent extinction.

Also in 1991 I commenced my editorship of the volume *Easter Island Studies,* to which 36 international experts would eventually contribute 45 essays. It turned out to be the most globally collective scientific book on Easter Island ever published. (It finally appeared in Oxford, England, in 1993. The journal *New Scientist* in London called it "a timely volume and a classic study of an island culture.")

In May 1991, Taki and I flew to Salem, Massachusetts, to research for a week at the excellent Peabody Museum, which possesses a magnificent Polynesian archive. Then we flew on to Honolulu, Hawai'i, where I presented my paper on the Old Rapanui language—"Homogeneity in Old Rapanui"—at the Sixth International Conference on Austronesian Linguistics, revealing the linguistic discoveries I've detailed above. At the same time, I was permitted to work with the four original *rongorongo* fragments at the Bishop Museum, where Taki and I were graciously welcomed by the library staff and made to feel at home. The final week of the world journey was spent with my cousin's family on the Big Island of Hawai'i, touring Kilauea, Mauna Kea, and the Hilo and Kona coasts—a breathtakingly beautiful island with a long and bloody human history.

In September of the same year, 1991, after two years of frustrating applications, I was finally granted permission to work with the "Berlin Tablet" at the Museum für Völkerkunde in Dahlem, a suburb of Berlin. In the end, the folks in Berlin couldn't have been nicer. But imagine my chagrin when the *rongorongo* tablet, one of the largest in existence, literally began crumbling in my hands! I hurriedly finished my transcription and handed it back to the curator, voicing my professional concern. I fear it will be a long time before anyone is again allowed the rare privilege of handling the fragile "Berlin Tablet."

The next year, in April 1992, Taki and I joined Thomas and Maria Barthel and a group of other Easter Island enthusiasts in St. Petersburg, Russia. The once-glorious capital of the Czars was then locked in the chaotic throes of the dying Soviet empire: Crime and street peddling were rampant, and there was an ever-present, tangible sense of danger. Here at the Museum of Anthropology and Ethnology, generally known in Russian (from the German) as the "Kunstkammer," I met the decipherer of the Maya script Yuri Knorozov—an old, grey, fierce Cold Warrior—and his colleague Nikolai Butinov, tall and aloof, both of whom had studied and published on the *rongorongo* script in the 1950s. The special find of this memorable journey to work with the two St. Petersburg *rongorongo* tablets had to be Irina Fedorova—small, thin, timid, and utterly dedicated to Easter Island. Irina Fedorova is the Slavic world's foremost expert on the ancient Rapanui culture, having published voluminously on this subject and on the *rongorongo* inscriptions since the early 1960s. She and I were to correspond often in the years to come, and she and her daughter Olga became very close to Taki and me.

After the St. Petersburg trip, we visited Thomas and Maria Barthel in Tübingen at least once every three months, sharing strolls through the wintry forests and summer meadows overlooking the old university town and castle, talking of *rongorongo* and deciphering, reciting German poetry, and philosophizing on the meaning of growing old. Thomas confided to me on one of these many walks in pensive acquiescence, *"Altwer-den heißt loslassen"* ("Growing old means letting go"). This was a time that meant much to all four of us.

August and September of 1992 found Taki and me and another couple pedaling our way to Vienna, Austria. For Taki and I had chosen to see the two Vienna tablets in the Hofburg, Austria's former Imperial Residence, by way of the Danube on our new bicycles. And so we set off, together with our two friends, from Sigmaringen on the Danube, just 30 kilometers north of Meersburg, on four bicycles loaded down with large double sidepacks. We proceeded to pedal, glide, and push our way a thousand kilometers to the east ... an adventure that took us over two weeks and had us gaping in awe at scores of Baroque churches along the way, each of which seemed to vie with the preceding in overweening opulence. In the end I was able to inspect the two Vienna tablets in comfort in the Hof-burg, through the kind assistance of the expert museum staff, who seemed pleasantly amused that a New Zealand scholar had come all the way from western Germany by bike just to see their Easter Island tablets. Whereupon the four of us took the train back to Austrian Bregenz at the southern end of Lake Constance and then pedaled leisurely back up to German Meersburg 40 kilometers northwest along the two countries' shared shoreline.

Two *rongorongo* pieces were inaccessible. The small tablet "Echancrée" in the Tahiti Museum, once part of Bishop Tepano Jaussen's collection and precipitously brought to Tahiti from the Sacred Hearts in Rome in 1975, was simply too far away for us to afford the trip. And the "Chauvet Fragment"— once also Bishop Jaussen's—now graces a private collection in New York City.

I tried for the longest time to see the two *rongorongo* tablets in the Smithsonian Institution, the National Museum of the United States in Washington, DC, but this was the only institution in the world to hamper my access to its Easter

Island artifacts. When I complained to the Director of the Smithsonian that access was being denied me by his well-known Pacific curator, pointing out that international museums and institutions all over the world had kindly facilitated my inspection of their respective *rongorongo* inscriptions, his chairman of the Department of Anthropology replied that I would be welcome to study the tablets if I could arrange to visit the museum before the end of the month. His letter arrived in Germany on the 22nd. This effectively put an end to the proper scientific documentation of the Washington tablets, two of the most important in the *rongorongo* inventory. It has left a bitter taste to this day.

However, at about the same time, I was able to gain access to a veritable gold mine of early Easter Island information. This was the field notes of the British ethnologist Katherine Pease Routledge who, together with her husband Scoresby Routledge, from 1914 to 1915 visited Rapanui and collected information from the last Easter Islanders to remember life on the island before the Great Death and the arrival of the Catholic missionaries in the 1860s. For a long time Katherine Routledge's field notes were considered lost. Only in the 1980s was it discovered that they had merely lain forgotten in the library of the Royal Geographical Society in London. I was granted permission to purchase microfilms of these from Canberra, Australia. And it was in this way that I retrieved many hitherto unsuspected insights into *rongorongo* customs and practices, which I incorporated into my growing documentation of the script. I also came to appreciate the unique role that the old Rapanui Daniel Ure Va'e Iko played in the *rongorongo* story, clearly the last person on the island to possess an intimate knowledge of the *rongorongo* texts.

This appreciation, won through the recently rediscovered Routledge notes, eventually led to the first important breakthrough in reading the *rongorongo* tablets.

In January and February 1993, Taki and I finally flew down to Santiago, Chile, to work with the two important Santiago tablets and with the unique "Santiago Staff." It was our first visit to South America. We were most impressed by Chile's friendly people, breathtaking landscape, and unexpected affluence. The inspection of the *rongorongo* artifacts at the Museo Nacional de Historia Natural in Santiago's large public park went very well; the staff were amicable and helpful, as indeed nearly all museum staffs had been throughout the world. The successful research was followed by marvelous days at the resort of Reñaca on the coast by Viña del Mar. Here we were hosted by the energetic and brilliant William Liller and his vivacious Chilean wife Matty at their sumptuous villa on the high cliffs overlooking the Pacific Ocean. William Liller, retired Professor of Astronomy at Harvard, is also a vice-president of the Easter Island Foundation and an expert on the ancient Rapanui culture who has since established the Mulloy Research Library for Easter Island at the Fonck Museum in Viña del Mar, now the leading center for Easter Island research.

Taki and I were soon joined at the Liller home by Georgia Lee and Joan Seaver Kurze, the latter the first president of the Easter Island Foundation and likewise a close and trusted friend—like Georgia and me a Ph.D. alumna from UCLA. Together with Georgia and Joan, we then flew on LAN Chile at the end of January to distant Rapanui, Chile's possession five hours to the west, where we would indulge our archaeological and linguistic passions for nearly a month.

It was the fulfillment of a life-long dream. After having read so much about Rapanui, after having scaled the summit of its scholarship, nothing could have prepared me for the Rapanui of 1993. This is because nothing—but nothing—of the ancient culture of Easter Island has survived the twentieth century ... except the stone ancestors standing silent sentinel. Rapanui's landscape is incredible: vast volcanic fields strewn with wild scrub and hundreds of toppled *moai* in ignominious scatter. Wide vistas of treeless, rolling country. Isolated hills here and there, bare and alone. And dominating this dirge of bleak obsolescence are the three large volcanoes that formed the island in three successive stages: Tere Vaka, Poike, and Rano Kau.

Today's Rapanui people, now full-fledged citizens of the technoglobe, appear neither to understand nor to cherish their ancient past for its own merit. It shocked and disturbed me particularly to find the Rapanui language in its last stages of senility, a Rapanui–Tahitian hybrid that will soon succumb to continental Spanish. Its fate has been sealed by the recent arrival on the island of Chilean television and by a rabid and insensitive tourism that has brought new affluence along with alien influences, values, and problems.

In our several weeks on Easter Island, Taki and I wandered everywhere on foot, communed in Old Rapanui with the stone ancestors, tried to sound out the latter-day Rapanui in their own dying language, too—including Thomas Barthel's two informants from the 1950s, old Juan Haoa and Leonardo Pakarati. We tried desperately to understand this disinherited people of the Pacific, once Polynesia's greatest carvers and the masters of *rongorongo*, Oceania's only indigenous literature. It was difficult. It was also rather sad.

At the same time, I was reflecting on the greater historical picture that I was putting together about the *rongorongo* past. In the end I was able to furnish a credible and logical answer to two of my key questions: I was able to propose where the *rongorongo* artifacts of Easter Island came from and how old they are.

The many years of research had by this time forged firm conclusions. I could effectively exclude the possibility of any foreign provenance for the *rongorongo* script. It was clear to me that *rongorongo* had been the product of the Rapanui people's own enduring genius. Those elderly witnesses still alive at the beginning of the twentieth century (like the Frenchman Eyraud in 1864) recalled seeing *rongorongo* being manufactured on Easter Island. They even remembered the names of their grandfathers, who, they claimed, had been the first to manufacture the incised staffs and tablets. Among the scores of writing systems in the world, past and present, not one can be found that might qualify beyond reasonable doubt as the source of Easter Island's *rongorongo* script.

The *rongorongo* inscriptions had to be of recent manufacture, too. Contrary to the claims of so many in the past, the incised artifacts of Easter Island were anything but ancient. The loveliest and perhaps most "classical" *rongorongo* inscription—the tablet "Tahua" in Rome—is incised on a European or American oar. No *rongorongo* inscription is found among the island's rock art. No inscribed artifact has been discovered in an archaeological context. Each surviving artifact reveals a shared text or structure; if this were an ancient tradition, it would have generated many texts with differing structures. The script's extreme standardization bespeaks a recent, very brief, and localized tradition of writing. Every bit of space on the rare driftwood tablets has been filled with glyphs; this dearth of wood occurred only in the latter part of the island's human history. The Rapanui at the beginning of the twentieth century remembered seeing the tablets being incised only decades before. The Frenchman Eyraud actually witnessed them being incised with *rongorongo* glyphs in 1864.

The message is clear: The *rongorongo* inscriptions of Easter Island were the product of the end of the eighteenth and the first half of the nineteenth century.

Of course, this evokes the hitherto unvoiced question: *Why?* The Rapanui people had no need for a script. No Polynesian—indeed none of the three-million-odd inhabitants of Oceania in the eighteenth century—needed a writing system. Oral traditions and knot records had served these peoples well in this regard for thousands of years. Why then did the Rapanui of all people suddenly develop a script in the latter decades of the 1700s?

The answer to this can only lie in foreign intrusion. The *idea* of writing was introduced to the Rapanui by outsiders who possessed writing. And the only documented occurrence of this happening was with the Spaniards in 1770, who urged the

Rapanui to apply their marks in pen and ink to the Spanish deed of cession (as here described on page 140).

This was the moment when the wonder of writing arrived on Easter Island.

Evidently the Rapanui sensed here the *mana,* the supernatural power, of transposing human speech onto a physical surface. They apparently believed that in emulating this act in the medium of wood, reproducing the isolated signs of their rock art in row after row of ever more elaborately detailed glyphs, they might take on the miraculous power that the visiting aliens possessed. The first *rongorongo* inscriptions were on long wooden battle staffs called *kouhau.* Later, flat pieces of driftwood were also used for incising. Soon an elaborate rite evolved about this practice that became the privilege of a few. Ritual readings were performed at the holiest of occasions. *Rongorongo* eventually grew to represent the sovereignty of the *'ariki mau,* or paramount chief, of Easter Island.

The idea of writing, its left-to-right reading direction, and its linearity were clearly the legacy of the Spaniards in 1770. However, the incised glyphs themselves, their functional modifications, the tablets' continuous reading with every other line upside down, and the entire social complex that evolved around this remarkable phenomenon were wholly the product of the indigenous Rapanui themselves.

But what did the *rongorongo* inscriptions say?

This final question still remained unanswered as I stood embracing Taki in the blustering wind atop Tere Vaka in February 1993, breathlessly contemplating both the peerless island and its extraordinary story ...

And wholly unaware that I would break the *rongorongo* code not one fortnight later.

CHAPTER 10

"ALL THE BIRDS..."

Every historic decipherment has its bingo! moment.

For Jean-François Champollion's decipherment of the ancient Egyptian hieroglyphs, it was in 1821—when Champollion realized that those curious oblong cartouches on the Rosetta Stone and the Philae Obelisk actually held the phonetically spelled names of Pharaoh Ptolemy and Queen Cleopatra. For Michael Ventris it was in 1952, when the cumulative weight of evidence finally convinced the Briton that the Linear B glyphs could only be written in a form of very early Greek. With my decipherment of ancient Crete's Phaistos Disk, it was that winter evening in 1984 when I understood with sudden clarity that *pu-da te ri-pu ni-si* had to mean "Pudaan and Libyan immigrants" in the Minoan Greek language ...

And for the decipherment of Easter Island's *rongorongo* it was March 2, 1993—the day I realized that the famous "Santiago Staff" had to consist of hundreds of three-glyph procreations: X mates with Y and their offspring is Z.

Taki and I had returned home to Meersburg from Easter Island and Santiago not two weeks before. I recall vividly that I was sitting on the couch studying our newly acquired museum replica of the "Santiago Staff"; Taki was tending to the houseplants and watching me with curiosity. I was reviewing the sequences of glyphs on the "Staff," noting their repetitions and distribution, analyzing the frequent and mutually exclusive appendages to the signs—and in particular scrutinizing the unique feature on the "Staff" that isn't to be found on any other object incised with *rongorongo* glyphs.

Scientific discoveries do not just happen. They are the harvest of years of patient cultivation. Epigraphic discoveries, like all discoveries, can also be brought to season by fortuitous anomalies in the object of investigation. For Champollion it had been those pharaonic cartouches holding proper names.

For me it was the vertical lines on the "Santiago Staff."

The "Staff" is the only *rongorongo* artifact to mark segments of text. It does this using as many as 103 irregularly spaced vertical lines (Figure 10.1). Scholars of *rongorongo* had been aware of this idiosyncrasy of the "Staff" since the 1870s but had hitherto not attached any significance to it. However, as I sat there on the sofa—home at last after an argosy halfway around the globe in search of the key to solve the perennial *rongorongo* riddle—I noted something most peculiar in conjunction with these scores of vertical lines on the "Staff."

Reading from left to right, as one must do with the *rongorongo* script, I perceived that the first sign after each of these 103 vertical lines invariably displays what appears to be a large phallus-like appendage (Figure 10.2). This appendage had been called an "erection" on the human-like *rongorongo* signs by Bishop Jaussen's young Rapanui informant Metoro Tau'a Ure back in 1873—though the same appendage is frequently attached to fishes, plants, and geometric figures in the *rongorongo* script, too. In the 1950s Thomas Barthel had acknowledged this glyphic appendage indeed to be a male member, but he then assigned to it the autonomous phonetic reading of *ure*, a Rapanui word meaning both "penis" and "lineage." That is, Barthel believed this phallic appendage to be an independent glyph that held a functional value equal to that of the much larger glyph to which it is attached.

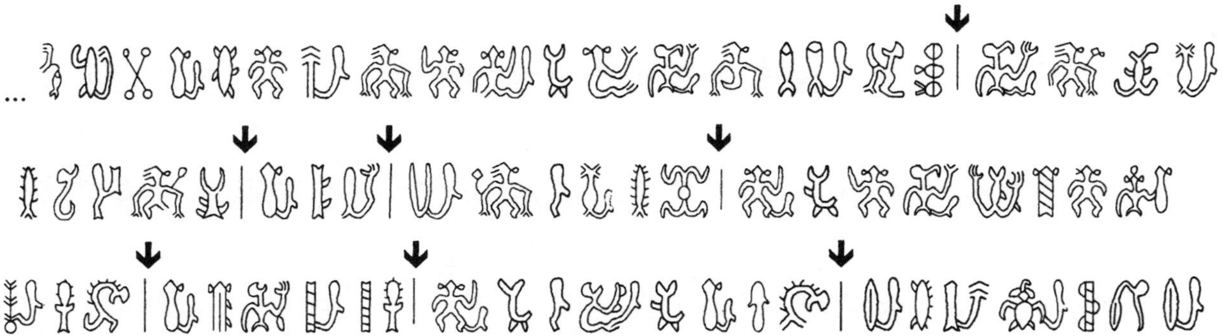

FIGURE 10.1

The "Santiago Staff" is the only *rongorongo* inscription that divides segments of text by using irregularly spaced vertical lines.

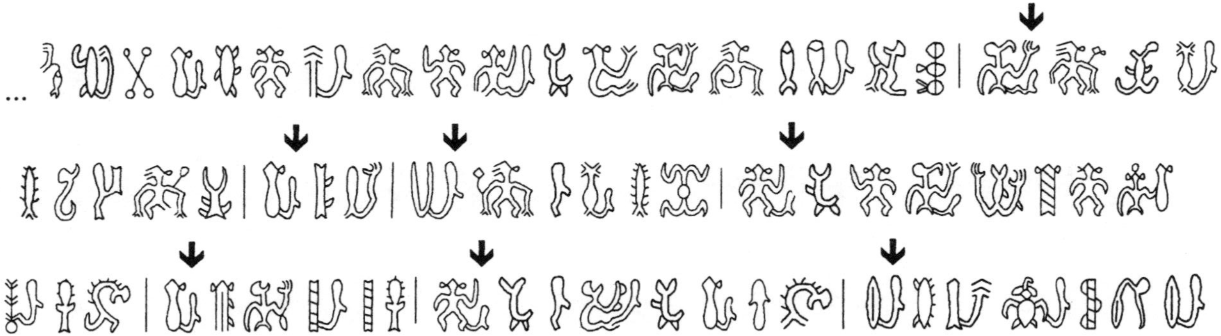

FIGURE 10.2

The first glyph after each vertical line on the "Santiago Staff" displays a phallus-like appendage.

Detecting a significant pattern in connection with this appendage, I now wondered whether this supposed phallus might express something altogether different from mere object identification.

This is because it had struck me how nearly every fourth, seventh, tenth, and thirteenth (and so forth) *rongorongo* glyph after a vertical line on the "Staff" also displays an identical erect phallus—one that seems to be "aimed" at the following glyph (Figure 10.3). What is more, I saw that not one of the 103-odd divisions on the "Staff"—that is, all those sequences of *rongorongo* glyphs that appear between two vertical lines—ever ends with a glyph with such a phallus on it. Even more striking, no penultimate glyph—the sign before the last sign of one of these divisions—sports one of these phalli (Figure 10.4). I registered only sequence after sequence of *rongorongo* triads of one glyph appended with a phallus followed predominantly, but not exclusively, by two glyphs without the phallus.

At the same time, I observed that many textual divisions on the "Santiago Staff" comprise only three glyphs and that there never occurred sequences consisting of fewer than three glyphs between vertical lines (Figure 10.5). And the first glyph of each of these sequences of three glyphs always displays a phallus.

This was significant. The *rongorongo* text was speaking to me. Maybe not in Old Rapanui yet, but the "Staff" was communicating in a larger structural voice—as important to an epigrapher as audible speech. I could immediately appreciate that the triad structure of *rongorongo* glyphs—the repeated sequences of three glyphs, the first of which invariably bears a phallus—has to constitute the minimum textual statement of the "Santiago Staff." This means that each sequence of three glyphs must have held a special and autonomous meaning to the erstwhile Rapanui scribes and priests. Each of these sequences of three is a significant unit, in other words. Each would have stood alone for its sound value ... and its meaning.

"I think I've found something important here," I told Taki, and when she came over and sat down, I carefully ex-

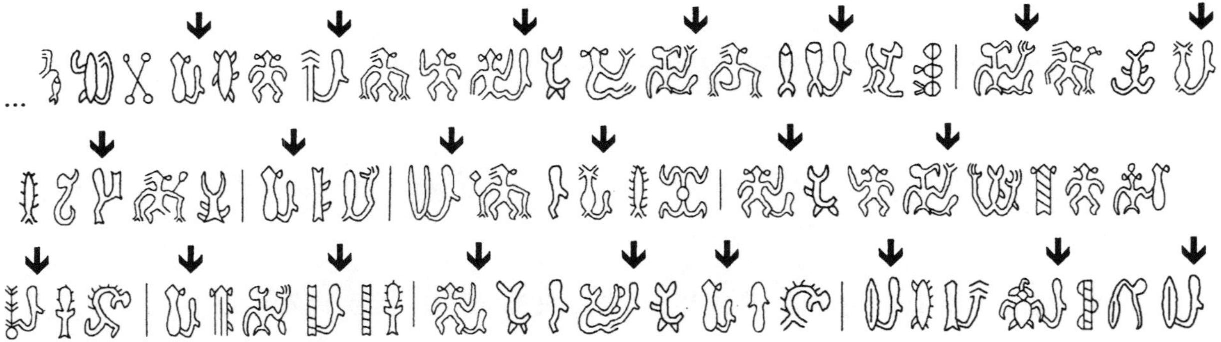

FIGURE 10.3

On the "Santiago Staff," nearly every fourth, seventh, tenth (and so forth) glyph after a vertical line displays a phallus-like appendage.

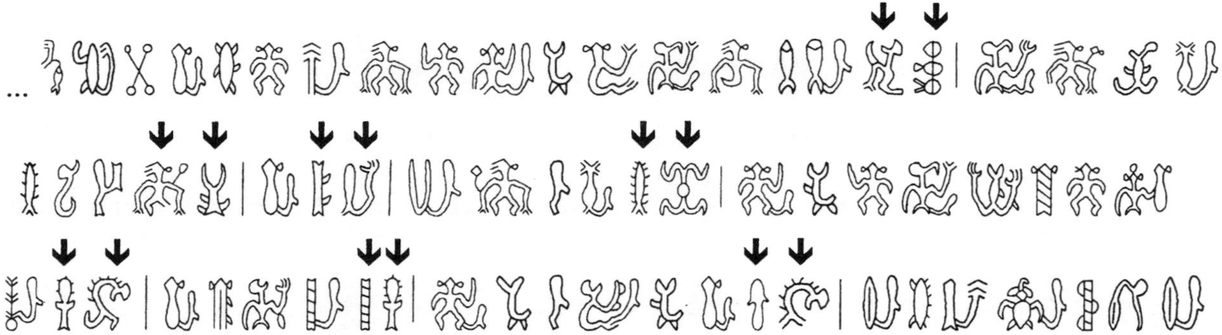

FIGURE 10.4

The ultimate and penultimate glyphs of the 103-odd divisions on the "Santiago Staff" never display a phallus-like appendage.

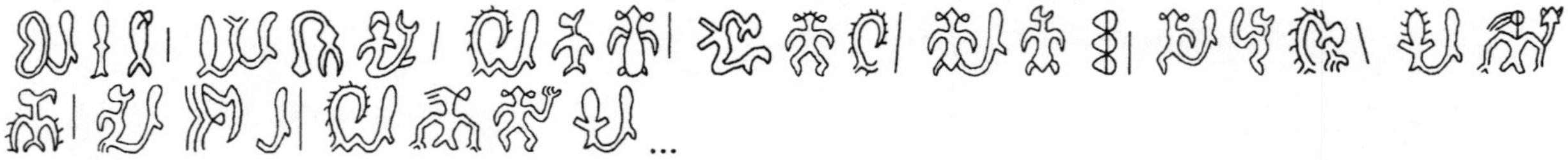

FIGURE 10.5

On the "Santiago Staff," no sequences of signs between vertical lines comprise fewer than three glyphs.

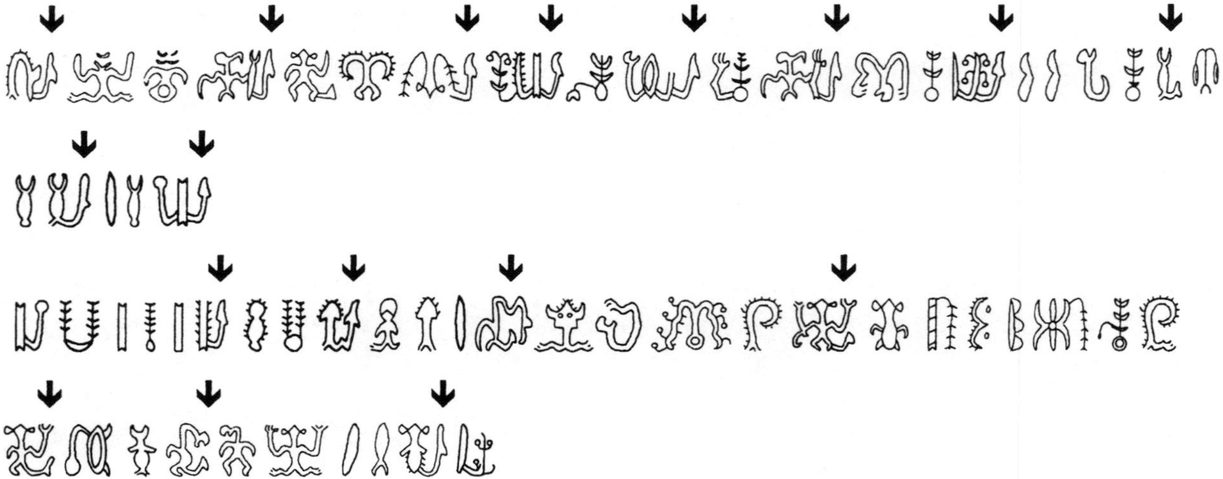

FIGURE 10.6

Every third glyph or so on the reverse of the "Small Santiago Tablet" (RR 8v) often displays a phallus-like appendage, as here in its first two lines.

plained to her what I had observed, pointing out these units, these triads, on the "Staff" replica.

"What does it mean?" she asked.

"I'm not sure, but I think this reminds me of something."

I immediately checked another *rongorongo* inscription on which such a phallus is observable: the "Small Santiago Tablet" (later I found the same on "Honolulu 3629," too). This inscription lacks the vertical division marker that the "Santiago Staff" displays so frequently. However, its glyphs repeatedly flaunt the phallus, just as on the "Staff" (Figures 10.6 and 10.7).

On the basis of this discovery, I devised an epigraphic formula: X^1YZn (Figure 10.8). It most succinctly epitomizes the repeating triad structure of glyphs on these three *rongorongo* artifacts. X signifies the first glyph of a triad, the one displaying

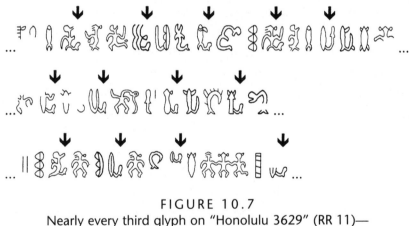

FIGURE 10.7
Nearly every third glyph on "Honolulu 3629" (RR 11)—
as here in lines six, seven, and eight—displays a phallus.

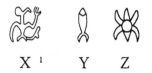

$$X^1 \quad Y \quad Z$$

FIGURE 10.8
The triad structure of *rongorongo* glyphs reduces to
the epigraphic formula X^1YZn.

the phallus, which is represented here by the raised ^{1}. Y is the second glyph of the triad. Z is the third glyph. And n denotes the constant, here signifying an unspecified number of repetitions of the identified triad structure of glyphs.

This was a major epigraphic breakthrough, I realized almost at once. It was the first time that the underlying structure of a complete *rongorongo* text had been isolated—and not on one but on three separate *rongorongo* artifacts! In the absence of external evidence, the formula might allow any number of promising philological speculations.

However, there was external evidence.

Intimately acquainted with Old Rapanui literature, I recognized that the formula X^1YZn also epitomizes the procreation chant "'Atua Mata Riri" ("God Angry Eyes"). This was one of several chants that the patriarch Rapanui Daniel Ure Va'e Iko had sung for the Americans in 1886. It was also the only chant that later Rapanui informants had identified to the British ethnologist Katherine Routledge as an authentic *rongorongo* text. She had further been told by the oldest Rapanui in 1914–1915 that Daniel Ure Va'e Iko had been the last person on the island to have had an intimate knowledge of the *rongorongo* texts.

In this notable chant, Ure had furnished the Americans with a list of 41 copulations and issues, such as: "God Mata Riri copulated with Sweet Lime: there issued forth the *poporo* plant" and "God Parent copulated with Compacted Sand: there issued forth the tree." Though parts of the 41 items had been recently invented by Ure or contaminated by Tahitian words, the structure of Ure's procreation chant is undeniably ancient and indigenous. And it reproduces the Old Rapanui oral formula X^1YZn. With this, each sire of a procreation is X. The following phrase that is repeated 41 times—"copulated with"—is the raised, or superlinear, ^{1}. The mate of each procreation is Y. And the issue is Z. (See Figure 10.9.)

It is the most common structure for Polynesian genealogies and procreation myths. The male mates with the female, and the result of the mating is the offspring. Not only important lineages were created in this way, but, according to ancient Polynesian thought, all of creation itself began with such copulations.

I had to conclude, then, that the three *rongorongo* artifacts whose textual statement I had formulated as X^1YZn constituted procreations that are structurally identical to those listed in Daniel Ure Va'e Iko's chant " 'Atua Mata Riri." That is, each triad of *rongorongo* glyphs depicts a sire (X) that is copulating (^{1}) with a mate (Y) and producing an offspring (Z). Ure's exact text wasn't being replicated in any of the three *rongorongo* inscriptions, of course. But the genre of a procreation chant—reproducing the ancient structure—underlay all four examples.

The three *rongorongo* inscriptions couldn't be genealogies, I reasoned. If they were, then the offspring (Z) would be the sire (X) of each subsequent triad of glyphs. This occurs only three times in the hundreds of triads on the "Santiago Staff" and not at all in either of the two other inscriptions that display the same structure. No, the inscriptions were clearly procreations. Just as in Ure's chant.

There was further proof, too.

Sometimes Daniel Ure Va'e Iko repeated the sire X in the Z, or offspring, position of a triad. This repetition is rare in Polynesian genealogies. However, it is frequent in Polynesian procreation chants. It means, for example, that the palm tree mates with the sand and the offspring of the mating is another palm tree. This would yield the alternative formula X^1YXn (Figure 10.10). There are several triads of glyphs on the "Santiago Staff," the "Small Santiago Tablet," and "Honolulu 3629" that reproduce this formula X^1YXn (Figure 10.11). Juxtaposing this structure from Ure's chant (left) with one of the *rongorongo* inscriptions (right), as shown in Figure 10.12, reveals very little difference between the two. Only Ure's second repetitive sequence *ka pū te* ("there issued forth the") is missing in *rongorongo*'s graphic text. This is probably because the Rapanui scribes and priests felt no need to mark this repetitive

'Atua Mata Riri   ki 'ai ki roto ki 'a   Taporō: ka pū te   poporo.

God Angry Eyes copulated with Sweet Lime: there issued forth the *poporo* plant.

X   Y   Z

FIGURE 10.9

The X^1YZn structure also describes the Old Rapanui chant "Atua Mata Riri," or "God Angry Eyes."

'A he roe   ki 'ai ki roto 'o   'uhi pura: ka pū te   roe.

Ant   copulated with   Pura Yam: there issued forth the ant.

X   Y   X

FIGURE 10.10

The alternate structure X^1YXn occurs in Daniel Ure Va'e Iko's procreation chant "'Atua Mata Riri."

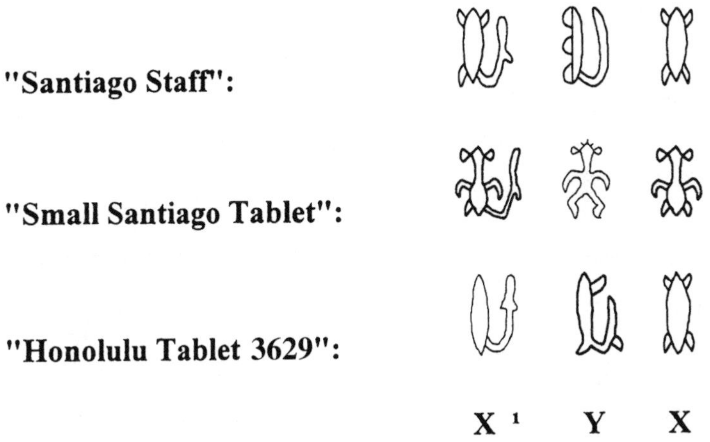

"Santiago Staff":

"Small Santiago Tablet":

"Honolulu Tablet 3629":

$$X^1 \qquad Y \qquad X$$

FIGURE 10.11
There are several triads of *rongorongo* glyphs on the
"Santiago Staff," the "Small Santiago Tablet," and
"Honolulu Tablet 3629" that reduce to the formula $X^1YX n$.

phrase with a special symbol, knowing that it automatically had to follow each Y-glyph of a procreation.

On the other hand, the Rapanui scribes and priests would certainly have understood that the appendage on each X-glyph of a procreation triad—the erect phallus that each time means "copulated with"—was a similar repetition. However, it was not meaningless redundancy. Probably to emphasize virility and the act of copulation, the verbal message "copulated with" was marked with the erect phallus, a symbol of life-giving importance to all ancient Polynesians. It also identified the sire of each triad of *rongorongo* glyphs, facilitating the reading of such long lists of copulations and issues.

Here the X-, Y-, and Z-glyphs function as *logoglyphs*; each sign designates the object whose name is to be spoken aloud. In contrast, the phallus attached to each X-glyph serves as a *semasioglyph*; it depicts an idea beyond the name of its symbol (in this case, the act of copulation). This division of glyph function proves *rongorongo* to be a mixed writing system. It also reflects an astounding grammatical perception by the premissionary

Rapanui people and characterizes their *rongorongo* script as being functionally far more sophisticated than scholars hitherto have generally assumed.

My identification of procreation chants in the three *rongorongo* inscriptions of the "Santiago Staff," the "Small Santiago Tablet," and "Honolulu 3629" also enabled me to suggest a phonetic reading of these inscriptions. That is, sound could finally be put to sign. The rhetorical pattern of Daniel Ure Va'e Iko's chant meant that each of the three *rongorongo* inscriptions of repeating copulations and issues reads as "X *ki 'ai ki roto 'o te* Y: *ka pū te* Z" or "X copulated with Y: there issued forth Z" (Figure 10.13).

Minutes after I had told Taki about my discovery, I penned a work note, dated March 2, 1993:

> *I believe RR 10 [the "Santiago Staff"] to be a "Creation Chant" of the sort "X ki 'ai ki roto ki Y, ka pū te Z" where X is a glyph (or multiple), ⅄ is the "ki 'ai" suffix, Y a glyph, Z a glyph. Important insight into mechanism of RR [rongorongo].*

I didn't know at the time that this was the decipherment of the *rongorongo* script.

The breakthrough soon yielded the first successfully deciphered *rongorongo* sentence, here from line one of the "Santiago Staff." The triad of glyphs "bird with grasping hand + phallus," "fish," and "sun" could be read as, "*Te manu mau ki 'ai ki roto ki te ika: ka pū te ra'ā*" or "All the birds copulated with the fish: there issued forth the sun." (See Figure 10.14.) This is very close to item number 25 from Daniel Ure Va'e Iko's procreation chant, recorded on Easter Island in 1886: "Land copulated with the fish *Ruhi* Paralyzer: There issued forth the sun."

Easter Island's *rongorongo* was speaking again at last ...

After 128 years of silence.

Over eighteen months would pass before I felt ready to announce this historic breakthrough in reading the *rongorongo* inscriptions of Easter Island. This is because I first wanted to be sure that what I had ferreted out was indeed the correct struc-

Daniel Ure Va'e Iko:

"Small Santiago Tablet":

'A he _roe_ ki 'ai ki roto 'o '_uhi pura_: ka pū te _roe._
  X   ¹   Y   X

FIGURE 10.12

A comparison of the X¹YX*n* alternative structure of Daniel Ure Va'e Iko's procreation chant with that of the "Small Santiago Tablet."

"Santiago Staff":

"Small Santiago Tablet":

"Honolulu Tablet 3629":

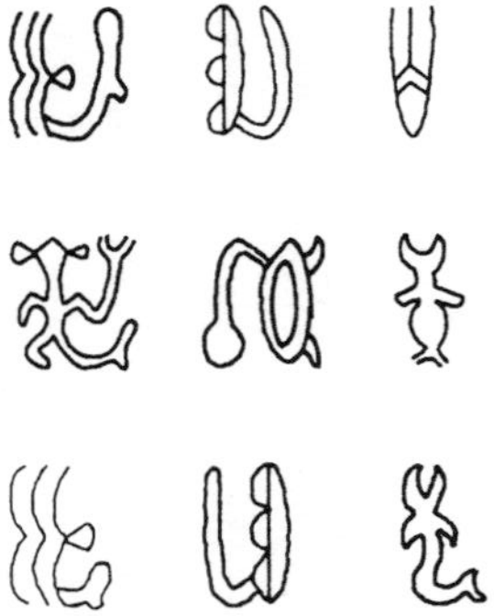

X ki 'ai ki roto ki 'a Y: ka pū te Z
X   ¹   Y   Z
X copulated with Y: there issued forth Z

FIGURE 10.13

The deciphered structural statement of the "Santiago Staff," the "Small Santiago Tablet," and "Honolulu Tablet 3629."

199

X ¹ **Y** **Z**
manu/mau + phallus   *ika*   *ra'ā*
birds/all + phallus   fish   sun

Te manu mau ki 'ai ki roto ki te ika: ka pū te ra'ā
"All the birds copulated with the fish: there issued forth the sun."

FIGURE 10.14
A phonetically deciphered procreation triad from
the first line of the "Santiago Staff."

tural reading of these three *rongorongo* artifacts. To obtain this certainty, I subjected my X^1YZn formula to numerous internal tests ... all of which confirmed beyond reasonable doubt that what I had retrieved were indeed hundreds of procreations of a type identical to those chanted on Rapanui by Daniel Ure Va'e Iko in 1886.

At the same time I took ill. On Rapanui I had suffered terrible cholic attacks that had kept me up for most of the night. On my return to Germany, my house doctor had put me on enzymes, but these had done little good. Months later I returned to my doctor, and, scanning my stomach region to determine the cause of my cholic, he discovered to his horror a lapidary's own collection of gallstones. Into the hospital I went that same week, in July 1993. It was the first time I had ever been hospitalized.

The following week saw me flying from Germany to Laramie, Wyoming, for the second international congress on Easter Island and the East Pacific. I felt like death warmed over and looked it, too. My paper on Easter Island settlement tradition was well received. (I proposed the heresy that the name of Rapanui's traditional settler Hotu Matu'a had been borrowed in the 1860s from Mangareva, having replaced the indigenous mythical settler Tu'u ko Iho.) And it was here among my international colleagues, most of whom had been contributors, that I was finally able to introduce publicly the voluminous collection of scientific essays I had edited, *Easter Island Studies*, which had been published the same week in Oxford, England. The two hundred volumes designated for sale at the Laramie congress miraculously arrived in Wyoming on the very day the congress commenced!

Once back in Meersburg, I tested my *rongorongo* discovery further as I continued writing my new book based on the many years of documentation: *Rongorongo: The Easter Island Script. History, Traditions, Texts.* No one but Taki knew of the *rongorongo* breakthrough. It was still too early to announce it, I firmly believed.

This was a time of personal frustration and irresolution, financial worry, and physical lassitude. As I confided to my journal on September 10, 1993, two days after my forty-sixth birthday,

> *Weak, weak, weak. A torpidness of body and mind. Each day I should like to accomplish so much, and end up doing nothing. It is a great strain even to dispatch a small handful of correspondence.... And the weakness, in body and mind. It's a strain to attend to any duty, and I can concentrate as well as a sieve. I have so many ideas for articles which must be written, I have to get back to the* rongorongo *book (hitherto 75 pp. only), and I really have to exploit my discovery of cosmogonical texts in the Santiago Staff and Small Santiago Tablet. But it is all too much at the moment. I can only read, sip tea, play with Kiwi [our parakeet], and regard the Lake.*

On the same afternoon, I added

> *Not one hour after I penned the above lines, I received my [volume]* Easter Island Studies *delivered by the postman. [Note: I couldn't afford to buy a copy at Laramie, but had to wait for the free editor's copy from my Oxford publisher.] It looks beautiful. Some-*

times one almost has the feeling that the struggle is worthwhile. A dim light of joy in a long, dark night of doubt.

Despite my continuing reluctance to mention the *rongorongo* breakthrough, word somehow got out that I had been making advances with the potential decipherment of the Easter Island script. To supplement a feature article about Easter Island, the associate editor of the popular scientific magazine *Bild der Wissenschaft*—Germany's version of *Scientific American*—arrived at Meersburg in December 1993 for a personal interview. We met in a shoreline cafe as the winter sun mirrored in Lake Constance set the vineyards aglow. Eventually, in February 1994, the published article highlighted the results of my years of documenting *rongorongo* and quoted my flamboyant revelation of the arcane script's solution:

"I am gradually gaining insights."

Taki and I by this time had accumulated enough frequent-flier points to squeeze in a long-overdue jaunt to London at the end of January 1994. Here, on our Silver Wedding Anniversary, the assistant keeper of the Museum of Mankind and faithful correspondent of many years Dorota Starzecka kindly assisted us in our documentation and transcription of the three *rongorongo* inscriptions in the British Museum. Of course, a pilgrimage to the Rosetta Stone had to follow the next day, and we also delighted in three evenings of spectacular musicals and plays, the second-greatest delight London can offer its devout pilgrims.

Two months later, without warning, Taki's position at the firm was eliminated. We turned our initial panic into positive action by immediately resolving to invest her generous separation payment in a move back to New Zealand. By then we'd been living in Germany for fourteen years. In the last two of these, we had been toying with the idea of establishing an Institute of Polynesian Languages and Literatures to preserve the indigenous languages of Polynesia and to foster their study. Here was our golden opportunity to realize this goal. The only

logical location for such an institute was the world's Polynesian capital: Auckland, New Zealand. The next seven months
saw us busily making the arrangements for this major uproot-
ing, which both Taki and I regarded as probably the last we
would undergo in our lives. At the same time, I continued writing my book *Rongorongo*, which filled each day.

Only now, a year and a half after the initial breakthrough,
did I finally feel ready to announce my discovery. The venue
chosen for this historic announcement was the Seventh International Conference on Austronesian Linguistics that was held
in Leiden, Holland, in August 1994. Here before a small audience of international experts, I revealed, in a 20-minute lecture
that made generous use of overhead illustrations, the unmis-
takable evidence for the successful reading of the structure—
and part of the text—of at least three *rongorongo* inscriptions
from Easter Island. The reaction of my peers was overwhelming endorsement. Several urged me to publish my results at
once.

Two months later—and only two weeks before our departure from Germany—the editor and film team of Austrian TV's
own popular science series "Nova" arrived at Meersburg. The
editor had heard through the grapevine about my *rongorongo*
advances and wanted a taped interview of me telling about the
breakthrough in German. We filmed the interview in the historic restaurant "Bären" alongside Meersburg's Upper Gate-
tower, which dates from the end of the thirteenth century. I
commenced by explaining the discovery as announced at Leiden. Then, using the replica of the "Santiago Staff" that I had
resting on the dining table, I showed and read out *rongorongo*'s
first successfully deciphered sentence—"All the birds copulated with the fish: there issued forth the sun." The camera-
man dramatically zoomed in on it. The program aired in the
middle of November, weeks after our departure.

One week before our flight to New Zealand, Thomas
Barthel arrived at Meersburg to bid us a scholar's adieu. The
three of us enjoyed a memorable tea on the terrace of Meers-

burg's medieval castle as the sun burned low over Lake Constance. It was a sad farewell. We had grown very close over the long years. Taki and I wondered if we would ever see Thomas again.

On October 19, 1994, we left Meersburg—and Germany—forever. It was the end of an important chapter in our lives.

And the beginning of a miracle.

CHAPTER 11

SURFING THE RONGORONGO

"I don't believe it.... Come on over here quick! Take a look at this!"

It was three months after Taki and I had found a small townhouse to rent in the Auckland suburb of Parnell just one kilometer east of the towering skyscrapers of the city. We had had three difficult months of job hunting, uncertainty, and the shock of what New Zealand had experienced in the intervening fifteen years—a drastic inflation, rejection of its British heritage, and virulent North American and Asian commercialization. I finally had found time to get back to my investigation of those triads of *rongorongo* glyphs I had identified. Yet I'd hardly expected to discover what I did this February evening of 1995.

"What is it?" asked Taki, sitting down on the sofa beside me.

"Here, take a look at this triad. Does it remind you of anything?" I was grinning.

She took the replica of the "Echancrée" tablet in her hands, the first *rongorongo* tablet that Bishop Jaussen had rediscovered for science.

"Look at these three glyphs carefully."

She did. Then she saw it.

"Isn't it the same bird, fish, and sun as on the 'Staff'?" she asked. "The one you pointed out in your talk in Holland? But it's different somehow. I don't see any thingy on the bird sign. Shouldn't it have a phallus on it, like on the 'Staff'?"

Precisely.

Taki was confirming that my original breakthrough in 1993 had been the long sought-after key. The second breakthrough of February 20, 1995, now completed the glyphbreaking process for Easter Island's *rongorongo* script.

What was this second breakthrough?

Well, the chances are about 1 in 14,400 that a sequence of three different *rongorongo* glyphs would arbitrarily recur on another tablet. It's theoretically possible but statistically unlikely. A Rapanui scribe would repeat such a sequence of three different *rongorongo* glyphs only if the grouping of three weren't arbitrary—that is, if the sequence of three signs constituted a meaningful *triad* of glyphs, grouped together by the scribe for a purpose.

Here Taki and I were reading on the tablet "Echancrée" that same sequence of three *rongorongo* glyphs—the bird, fish, and sun—from the "Santiago Staff" that I had highlighted as the first successfully deciphered sentence from the Easter Island literary corpus (Figures 10.14 and 11.1). In other words,

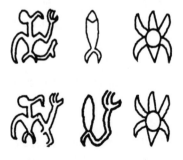

FIGURE 11.1
The procreation triad "bird—fish—sun" from the "Santiago Staff" (top) recurs on the *rongorongo* tablet "Echancrée" (bottom)—without the phallus on the X-glyph. (The "hand" is a pluralizing suffix meaning "all.")

here was apparently a procreation triad on a tablet that no one had guessed contained procreations. There shouldn't be procreations: None of the *rongorongo* glyphs on "Echancrée" displayed the phallus.

But I had just discovered that in the *rongorongo* script, $X^1YZn = XYZn$.

That is, the phallus was dropped on later *rongorongo* inscriptions. The erect phallus (^{1}) that always marked the X-glyph of a procreation triad? The symbol identifying the sire of each copulation in the oldest surviving *rongorongo* inscriptions? It was apparently dispensed with as superfluous by later Rapanui scribes.

The "Staff" never omits a phallus on its X-glyph; the sire of each procreation is marked with the phallic symbol. "Honolulu 3629" is just as faithful in this. For this reason, these two artifacts are likely to be the oldest *rongorongo* inscriptions of the 25 that have survived the ravages of history. The "Small Santiago Tablet" is more irregular in marking each X-glyph with a phallus; this suggests that the "Small Santiago Tablet" was carved later than the first two, probably in a transition period when the Rapanui scribes no longer considered the depiction of the phallus absolutely essential for reading. Later scribes omitted the phallus altogether. However, the appendage still appeared now and again, as isolated texts reveal. (These are the so-called "vestigial phalli.")

What does this mean? Nearly all the surviving *rongorongo* inscriptions—not just those first three inscriptions that I identified for the Holland paper—are procreation chants of the type X^1YZn or $XYZn$. In fact, only some 15 percent of the *rongorongo* corpus seems *not* to constitute procreation chants of this type.

It demanded several months of further study to understand fully what had happened on premissionary Rapanui. Later Rapanui scribes had obviously come to treat the repetitive phrase "copulated with" the same as the repetitive phrase "there issued forth." That is, a graphic representation of the phrase "copulated with" was deemed unnecessary. And the scribes eventually gave up carving the phallus altogether, with only rare exceptions. Nevertheless, each reader of a *rongorongo* inscription knew that after each X-glyph, he still had to chant aloud the phrase "copulated with," just as though the phallus were still there.

The omission of the phallic appendage with each X-glyph of a procreation triad by later Rapanui scribes constituted an evolution in the *rongorongo* script. *Rongorongo*'s initial "complexity"—humble as it was—underwent simplification within only one or two generations of the script's inception. The omission also freed that much more space, allowing more *rongorongo* text to be written on the rare wooden artifacts.

On treeless Easter Island, wood was gold.

In May 1995 Taki and I moved to Waiheke Island in the Hauraki Gulf, just seventeen kilometers off Auckland's shore. With a population of only six thousand, many of whom commute daily with the jet ferry into the city, Waiheke Island enjoys a reputation as the weekend getaway for the sprawling megalopolis that Auckland, Polynesia's largest city, has become. Yet Waiheke still retains the charm and leisure and backwardness of the old New Zealand that both Taki and I had come to know and love in the 1970s. Waiheke also is popular with international tourists who have several days to spare in greater Auckland. We rented a house commanding a bird's-eye view over the Tamaki Strait and coast of New Zealand far away … which reminded us so much of our Meersburg view over Lake Constance, the Swiss shore, and the Alps.

We felt we were home at last.

I was very fortunate in incorporating, with a minimum of time and trouble, the Institute of Polynesian Languages and Literatures as a registered Charitable Trust with New Zealand's Ministry of Justice. Our dream had come true.

At the same time, the successful decipherment of Easter Island's *rongorongo* yielded valuable insights into the nature of Polynesia's arcane script.

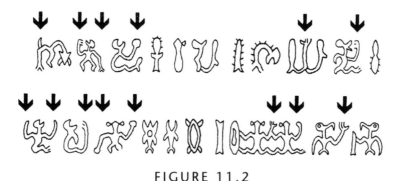

FIGURE 11.2

Several different plural markers—meaning "several," "all," "many," and
so forth in the Old Rapanui language—appear as prefixes or suffixes to
the main glyphs in the form of various wings, arms, grasping hands, or
bulbous fists. These examples are taken from the "Santiago Staff" (top,
with phallus) and the "Large St. Petersburg Tablet" (bottom, without phallus).

Continuing to isolate more procreation triads, I noticed
that several different plural markers—meaning "several,"
"all," "many," and so forth in the Old Rapanui language—
attach before or after the main glyphs as various wings or arms
or grasping hands or bulbous fists (Figure 11.2). Sometimes the
procreation lists yield telling combinations; for example, birds
are often mentioned as the offspring of fish, and fish as the
issue of birds (Figure 11.3). Sometimes the X- and Y-glyphs

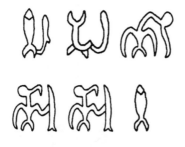

FIGURE 11.3

In the *rongorongo* inscriptions, birds are often mentioned as the
offspring of fish, and fish as the issue of birds. These examples
are from the "Santiago Staff" (top, with phallus) and the
"Small Washington Tablet" (bottom, without phallus).

FIGURE 11.4
Sometimes the X- and Y-glyphs of procreation triads produce offspring
that incorporate both parents or elements of both. These examples are
from the "Large Washington Tablet" (top, with vestigial phallus).
and the "Large Santiago Tablet" (bottom, without phallus).

combine to produce an offspring that incorporates both parents
or elements of both (Figure 11.4).

In fact, the triad structure of procreations proved to be the
most economic explanation for glyph frequency and variety. It
solved the riddle of why there were so many birds and fish and
plants and human-like figures in the *rongorongo* texts, all
seemingly jumbled together. It also explained why one particular sign was repeated so often after every third sign: because it
occupies the X-position of procreations as the repeated sire
(Figure 11.5). The identification of procreation triads on most
of the *rongorongo* inscriptions finally made possible the logical
segmentation of many sequences of glyphs on a scientifically
verifiable basis. Reading *rongorongo* was no longer ethnologi-
cal speculation. It was structural certainty.

FIGURE 11.5
The curve-backed sign with head and open mouth
is the repeated sire of the procreation sequences in
this example from line eleven of the "Santiago Staff."

FIGURE 11.6
Most *rongorongo* inscriptions frequently segment into natural groups of three glyphs. These contrasting examples are taken from the "Santiago Staff" (top), the "Large Washington Tablet" (middle), and "Aruku Kurenga" (bottom).

Perhaps the strongest evidence for procreation triads lacking the phallus on their X-glyph was the frequent segmentation of most *rongorongo* inscriptions into natural groups of three glyphs (Figure 11.6). This segmentation often reveals the structure XYXn that repeats the sire as the issue of the mating (Figure 11.7), a structure already known from the "Santiago Staff," the "Small Santiago Tablet," and "Honolulu 3629" and from

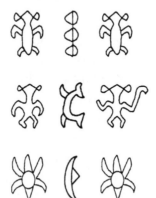

FIGURE 11.7
The segmentation of the *rongorongo* inscriptions into natural triads of glyphs often reveals the structure XYXn that repeats the sire as the issue of the mating.
These examples are from the "Large Washington Tablet" (top), the "London Tablet" (middle), and the tablet "Mamari" (bottom).

Daniel Ure Va'e Iko's procreation chant (see page 195 and Figures 10.10, 10.11, and 10.12).

As I was analyzing these many structures in the different *rongorongo* inscriptions, confirming that *rongorongo* consists primarily—but not exclusively—of procreation triads, I was in effect finally riding the waves of significant patterns of *rongorongo* glyphs that I had perhaps always felt but until now had failed to catch. At last I was epigraphically surfing the *rongorongo*.

This afforded a new understanding.

I understood, for example, what the Rapanui people were telling their Chilean visitors in 1870 when they were asked the meaning of the "Santiago Staff." The newly baptized Rapanui had pointed to the "Staff" and to the sky and then back to the "Staff" again, indicating to the Chileans that there was a connection between Heaven and this wooden staff covered with more than 2300 strange hieroglyphs. From this demonstration, the Chileans had been "inclined to believe that these hieroglyphs recalled something sacred." Now I was able to show that the hieroglyphic text was nothing less than the Rapanui people's explanation for all of creation.

It was the Rapanui Genesis.

I also understood more readings. These were procreation triads that recurred on two or more tablets. They frequently involved artifacts that dispensed with the phallus on the sire. This provided such provisionally translated texts as "All the birds copulated with the sea: there issued forth the shellfish"; "The many birds copulated with the (kind of) birds: there issued forth the fish"; "The shark copulated with the male deity: there issued forth the shark"; and "The plural male deities copulated with the (qualified) female deities: there issued forth the (kind of) bird." (See Figure 11.8.)

Exact phonetic values for the *rongorongo* glyphs in the Old Rapanui language will probably remain points of contention among *rongorongo* scholars for some time to come. Only a few, such as those for "bird," "fish," and "sun"—in

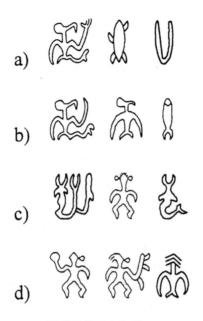

FIGURE 11.8
Provisionally translated *rongorongo* texts.
a) "All the birds copulated with the sea: there issued forth the shellfish"
("Santiago Staff," "Paris Snuffbox"). b) "The many birds copulated
with the (kind of) birds: there issued forth the fish" ("Santiago Staff,"
"Aruku Kurenga," "Large Santiago Tablet," "Large St. Petersburg
Tablet"). c) "The shark copulated with the male deity: there issued
forth the shark" ("Small Santiago Tablet," "Berlin Tablet"). d) "The
plural male deities copulated with the (qualified) female deities: there
issued forth the (kind of) bird" ("Large Santiago Tablet," "Small St.
Petersburg Tablet," "Large St. Petersburg Tablet").

other words, the main glyphs that probably represent generic
terms—are relatively self-evident and are therefore already
accepted by a number of scholars. Most *rongorongo* glyphs are
less transparent than this.

Let's look at two examples of the latter. Because it often
shows plural suffixing, the glyph for "male deity" &, one of
the most frequent in the *rongorongo* inventory, probably signifies the generic term *'atua,* Old Rapanui for "god, deity," rather
than the specific name of premissionary Rapanui's supreme
god Makemake. In similar fashion, the glyph for "female deity"

🐦—one that, logically enough, most frequently occupies the Y-position of a procreation triad and that also displays plural suffixing—probably represents *'atua vī'e,* Old Rapanui for "female deity," rather than the proper name of the goddess Hina. It is always wise to propose the generic term for such glyphs until a specific identification can be cogently argued. Nearly all of these sound values for the glyphs—whether from native informant or modern scholar—are still only provisional, pending final confirmation or rejection.

The important thing at this early juncture is that we finally know what nearly all the *rongorongo* inscriptions say; they are lists of copulations and issues of the type "X copulated with Y: there issued forth Z." We also know from the general forms of the glyphs themselves whether the procreations involve flora, fauna, deities, or "geometrics"—the latter probably including such natural phenomena or objects as clouds, rain, waves, and stars. In this way we can at least state, for example, that "This kind of bird copulated with this other kind of bird: there issued forth this third kind of bird." In time each kind will be identified with its Old Rapanui name.

This is the challenge that awaits future scholars of Easter Island's extraordinary script.

One month after our move out to Waiheke Island, I finally finished the book *Rongorongo: The Easter Island Script,* which I had been documenting and writing for over six years. This first compilation of the complete *rongorongo* story, including the unique insights I had gained into the script's mechanism from its successful decipherment, made it possible to draw a wealth of new conclusions about the nature and meaning of Easter Island's primitive writing system:

- The *rongorongo* script of Easter Island probably originated after several Rapanui were made to witness, in pen and ink, the Spaniards' deed of cession on November 20, 1770.

- Though there was no need for writing on Rapanui, the *tuhunga,* or priests, who from time immemorial had officiated over all rites on the island, apparently sensed the *mana*—the spiritual power—that lay in this act the power-ful foreigners demonstrated. Their comprehending the abstraction of human speech gave rise to a wholly unique script, the only Oceanic script predating the twentieth century ... one that eventually came to be called *rongorongo*.

- In appearance and function, Easter Island's *rongorongo* script is a Rapanui creation, owing nothing to Western writing but its inspiration, linearity, and left-to-right reading direction.

- The corpus of *rongorongo* glyphs originated in the inventory of Easter Island's rock art, Polynesia's richest.

- *Rongorongo* is written in the Old Rapanui language that was spoken on Easter Island at the end of the eighteenth and the first half of the nineteenth century.

- *Rongorongo* soon became a franchise of Rapanui's elite, probably for specific socio-political reasons. Following the end of the protracted wars between the island's two major descent groups—the western Tu'u and eastern 'Otu 'Iti—and during the period of gradual consolidation and reassertion of the ancient royal prerogative, the *rongorongo* script appears to have assumed the greatest "cohesive" role in Easter Island society. The peerless champion of *rongorongo* was the paramount chief Nga'ara, who died at the end of the 1850s.

- Schools for *rongorongo* instruction had been created on pre-missionary Easter Island for the elite families' pubescent sons. The instruction by priests ensured the continuation of *rongorongo*'s recitation and production.

- *Rongorongo* enjoyed the exclusivity conferred by the royal *tapu*, or sacred prohibition. The incised artifacts were accessible only to a small number of socially prominent males.

- The writings on the *rongorongo* artifacts were publicly and privately chanted at various rituals and festivities during the year, including the celebrated 'Orongo Birdman competition.

- All *rongorongo* texts were performed in a singing (chanting) voice.

- The most prominent *rongorongo* genre appears to have been the procreation chant of the type X^1YZn (whereby X^1

represents a procreator glyph with phallus) or XYZ*n*; both reproduce the formula "X copulated with Y: there issued forth Z." This structure adorns, in whole or in part, no fewer than 14 confirmed (and perhaps 4 unconfirmed) inscriptions on the 25 randomly preserved *rongorongo* artifacts. By volume it constitutes 85 percent of the surviving *rongorongo* texts, which one may consider representative. The procreation chant—repeatedly listing names, flora, fauna, and heavenly phenomena—dominates the *rongorongo* complex.

■ It appears that in graphically depicting thousands of procreations, the Rapanui people were attempting through writing to encyclopedize all of creation as they understood it. The origin of every visible object on Easter Island was explained in this way. Doubtless this act of describing the origin of everything, and memorializing it in thousands of signs that abstracted human speech in wood, fulfilled an important social and psychological need in premissionary Rapanui society.

■ As Thomas Barthel discovered in the 1950s, one *rongorongo* inscription, "Mamari" (RR 2), includes a lunar calendar of some kind.

■ Each surviving *rongorongo* inscription reproduces either partial glyphic sequences from other surviving inscriptions or glyphic structures revealing shared genres. This testifies to a limited number of original *rongorongo* texts and to an active copying tradition on premissionary Rapanui.

■ The Rapanui scribe used main glyphs (with numerous variants and arbitrary orientations) such as 𝄞. These could be prefixed 𝄞; suffixed 𝄞; prefixed and suffixed 𝄞; suprafused 𝄞; subfused 𝄞; or compounded with other glyphs, alloglyphs, or (allo-)glyphic parts 𝄞. The practice was subject to the whim of the scribe and/or to the amount of available space on the rare wood he was using. As Bishop Jaussen learned from Metoro Tau'a Ure in 1873, "In addition to the word and the proper meaning of the sign, this [*rongorongo*] chant contains a grouping of other words added by the artist's fancy, and which it costs the pupil infinitely more work to retain in his memory than the mere meaning of the sign."

■ Despite the superficial complexity of the *rongorongo* script, it could evidently be taught to the Rapanui youths in several months of instruction. This is because there were apparently only some 120 main glyphs to learn; a limited number of rules for affixing, fusing, and compounding these glyphs; and only a small corpus of (largely) procreation texts that made use of repetitive phrases.

■ The Rapanui scribes' choices among the alternatives open to them were apparently arbitrary. This resulted in a "system" that was both sloppy and contradictory. As the British ethnologist Katherine Routledge correctly judged in the early twentieth century, *rongorongo* is a "rude system of writing."

■ Even so, there exists a remarkable amount of standardization among *rongorongo*'s main glyphs and affixes. As a result of widespread copying and a rigorous centralized control (probably exercised by the *'ariki mau* Nga'ara himself), this standardization occurs also in the writing of fusions and compounds. Nearly every *rongorongo* glyph can easily be attributed to one of the approximately 120 main glyphs, as the Swiss Alfred Métraux first discovered in the 1930s and as the German Thomas S. Barthel described in the 1950s.

■ Such glyphic forms, as both internal analysis and informant data suggest, doubtless corresponded to a fixed inventory of sound values. Hence, for example, the glyph 🌀 probably reproduces the sun and embodies the value *ra'ā*, the Old Rapanui word for "sun, day, time, name of sub-tribe." Metoro Tau'a Ure's identification of the frequent glyph ⍦ as Old Rapanui *rangi* ("sky") with an accuracy of 95 percent belies spontaneous invention; the glyph might indeed have held this fixed sound value on premissionary Rapanui.

■ *Rongorongo* affixes, or appendages, also appear to have represented fixed sound values. For example, it is likely that prefix ⍦ and suffix ⍦—ostensibly derived from Old Rapanui *ma'u* ("grasp, take")—were used to reproduce the Old Rapanui adjective *mau* ("all, a general plural marker") in near-homophonous association.

■ If this is true, then affixes in the *rongorongo* script could, among other functions, represent descriptive elements qualifying the main glyphs to which they are almost always attached. There are also examples of an affix detaching from its main glyph and standing before or after this glyph as an autonomous sign.

- A *rongorongo* suffix apparently can also be semasiographic—that is, it can be used to indicate ideas directly. An example of this is the phallus ⟫ that is regularly appended to the X-glyph in the procreation triads of the earliest *rongorongo* artifacts. The phallic suffix evidently reproduces the act described by the Old Rapanui phrase *ki 'ai ki roto ki/'o* ("copulated with").

- Thus *rongorongo* is a mixed script, consisting of glyphs that are both logographic (the sign is the object to be pronounced) and semasiographic (the sign provides visual communication that is not bound to the name of an object). It is a very primitive form of writing that basically suffices only to record a limited number of familiar genres and rhetorical structures. However, as Sir Hercules Read of the British Museum wrote at the beginning of the twentieth century, "The Easter Island writing has got some way [come a long way] from the pictograph."

- *Rongorongo* is not a simple mnemonic device, a mere memory aid that has nothing to do with the spoken word. The Rapanui priests read *rongorongo*. However, it was necessary to know what genre one was dealing with in order to fill in those repetitive phrases that usually were missing in *rongorongo*'s graphic statement.

- Unhappily, one looks in vain among the *rongorongo* corpus for truly ancient chants or texts that will reveal something substantial about the island's premissionary past. It is possible that nearly every inscription, except the isolated dedication, is a slightly modified copy or fragment of one or more whimsical lists created specifically for the *rongorongo* artifacts themselves at the end of the eighteenth and in the first half of the nineteenth century.

- *Rongorongo* evidently flourished from the 1770s until 1865, one year after the first temporary lay missionary landed and one year before the first permanent missionaries descended. Its use probably spanned no more than three full generations.

- The *rongorongo* custom died out because of slave raids, pandemics, Christianity, the loss of *tapu* and of the royal legitimization, and the sudden abandonment of the so-called "*rongorongo* schools."

- In 1865 and thereafter, the "hundreds" of *rongorongo* artifacts that existed were burnt, concealed, cannibalized, sold, exchanged, thrown away, or given away.

- The last Rapanui to hold a real, if limited, knowledge of the *rongorongo* texts was Daniel Ure Va'e Iko, who died in the 1890s.

- Today there remain only 25 genuine *rongorongo* inscriptions in museums and institutions throughout the world. (Rapanui possesses none.) Of these 25, there are only 7 large and intact inscriptions that permit an adequate scholarly analysis. These 7 contain about 9700 glyphs, or approximately 80 percent of the entire *rongorongo* corpus.

- In the 1960s Ignace Gelb—the "father of American epigraphy"—dismissed *rongorongo* as "pictorial concoctions for magical purposes." This he did principally because, "if we were to assign the Easter Island 'inscriptions' to a stage of writing, any stage of writing however primitive, we would have to reckon with the existence of a completely unique type of writing from the point of view of the form and composition of its signary." However, because *rongorongo* has now been proved indeed to comprise a script, we must acknowledge *rongorongo*'s singular position among the scripts of the world. The Rapanui reinterpreted writing in their own fashion, and the unique way they did this invites wonder and admiration.

- Because the idea for Easter Island's *rongorongo* derived from eighteenth-century contact with Europeans, one can now state categorically that there existed no writing system in all of Oceania before contact with outsiders.

This is the extraordinary *rongorongo* of Easter Island. At the beginning of the twentieth century, virtually nothing had been known about this script beyond Rapanui's shores. By the end of the twentieth century, the *rongorongo* story was an open book.

It didn't take long for the world to learn of this decipherment of the Easter Island script.

During the eight months it now took me to draw by hand all the *rongorongo* inscriptions for the finished book *Rongorongo: The Easter Island Script*—the curious will appreciate that the graphic program of my newly acquired first computer masked my tremor—my two scientific papers describing the successive breakthroughs appeared in print. The oldest and most prestigious journal of Pacific research, *The Journal of the Polynesian Society*, published in its September 1995 issue my initial breakthrough as it had been announced at the Holland conference the year before. This was followed in December 1995 by an article in the *Rapa Nui Journal* that detailed the second breakthrough and explained how nearly all the surviving *rongorongo* inscriptions comprise procreation chants of the type XYZn.

At this point, the well-known British archaeological author and Easter Island expert Paul Bahn—without my knowledge—approached England's foremost scientific journal, *Nature*, proposing to write an article about the recent decipherment of Oceania's only indigenous writing system. "An Oceanic writing system called *rongorongo?*" asked the *Nature* staff, incredulous. "Is this by any chance a joke?" After Paul Bahn finally managed to convince them that, yes, there was an Oceanic script called *rongorongo*, and yes, it had just been successfully deciphered, the staff at *Nature* grew enthusiastic. They agreed to publish at once. Bahn's article "Making Sense of Rongorongo," which appeared in the January 18, 1996, issue of *Nature*, summarily described the process that led to both breakthroughs in the *rongorongo* script's decipherment. It was a model of scientific precision ...

And it kindled excitement around the world.

The *Corriere della Sera* in Rome, *Sciences et Avenir* in Paris, and the *Süddeutsche Zeitung* in Stuttgart soon followed with their own versions of Bahn's *Nature* article. My phone starting ringing day and night. Impromptu radio interviews were hastily arranged for national and international broadcast. I described the decipherment on New Zealand television, using a *rongorongo* replica as I had done for Austrian TV in 1994. Whereupon a Reuters reporter, accompanied by a contract photographer, came to Waiheke Island for an interview and photos; the international feature that was released three weeks later appeared in newspapers and radio broadcasts throughout the world—in thirty languages, I was told. My aunt wrote from Corona del Mar, California, that as she was waiting in her car at a red light, she was transfixed by a lengthy radio report all about the decipherment of the "mysterious *rongorongo* script of Easter Island" by a linguist in New Zealand called Steven Roger Fischer. *Rongorongo* was now the topic of the day.

The popular scientific magazine *New Scientist* in London published the feature article "Cracking the Easter Island Code" in its issue of June 15, 1996. "Fischer seems to have found the key to reading rongorongo inscriptions," the article proclaims, "and that in itself constitutes a successful decipherment. It also makes Fischer unique among linguists." Because of the tremendous reader response to this article, *New Scientist* included in its issue of July 20, 1996, a short explanation of the decipherment of the Phaistos Disk, accompanied by a cartoon showing a scientist studying the Disk while a Greek-helmeted, sword-wielding apparition looms over him crying, "Your country needs you!" At the same time, journalists from around the world continued to ring me here on Waiheke Island for more information and even further radio interviews, from "Monitor" in America to the BBC—for two separate programs—in England.

Even as I was writing these very lines in New Zealand, the phone rang again, and yet another journalist in England wanted to know whether I could supply information about "the *rongorongo* writing from Easter Island."

And so it goes. This deluge of international queries does not disturb me. On the contrary. I'm happy to see such a great interest throughout the world in the Rapanui people's work of wonder. It deserves the world's admiration. *Rongorongo* itself, that is. Not its latter-day disciple.

The enthusiastic way in which my work with *rongorongo* was received was especially welcome by comparison with the hostile reception my decipherment of the Phaistos Disk had met with in some quarters. One of the most pleasant notices during this particularly hectic time had nothing to do with the popular media. After eight months of reviewing my voluminous manuscript, Oxford University Press in Oxford, England, wrote to inform me that Oxford had decided to publish *Rongorongo: The Easter Island Script.* My 700-page academic monograph should appear by August of 1997, the communication said. I was elated by the news.

More moving, however, was the letter that arrived from Thomas S. Barthel in Germany. For over forty years the dean of international *rongorongo* research, Thomas now wrote in his customary terse fashion that "with your basic triad (*with* ure ["phallus"] in the sense of ai ["copulated with"]) there can no longer be any doubt; for I, G, T ["Santiago Staff," "Small Santiago Tablet," "Honolulu 3629"] therefore unlimited endorsement."

I felt honored. Such an endorsement of a *rongorongo* decipherment—from a professional in the field—had never occurred before in the 132-year history of *rongorongo* scholarship.

Out of the many congratulatory letters and phone calls that I received almost daily from colleagues and strangers throughout the world in these many months, one looms large in my mind: two handwritten pages from a very special gentleman in Surrey, England, whom I have always held in the highest esteem:

> "Dear Dr Fischer. . . . I congratulate you most heartily. What a magnificent achievement and how satisfying it must be to solve a problem that has baffled so many able minds for so long."

Signed: Sir David Attenborough.

For the first time in history, one person had deciphered two wholly different historical scripts.

SUGGESTED READING

Bahn, Paul, and John Flenley. 1992. *Easter Island, Earth Island*. London: Thames and Hudson.

Barber, Elizabeth J. 1974. *Archaeological Decipherment: A Handbook*. Princeton: Princeton University Press.

Barthel, Thomas S. 1958. *Grundlagen zur Entzifferung der Osterinselschrift*. Hamburg: Cram, De Gruyter & Co.

———. 1978. *The Eighth Land. The Polynesian Discovery and Settlement of Easter Island*. Honolulu: The University Press of Hawaii.

Brice, W. C. 1961. *Inscriptions in the Minoan Linear Script of Class A*. Oxford: Oxford University Press.

Callender, Gae. 1987. *The Minoans*. Drummoyne (N.S.W., Australia): Shakespeare Head Press.

Chadwick, John. 1958. *The Decipherment of Linear B*. Cambridge: Cambridge University Press.

———. 1976. *The Mycenaean World*. Cambridge: Cambridge University Press.

Coe, Michael D. 1992. *Breaking the Maya Code*. London: Thames and Hudson.

Dickinson, Oliver T.P.K. 1994. *The Aegean Bronze Age*. New York: Cambridge University Press.

Diringer, David. 1962. *Writing*. New York: Praeger.

———. 1968. *The Alphabet. A Key to the History of Mankind*. 3d ed. 2 vols. London: Hutchinson.

Duhoux, Yves. 1977. *Le Disque de Phaestos. Archéologie, Epigraphie. Edition critique. Index*. Louvain: Peeters.

———(ed.). 1978. *Études minoennes I*. Bibliothèque des Cahiers de l'Institut de Linguistique de Louvain 14. Louvain: Peeters.

Evans, Arthur. 1909. *Scripta Minoa I*. Oxford: Oxford University Press.

———. 1921–35. *The Palace of Minos*. London.

———. 1952. *Scripta Minoa II*. Oxford: Oxford University Press.

Faure, Paul. 1973. *La vie quotidienne en Crète au temps de Minos*. Paris: Librairie Hachette.

Fischer, Steven Roger. 1988a. *Evidence for Hellenic Dialect in the Phaistos Disk*. Berne: Peter Lang.

———. 1988b. *Meersburg im Mittelalter. Aus der Geschichte einer Bodenseestadt und ihrer nächsten Umgebung*. Meersburg: List & Francke.

———. 1992. Homogeneity in Old Rapanui. *Oceanic Linguistics*, 31: 181–90.

———(ed.). 1993. *Easter Island Studies: Contributions to the History of Rapanui in Memory of William T. Mulloy*. Oxbow Monograph 32. Oxford: Oxbow Books.

———. 1995a. Preliminary Evidence for Cosmogonic Texts in Rapanui's *Rongorongo* Inscriptions. *Journal of the Polynesian Society*, 104: 303–21.

———. 1995b. Further Evidence for Cosmogonic Texts in the *Rongorongo* Inscriptions of Easter Island. *Rapa Nui Journal*, 9: 99–107.

———. 1997. *Rongorongo: The Easter Island Script. History, Traditions, Texts*. Oxford Studies in Anthropological Linguistics 14. Oxford: Oxford University Press.

Gelb, Ignace J. 1952. *A Study of Writing*. Chicago: University of Chicago Press.

Godart, Louis, and Jean-Pierre Olivier. 1976–1985. *Recueil des inscriptions en linéaire A.* 5 vols. École française d'Athènes, Études crétoises 21. Paris: Geuthner.

Hood, S. 1971. *The Minoans. Crete in the Bronze Age.* London: Praeger.

Hooker, J. 1976. *Mycenaean Greece.* London: Routledge & Kegan Paul.

Hutchinson, R. 1962. *Prehistoric Crete.* Harmondsworth: Penguin.

Jensen, Hans. 1970. *Sign, Symbol and Script. An Account of Man's Efforts to Write.* 3d ed. London: George Allen & Unwin.

Kahn, David. 1967. *The Codebreakers: The Story of Secret Writing.* New York: Macmillan.

Kober, Alice. 1948. The Minoan Scripts: Fact and Theory. *American Journal of Archaeology,* 52: 82–103.

Lee, Georgia. 1992. *The Rock Art of Easter Island: Symbols of Power, Prayers to the Gods.* Monumenta Archaeologica 17. Los Angeles: The Institute of Archaeology, University of California, Los Angeles.

Métraux, Alfred. 1940. *Ethnology of Easter Island.* Bernice P. Bishop Museum Bulletin 160. Honolulu: Bernice P. Bishop Museum Press.

Packard, David. 1974. *Minoan Linear A.* Berkeley: University of California Press.

Palmer, Leonard. 1965. *Mycenaeans and Minoans.* 2d ed. London: Faber.

Pope, Maurice. 1975. *The Story of Decipherment: From Egyptian Hieroglyphic to Linear B.* London: Thames and Hudson.

Pugliese Carratelli, G. 1945. Le iscrizioni preelleniche di Haghia Triada in Creta e della Grecia peninsulare. *Monumenti Antichi* (Rome) 40: col. 421–610.

Raison, Jacques, and Maurice Pope. 1971. *Index du linéaire A.* Incunabula Graeca 41. Rome.

———. 1977. *Index transnuméré du linéaire A.* Bibliothèque des Cahiers de l'Institut de Linguistique de Louvain 11. Louvain: Peeters.

————. 1980. *Corpus transnuméré du linéaire A.* Biblio-thèque des Cahiers de l'Institut de Linguistique de Louvain 18. Louvain: Cabay.

Routledge, Katherine Pease (Mrs. Scoresby). 1919. *The Mystery of Easter Island. The Story of an Expedition.* London: Hazell, Watson and Viney Ltd.

Ventris, Michael. 1940. Introducing the Minoan Language. *American Journal of Archaeology,* 44: 494–520.

Ventris, Michael, and John Chadwick. 1953. Evidence for Greek Dialect in the Mycenaean Archives. *Journal of Hellenic Studies,* 63: 84–103.

————. 1956. *Documents in Mycenaean Greek.* Cam-bridge: Cambridge University Press. Second and revised edi-tion, Cambridge 1973.

Warren, Peter M. 1989. *The Aegean Civilizations.* New York: Peter Bedrick Books.

Willetts, R. 1977. *The Civilization of Ancient Crete.* Berkeley and Los Angeles: University of California Press.

INDEX